D0209524

BITBURG
IN MORAL
AND POLITICAL
PERSPECTIVE

BITBURG

IN MORAL AND POLITICAL PERSPECTIVE

EDITED BY

Geoffrey H. Hartman

INDIANA UNIVERSITY PRESS
BLOOMINGTON

Manufactured in the United States of America

Library of Congress Cataloging-in-Publication Data
Main entry under title:

Bitburg in moral and political perspective.

Bibliography: p.
1. Holocaust, Jewish (1939–1945)—Anniversaries,
etc.—Addresses, essays, lectures. 2. Reagan, Ronald—
Journeys—Germany (West)—Addresses, essays, lectures.
3. Visits of state—Germany (West)—Addresses, essays,
lectures. 4. Holocaust, Jewish (1939–1945)—Public
opinion—Addresses, essays, lectures. 5. Bitburg
(Germany)—Addresses, essays, lectures. I. Hartman,
Geoffrey H.
D810.J4B497 1986   940.53′15′03924   85-45960
ISBN 0-253-34430-1
ISBN 0-253-20383-X (pbk).

1   2   3   4   5   90   89   88   87   86

*For all who have contributed to the Video
Archive for Holocaust Testimonies at Yale*

Contents

Acknowledgments

A sense of vigilance is with everyone who has some knowledge of the European catastrophe of 1933–45. Whether that vigilance can be translated into educational measures, and a less forgetful attitude toward history, is a long-range question. The forces arrayed against the memory of catastrophe include not only a natural need to allow new life to emerge but also further wars, catastrophes, and even—as "Bitburg" showed—well-meaning ceremonies. The conception of this book, and what made me wish to edit an informed series of essays, springs from this question of memory and its educability.

Without the devoted research help of Tom Keenan and Tom Levin, and earlier work by Barbara Browning and Karin Cope, this book could not have been. I am also grateful to a research grant from the A. W. Griswold Fund at Yale and a publication grant from the International Center for Holocaust Studies of the Anti-Defamation League of B'nai B'rith.

The following institutions and individuals have generously allowed me to use copyrighted materials: *Cleveland Plain Dealer*; Deutsche Presse-Agentur; Dow Jones & Company, Inc.; Chuck Fishman; Jürgen Habermas; *Jerusalem Post*; Miles Kington; Max Kohnstamm; Mark Krupnick; *Los Angeles Times*; Martin E. Marty; Charles William Maynes; Meir Merhav; *Le Monde*; *New Republic*; *Newsweek*; *New York Times*; Nathan Rapoport; Arthur Schlesinger, Jr.; Suhrkamp Verlag; *Time*; *U.S. News & World Report*; *Washington Post*; Avraham Weiss; *Die Zeit*.

Chronology

The information in this chronology has been assembled from a variety of sources, which have conflicted on some points. It is accurate to the best of our knowledge.

June 1984   Chancellor Kohl barred from participating in Allied ceremonies commemorating fortieth anniversary of D-Day landings at Normandy.

September 1984   Kohl and French President Mitterrand hold hands during ceremony of reconciliation at French-German military cemetery on Verdun battlefield.

30 November 1984   Kohl, meeting President Reagan in Washington, urges him to visit a German military cemetery during European visit in May 1985; also "broaches idea of a Dachau visit."

January 1985   President Reagan reportedly reluctant to include Dachau visit in itinerary. "I don't think we ought to focus on the past. I want to focus on the future. I want to put that history behind me."

28 January 1985   White House announces president will commemorate fortieth anniversary of V-E Day and confer with Chancellor Kohl during May trip to Europe.

14 February 1985   White House announces cancellation of plans to commemorate V-E Day in Germany; economic summit meeting and state visit will conclude prior to 8 May; president will address European Parliament in Strasbourg on that day instead.

February 1985   White House and German staff team surveys and approves planned sites, including Kolmeshöhe military cemetery at Bitburg, West Germany, near Luxembourg border and two miles from US air base, for Reagan's visit in May.

21 March 1985   At a White House news conference, President Reagan says that he will not visit a concentration camp site during his German visit: "I feel very strongly that . . . instead of reawakening the memories, . . . we should observe this day as the day when, forty years ago, peace began." He adds that "none of them [the German people] who were adults and participating in any way" in World War II are still alive, and "very few . . . even remember the war." "They have a guilt feeling that's been imposed upon them, and I just think it's unnecessary."

1 April 1985   President Reagan, in interview with *Washington Post*, explains that his decision not to visit a concentration camp site was based on a desire not "to take advantage of [the] visit" by reopening Germans' "great feeling of guilt . . . [about] what their nation did." Reiterates his "determination" that "we should never forget the Holocaust."

11 April 1985   White House announces itinerary of Reagan's trip to Europe, 30 April to 10 May; Reagan, accompanied by Kohl, plans to lay wreath at German military cemetery at Bitburg; ceremony described by spokesman as taking place "in a spirit of reconciliation, in a spirit of forty years of peace, in a spirit of economic and military compatibility."

12 April 1985   Facing immediate protests from Jewish and veterans' organizations against Bitburg visit, White House says plans are "under review."

14–21 April 1985   Nationwide "Days of Remembrance" of Holocaust, sponsored by U.S. Holocaust Memorial Council.

15 April 1985   U.S. Holocaust Memorial Council, meeting in emergency session in New York, considers but defers action on resolution calling for resignation of all of its members unless Bitburg visit is dropped from Reagan's itinerary.

Chancellor Kohl cables Reagan to recall that original German itinerary had included a stop at the site of the Dachau camp.

News reports reveal that Bitburg cemetery contains some graves, originally estimated to number around thirty, of soldiers in the Waffen SS. West German government spokesmen initially dodge question, calling it "of secondary importance." The number of SS graves is later determined to be forty-nine.

16 April 1985   President Reagan, in speech to Conference on Religious Liberty, reverses previous decision and announces he will lay a wreath at the site of a Nazi concentration camp, not as yet selected, but he does not change plans to visit Bitburg cemetery as well.

17 April 1985   Fifty-three U.S. senators write in petition to President Reagan that "a visit to Bitburg by an American President would be most unfortunate"; they "strongly urge" that he cancel the visit and include instead "an event commemorating the Holocaust."

18 April 1985   *Yom Hashoa*, Day of Holocaust Remembrance, is celebrated around the country amid expressions of protest at President Reagan's plan.

The president, in question-and-answer session with broadcasters and editors, defends Bitburg visit: ". . . there's nothing wrong with visiting that cemetery where those young men are victims of Nazism also. . . . They were victims, just as surely as the victims in the concentration camps." New protests erupt.

Elie Wiesel, speaking at National Civic Day of Commemoration of the Holocaust ceremony in U.S. Capitol rotunda, urges Secretary of State Shultz to "tell those who need to know that our pain is genuine, our outrage deep"; notes "pain and shame" felt "upon learning that the President . . . plans to visit a cemetery in which there are a good number of SS graves."

Holocaust Memorial Council, meeting in Washington in second emergency session, considers and tables motion on mass resignation; sends telegram to Mr. Reagan expressing "shock" at his "distortion of what took place during the Holocaust."

19 April 1985   White House announces Reagan will visit concentration camp site at Bergen-Belsen.

Wiesel, receiving Congressional Gold Medal of Achievement in White House ceremony, implores Reagan to cancel cemetery visit: "That place, Mr. President, is not your place. Your place is with the victims of the SS."

20 April 1985   Alfred Dregger, floor leader for Kohl's CDU party in West German Bundestag (parliament), in letter to Senator Howard Metzenbaum (who had circulated senators' petition to Reagan) responding to fifty-three senators, says that their request that Reagan cancel his "noble gesture" of visiting Bitburg was an "insult to my brother and his fallen comrades" who died on the eastern front in World War II.

21 April 1985   Chancellor Kohl, commemorating fortieth anniversary of liberation of Bergen-Belsen, says he accepts Germany's "historical responsibility for the crimes of the Nazi tyranny, . . . a responsibility reflected not least in never-ending shame."

Survivors of Holocaust, meeting in Philadelphia at the Inaugural Ceremony of the American Gathering of Jewish Holocaust Survivors, voice strong protests against planned Bitburg visit.

25 April 1985   257 members of US House of Representatives, in letter to Kohl, urge him to release president from commitment to visit Bitburg cemetery.

West German Bundestag votes down 398 to 24, motion by members of opposition Green Party asking Kohl government to eliminate stop at Bitburg. In debate, Kohl thanks Reagan for his "noble gesture." "Reconciliation is when we are capable of grieving over people without caring what nationality they are."

26 April 1985   US Senate passes, by voice vote, resolution sponsored by eighty-five Senators recommending that the president "reassess his planned itinerary."

28 April 1985   *New York Times* reports that Bitburg contains graves of soldiers from Second SS Panzer Division, "Das Reich," which committed one of the worst massacres of World War II, killing 642 villagers in Oradour-sur-Glane, France, in June 1942.

Simone Veil, former president of European Parliament, speaking at Dachau on fortieth anniversary of liberation, emphasizes singularity of the Holocaust ("Auschwitz is not Hiroshima") and rejects Reagan's "victims" comments as "impossible to accept."

30 April 1985   US House of Representatives, in 390 to 26 vote, passes resolution asking Reagan to "pay tribute to appropriate symbols of [Germany's] current democracy" and "reconsider the inclusion of the Bitburg cemetery" in his trip.

3 May 1985   Veterans of Waffen SS Death's Head Division gather at Schwabian ski resort of Nesselwang, West Germany. "We were soldiers, just like the others," one says.

5 May 1985   President Reagan, with Chancellor Kohl, lays wreath and speaks at Bergen-Belsen concentration camp, then visits Kolmeshöhe military cemetery at Bitburg and delivers address at US Air Force Base in Bitburg. Protest demonstrations are held at both locations.

8 May 1985   German President von Weizsäcker, in speech to Bundestag marking fortieth anniversary of V-E Day, says: "All of us, whether guilty or not, whether old or young, must accept the past. We are all affected by its consequences and liable for it. . . . We must understand that there can be no reconciliation without remembrance."

11–12 May 1985   First SS Panzer Corps reunion at Nesselwang.

13 June 1985   West German Bundestag passes so-called Auschwitzlüge law, making it an offense to deny that persecution was suffered "at the hands of the Nazi regime, or at the hands of another system of violent and arbitrary domination."

14–16 June 1985   In Hannover, West Germany, Chancellor Kohl addresses mass rally of Germans expelled by the Russians from Silesia (now part of Poland) at the end of World War II.

BITBURG
IN MORAL
AND POLITICAL
PERSPECTIVE

Geoffrey H. Hartman

Introduction
1985

The theme of memory haunts us increasingly. As events "pass into history," and they seem to do so more quickly than ever, are they forgotten by all except specialists? "Passing into history" would then be a euphemism for oblivion, though not obliteration. That something is retrievable in the archives of a library may even help us to tolerate the speedy displacement of one news item by another. The storage capacity of the personal memory is, after all, very limited. But what of the collective memory, with its days of celebration and lamentation, and the duty to keep alive a community's heritage?

The actual memories are likely to be what they have always been: joyful, painful, or both together. Yet recently the tonality of the word "memory" has darkened and moved toward lamentation. We complain, for instance, about the shortened memory-span of the young, and their refusal to extend personal experience by the study of history. One scholar has therefore talked of the "death of the past." Another has characterized the historian as a "physician of memory." Paradoxically, or so it seems, we plan more and more rites of memorialization, unveiling monuments and instituting days of remembrance that dot the calendar with new holidays. Is there a concern that the burden of the past on the individual consciousness will prove too heavy? Perhaps, then, the mechanics of commemoration are being used to achieve a disburdening of memory, to "construct" forgetfulness, and so—unfortunately—to forestall real, continuous thought about catastrophic events that mark our recent past.

Nineteen eighty-five was the fortieth anniversary of both the end of the Second World War and the liberation of the Nazi death camps. Public speakers remarked on the symbolism of the "forty years" that the Israelites were compelled to spend in the Wilderness. Only after the older generation had died out were they permitted into the Promised Land. But that parable for our time was applied in two very different ways. There were those, including the president of the United States, who felt that Germany, now a bulwark of democracy and NATO, had passed through its exile years and should be rehabilitated spiritually. (Its economic and political standing had been restored long before.) But there were also those who saw that the survivors of the Nazi camps were approaching the term of their life. Soon very few would remain. This occasion was a chance to become more aware of how *they* felt about past and present, including events the president wished to distance. The historians had documented in necessary and fearful detail the Nazi killing machine; the politicians had agreed to establish a Holocaust Memorial Council and annual Days of Remembrance; but the survivors' experience as experienced, their personal story and individual memories—everything too easily characterized as "Oral History"—was only beginning to be heard.

The "forty years," then, meant different things for these two groups that came into collision when the president agreed to honor a German military cemetery at Bitburg, having previously declined to visit a concentration camp memorial site. The full rehabilitation of a perpetrator nation by Mr. Reagan clashed with the survivors' sense (shared by the Jewish community) that they were passing from the scene with their message still unheard, though repeated many times.

Nineteen eighty-five may also have brought to consciousness a related, and more universal, conflict. Life is characterized by a contradictory effort: to remember and to forget, to respect the past and to acknowledge that the present is open to the future. Associated with this common tension are issues that reach into the most sensitive area of morality as it intersects with a nation's political agenda. However hostile the relation between states, a realignment of alliances can occur. It is always possible that a Sadat will fly to Jerusalem and begin a peace process that was unimaginable just months before. The ties between America and Germany, moreover, had grown and intensified over the space of thirty years, aided by a shared anxiety about the East.

Yet the moral question remained, because the guilt incurred by Germany during the war was exceptional. The war brought to light the crime of genocide. The Nazi regime had deprived its own Jewish citizens of profession and property, then of life itself. An entire people was hunted down in the Occupied Territories and slated for extermination. The War against the Jews was prosecuted with as much zeal as the military campaign against the Allies, and even interfered with it. An incredible obsession, it still has not found its explanation and may never find it. But the death camps altered forever the landscape of memory.

There could be no forgetting, then. By 1985, memorials to the victims of the Holocaust were going up everywhere in America. Yet by 1985, too, the memory of that era belonged primarily to the historian rather than to the general public. For the majority of citizens in America and Europe were born after the beginning of the war. For them knowledge about the war and the Holocaust comes primarily from history books and the media rather than from personal recall or contact with individual survivors. This is a turning point, then, and a crucial one. Education and ritual must supplement personal experience; and these, *in less than one more generation*, may have to carry the entire burden of sustaining the collective memory.

The prophets of an older time knew that ceremonies were not enough. Ceremonies would substitute for, rather than inscribe, what should be known and acted upon. Few will quarrel with the fact that to deal with the moral issues raised by the Holocaust, or to transmit a knowledge of it without causing new trauma, is basic. Yet many think they already know about the Holocaust, and that it has received too much attention. But their attitude is a sign that they have no direct memory of the events and learn about them mainly from ceremonies and the media.

This "I know, I know" is only one of many defenses. Saul Friedländer, in his essay on Germany's struggle with memory, lists others. The fact is that each new generation, German as well as American, has known *something*. The events of April–May 1985 are not unique. There are recurrent crises of consciousness involving the Holocaust.[1] But each crisis—triggered by the Eichmann trial revelations, for instance, or the full disclosure of how much American leaders (Jewish as well as Gentile) knew and how little they did—simply brings about new mechanisms of defense. If this pattern of disclosure and defense is allowed to continue, it will achieve nothing except an occasional catharsis. Each decade will have its "punctual agony," after which things return to normal. So Theodor Adorno (a German philosopher who survived the Nazis by spending the war years in America and whose essay is translated here for the first time) anticipated in 1959 what has become only too clear in 1985. It was also Adorno who raised the question of what education meant "After Auschwitz." The Holocaust should not be assigned to the history of the victims, as if it were not of the utmost consequence to every thoughtful person. This is where education enters as a responsibility that cannot be delayed.

It is an education, quite specifically, that will have to pose questions for which the answers are lacking, while not abandoning its obligation to find answers. Such questions as: how do we transmit so dark and debilitating a knowledge? There are righteous and kindly acts to be reported, but they stand out in their rarity. Can any culture, including that of pre-Holocaust Jewry, help us to absorb or integrate the damaging picture? Our concern for the human image, moreover, could extend itself to the divine image. For the Holocaust acts as an eclipse of the *imago Dei* (of the God in whose image man is said to be created), even if the faith of many survivors was unshaken. As we consider such large questions, we realize that they connect, as in the case of Bitburg, with something daily and immediate. What does "forgiveness" or "reconciliation" mean? Especially in circumstances where the offense may not be forgotten?

This issue of *response* cannot be separated, in short, from that of *responsibility*. How do we handle the imputation of collective guilt? Can the offended and injured evolve a statute of limitations, not of course toward individual criminals but toward the perpetrator nation, or bystanders (the church and others, not just the average German) who did so little to help? We surely cannot invoke a collective guilt of the kind that bloodied the record of history long before the Nazis translated it into their atrocious practices against the Jews.

Education must raise these issues formally. But there remains an ultimate question and the most subversive of all. Can a method be found to prevent the recurrence of genocidal regimes by instituting a more effective system of law and education? The question is subversive because we know all too well that Germany was a law-abiding and civilized country. The fact that the Holocaust occurred among an educated people, and where the Jews had achieved a remarkable symbiosis, requires us to rebuild our faith in education itself. It is not just a matter of gaining more space for the Holocaust (more textbook pages) in the curriculum. To have predicted the crimes against the Jews and other "racially inferior" groups by that cultured nation, Germany, was as impossible, one commentator wrote during the Bitburg turmoil, as imagining that Goethe ate human flesh.

President Reagan's decision to visit Bitburg during ceremonies marking the fortieth anniversary of Germany's "liberation" from the Nazi yoke may simply have been a blunder, caused by bad advance planning. Blunder or not, the story of that visit as it unfolded occupied the media for two months, from the end of March to the end of May.

It was a remarkably intense period. The anguish, especially though not exclusively within Jewish circles, and particularly among those who survived the Holocaust, has still not passed away.

Americans may have been ready for what Mr. Reagan called "reconciliation," but not in *that* form. All at once we realized again the crucial importance of symbols, as well as the difficulty of finding any symbol or ceremony that could have served Mr. Reagan's aim. The time had not come for so global an act of political absolution. Any place chosen for its symbolic value might therefore seem flawed—though some less than others, as Raul Hilberg points out. Even so moving a gesture as Willy Brandt's, when he fell to his knees before the Warsaw Ghetto memorial during a 1970 visit, was questioned by the press.

Every monument or ceremony seeking to honor the collective memory can be "forgetful" in the sense that its design is influenced by policy—James Young makes that restrictive relation between monument and memory quite clear. But the choice of Bitburg not only raised a question as to whether the ceremony was necessary, or what ceremonies really achieve—it gave the impression of wishing to recall *nothing* of the past except common sacrifices and a shared code of military honor. Yet was it not that very code which was breached by Nazi "crimes against humanity"?

Mr. Reagan treated the matter as if it were an internal American affair. There had been some fuss when Gerald Ford, after assuming the presidency, pardoned Nixon and asked the nation to heal its wounds. This time, on a divisive issue involving the international community, we were asked to accept a formal act of reconciliation that would take place not only on German soil but in a military cemetery of that nation.

When Elie Wiesel, in a phrase that became famous, told the president, "That place [Bitburg] is not your place," the emotional impact was amplified by a consciousness that the Jews had been a displaced people for too long—lacking their own place or haven until the establishment of Israel in 1948. If the soldiers buried in that German cemetery had won the war, the Jews would have disappeared from the face of the earth, and unlike the Wehrmacht or Waffen SS buried there, no place could have been found to honor them. Close to six million did perish, many in unmarked mass graves. "Here rest a thousand dead," one of the signs reads in the Bergen-Belsen memorial site. The Jews were to be remembered only in Nazi histories, where their extermination would be, Himmler said, "the most glorious page" in the annals of the Third Reich.

No wonder a sense of shock and betrayal swept the Jewish community. The head of a country that had given refuge to so many victims of the Nazis—a country they trusted and where, all things considered, they felt at home—did not seem to have a real sense of their history. Veterans' groups too protested, as did many church-related organizations with a more troubled view than the president about who had the right to forgive. William Bole documents that unusually massive support. Many pointed out with Lance Morrow that "forgiveness to the injured doth belong." Unfortunately, Mr. Reagan compounded his error by explanatory statements that made no distinction between the fallen German soldiers and the murdered Jews; indeed, he suggested that both were "victims" of a Nazi oppression whose responsibility he limited by laying it upon the madness of "one man."[2]

Those who mock official Soviet distortions of history (a sample of the Russian response to Bitburg will be found in the "East Bloc" section of the Press Commentaries) must have been embarrassed. This interpretation, surely, was equally bad, however benevolent its motive. Good intentions do not guarantee good history, any more than do revengeful ones. "1985," then, is not so far from "1984," despite the fact that George Orwell was evoking the danger of totalitarianism: how it would distort history and by its "newspeak" flatter and flatten the mind. Nor all that far from "1914," when Walter Lippmann foresaw that out of the unrest of democratic liberties there comes not disciplined thought but a penchant for easy and hopeful solutions. The "real American," he wrote, in *Drift and Mastery*, was actually a dreamer seeking a "Golden Age in which he could drift with impunity." But "this habit of reposing in the sun of a brilliant future is very enervating. It opens a chasm between fact and fancy, and the whole fine dream is detached from the living zone of the present."

That detachment in the president, that optimistic ability to overlook certain things in the past and so to counter drift by an appearance of mastery, is what everyone felt. Some were grateful; many were offended. A sense of history is particularly important in the era of the Holocaust. It was a vicious propaganda in the form of history that, if it did not bring Hitler to power, certainly helped to justify his excesses once in power. A similar libel comes today from the Soviet sphere, which sees the Holocaust as a conspiracy of Zionists and Nazis to create the conditions for the founding of Israel. There exists, moreover, a crude revisionism that claims that the death camps with their gas chambers and crematoria were merely unpleasant work camps (more like Gulags, say). Finally, a more subtle revisionism is all around us that mitigates the horror of the camps, not by denying it but by using equalizing comparisons. So Vietnam or the bombing of Beirut is dubbed a "holocaust." (On one aspect of this kind of revisionism, see Alvin Rosenfeld's essay in this volume.) The exceptionality of the Holocaust is diminished by such liberal yet vague analogies.

It should therefore be stated very clearly: Even if "nothing human is alien to us," the burden of the *Shoah* (the Hebrew word means "annihilation") cannot be overcome because it cannot be reduced to familiarity. The Holocaust remains human and alien at the same time. The worst attitude we could take is to persuade ourselves that it might not happen again *or* that it is something that happened before—that the Holocaust was one catastrophe among others.

It is true that such a perspective divides history by positing a caesura more decisive than a theophanic event. It makes of the Holocaust a *novum* (as Emil Fackenheim, among others, has argued); so that, for the time being, which may last some time, all that went before and all that presently befalls us must be seen in the ominous light of that destruction. The history of the Jews, Nikolai Berdyaev wrote, presents nothing but a perpetual crucifixion. This very fact, however, helped to deceive and decoy Hitler's victims, as Raul Hilberg has shown in his classic *The Destruction of the European Jews*. The Jews were used to pogroms, accustomed to those terrible yet temporary turns of fortune. Elie Wiesel has said of his youth: "Somehow I accepted persecution as a law of nature. I was convinced that this was how God created the world, that once a year we had to avoid being in the street because on that winter evening, or on that day in the spring, Christians attacked Jews. It was clear, it was normal. I didn't even protest." But the Nazi terror aimed at a "Final Solution."

In witness accounts by Holocaust survivors two phrases recur: "I saw it," and "I could not believe what my eyes have seen." It needs a particular courage not to overcome the past but to live with it still. Historians, we are told, instruct us in the uses of the past, yet it is hard to see what that means when the Holocaust is the issue. Education, in this case, cannot be equated with enlightenment. The universe of death we call the Holocaust or Shoah creates, as Claude Lanzmann has said, its own sacred and isolating wall of fire. The very fact that it happened repels us. Yet it also makes us aware how painful it is to stay with a knowledge that is about evil rather than about good, and so tempts us to simplify what happened or commemorate it merely ritually. The essays and articles that follow resist simplifying the historical record. They are not interested in fanning resentment or settling a score. Nor do they consider "Bitburg" as an isolated incident but rather perceive it as a symbolic and symptomatic event with high visibility, from which much can be learned.

I personally learned that despite the attention the Holocaust had received (at least since the TV series "Holocaust" was screened), one could not count on the facts being known or their significance being understood. Publicity, media exposure and Days of Remembrance have been less than successful in conveying the enormity of the Shoah. "Bitburg" disclosed that what understanding there was at the highest level of government led not to sensitivity, but only to sentimentality. For even if Mr. Reagan was being shielded from too close a contact with the emotional side of things, the straight historical truths also were not getting through; and this meant an astonishing ignorance or lack of interest on the part of his advisors.

Although journalism during the Bitburg episode was of very high quality, too many letters in the papers repeated charges about Jewish attempts to claim a monopoly on suffering. This makes me doubt that Holocaust studies have affected more than a very small portion of the public. My work with the Video Archive for Holocaust Testimonies at Yale suggests the same conclusion. There has to be a will to talk, but also a will to listen. The survivors are finally talking, but are we ready to listen?

An anecdote can illustrate the difficulty of speaking about the Holocaust experience—or taking it in. I had addressed a small group of survivors for some fifteen minutes, setting forth the reasons why they should give their testimony. When I finished an old—a very old— woman turned her arm over, disclosing the bluish tatoo, and said simply: "I was there."

It comes to that, first and last, to that evidential, sorrowful "I was there" spoken by those who were in the camps. I felt unnecessary, and yet I had to be "there" myself as a belated witness to that act. Those who complain about the attention the Holocaust is receiving are right that no one should make a platform out of the suffering of others. And we have seen young people with political ambitions who are falling into that temptation, and whose rage in denouncing Mr. Reagan's mistake gave the impression of seeking a constituency.

Yet the political brouhaha does not excuse those who say, Enough. They have forgotten two things. That the survivors must be heard now, if at all; and that for a long time they were not heard, or not believed. The Holocaust is such Bad News that even now teachers and researchers who take up the task of telling what they know face all kinds of psychological obstacles. The bereaved too are not always exempt from subtle forms of denial, as Primo Levi tells us in his remarkable "The Memory of Offense." We have to reconcile ourselves to the fact that an utterly inhumane event like the Holocaust occurred, before we demand another kind of reconciliation—a forgiving spirit on the part of those who survived, and who represent not only themselves but their murdered families.

Mr. Reagan's initiative, as William Safire points out, at least had the virtue of eventually adding thoughtfulness to ritual. He was led by an invisible "pedagogical hand." The initiative, in other words, did the opposite of what it intended, and so gave us a chance—however unfortunate the occasion—to think matters through more honestly. It produced, for example, a speech by Richard von Weizsäcker (president of the Federal Republic of Germany) that is really a public confession never before uttered at that level. Yet from the letter-debate in the London *Times*,[3] it is equally certain that the so-called Christian-Jewish dialogue has not advanced very far.

The letters suggest that Jewish ethical thinking is not known or appreciated, and that Christian attitudes about forgiveness approach at times old anti-Semitic stereotypes concerning the obstinacy and hardheartedness of the Jews. This is an unhappy theme. Clearly, ecumenical assemblies are not enough: as A. Roy Eckardt's essay suggests, it is time to broach more forcefully the issue of Christian anti-Semitism, and the related question of prejudicial Gospel texts from Matthew and John that remain an integral part of the lectionary. They support, and have done so for centuries, an anti-Jewish mentality and the idea of collective guilt. Vatican II's declaration, modifying the charge of deicide and collective guilt, at least officially recognized the problem without being as decisive a statement as one would wish. And it certainly has not sunk in. Claude Lanzmann's epic film *Shoah* contains a chilling sequence in which the filmmaker's patient questioning of people in front of a Polish Catholic church (a colorful ceremony honoring the birth of the Virgin forms its background) leads finally to a startling change of mood, as the crowd goes from good-hearted professions of ignorance as to why the Jews suffered the Holocaust, to excited explanations based on Matthew 15:27, with its climactic "His blood be on us and on our children!"

The Bitburg affair made American Jews feel vulnerable. Not because they doubted the soundness of the American system or the good will of the president. Yet they understood, again, their dependence on that good will—on how even in a democracy the tune is called on high, and "administration" means more than carrying out a mandate with efficiency. Those who do not see why there was so much agitation about Mr. Reagan's "modest symbolic gesture" are failing to analyze the immense importance that the impression of being fully in charge has in a pluralistic society. *E pluribus unum*: how is this unity to be maintained in so divided, so heterogeneous a country, without force, or the least amount of force? Think of the passions aroused by the silent or one-minute prayer controversy. An agreement on *symbols* is crucial if violent encounters are to be avoided. Hence there are no "modest" symbolic gestures.

Jews may be particularly sensitive to symbolic acts because they have often been humiliated by them. Forced baptism, forced gestures of obedience (Freud recalls his father's story of quietly retrieving his cap knocked into the gutter when a gentile wished him off the pavement) are among the more *benign* events of their history. The "forced reconciliation" of Bitburg, therefore, can suggest the possibility of further steps involving state power. The essay by Jürgen Habermas included here is a difficult yet important piece that suggests the closeness of *Verwaltung* (administration) to *Gewalt* (force), and the danger of the latter masking as the former. His radical conclusion is that politicians cannot be trusted to exert spiritual or moral leadership. They will always engage in "forced reconciliation," or what Kenneth Burke, recalling Hitler's era—which we still ponder, however far we are from it—characterized as "sinister unifying."

In this situation, then, an honest appraisal seems better than words of false comfort. The questionings of Job suit an age that nevertheless reaches out in the hope of *tikkun*—a Hebrew word that suggests a mending rather than reconciliation. The Bitburg turmoil did sometimes provide such a mending in the form of new coalitions (whether or not they will prove to be transitory) in America and France. One especially moving development is reported by Henry Rousso. Though the French community's response, like that of their government, remained muted, Bitburg provided the occasion for a march and a manifesto that united young Jews and immigrant workers, including Arabs. They discovered a common cause in protesting racism, whether anti-Jewish or anti-Arab (the latter a growing problem in France), and issued an eloquent statement affirming that "there are wounds and acts which can never be effaced from the collective memory."

This mending, as Emil Fackenheim has reminded us, also extends to the question of our speech, and its involvement in symbols.[4] In 1985, and perhaps every year, we begin to think anew about the symbols that are supposed to unite us, yet, like Bitburg, often reveal deep and unresolved points of difference. The memory of offense cannot be eradicated by the magic touch of benevolence. Not in the private mind, and not in the general consciousness of those who have been through the Holocaust or suffered other crimes of the Nazi era. "Pity and Love are too venerable for the imputation of guilt," William Blake has one of his grand, self-deluding figures declaim. For he knows these virtues too must be open to scrutiny. What he calls "mental fight" continues.

As I write this, six months after Bitburg, there are some who feel that an unfortunate incident was inflated into a *cause célèbre*. Bitburg, they say, cannot retain its significance. Yet Bitburg was meant to be significant, was meant to create a symbolic occasion, and therefore relied on image-making and the media—on the very forces that exposed a flawed thinking. "Reagan: F in History," a French newspaper headline declared. The president and his advisors, however, were not alone in finding it difficult to "master" history. America, as Walter Lippmann suggested, is a land that has made light of the past and sometimes taken pride in shaking off an unnecessary burden. The American Adam is a figure both mocked and admired. There was nothing covert in what happened: the media simply reflected an iconomania that is creating a "generation without memory."

Both the Germans and the French, in this light, are closer to a past that keeps returning. Even the people called by Shimon Dubnov "the veterans of history" are finding it harder to bring their past into the collective memory. It does not help to quote Santayana, that those who refuse to learn from history are bound to repeat it. For history sends mixed messages. Dubnov, a great historian, said that the nineteenth century promised the emancipation of the Jews, the full restoration of their civic rights, despite ominous regressions toward the close of the century in Russia and Austria. Yet our time has witnessed a Holocaust that took Dubnov's own life even as he was recording the deadly scene.[5] How then can remembrance lead to redemption, as a famous Hasidic master, the Baal Shem Tov, thought? The memorials we multiply reflect a universe of death, of which history is the record. In this regard, the survivors of the camps become a crucial generation for us. They are, often, the history we would rather forget; yet their memories, though traumatic, did not entirely displace in them a tradition of learning transmitted for two thousand years.

NOTES

1. The situation in France is much less clear. Even in talking about survivors, the word "déporté" is more common than "survivant," and Alain Resnais's famous *Night and Fog* avoids identifying the inmates of the camps as mainly Jewish. In an issue of the *Nouvelle Révue de Psychanalyse* entitled *Mémoires* (15, 1977) the Holocaust does not make an appearance. For the

complex reaction to Bitburg in France, see Henry Rousso's essay in this volume.

2. Jean Améry writes: ". . . death in battle and the [camp] prisoner's death are two incommensurables. The soldier died the hero's or victim's death, the prisoner that of an animal intended for slaughter. . . . The decisive difference lay in the fact that the front-line soldier unlike the camp inmate was not only the target, but also the bearer of death." *At the Mind's Limits: Contemplations by a Survivor on Auschwitz and Its Realities*, trans. Sidney Rosenfeld and Stella P. Rosenfeld (Bloomington: Indiana University Press, 1980), p. 16.

3. Reprinted in *European Judaism* 19:2 (London), Spring 1985, 3–17. The controversy centered on a letter by Dr. A. C. J. Phillips, chaplain of St. John's College, Oxford, which contains the following sentences:.

. . . A theology unwilling to come to terms with the oppressors, however heinous their crimes, imprisons itself in its own past jeopardizing the very future it would ensure.

Without forgiveness there can be no healing within the community, no wholeness, holiness. The leopard cannot lie down with the kid. Indeed the opposite occurs. For failure to forgive is not a neutral act: it adds to the sum total of evil in the world and dehumanizes the victims in a way the oppressors could never on their own achieve.

In remembering the Holocaust, Jews hope to prevent its recurrence: by declining to forgive, I fear that they unwittingly invite it.

4. *To Mend the World* (New York: Schocken Books, 1982), especially chapter 4.

5. See Elie Wiesel, "In the Footsteps of Shimon Dubnov," in *Against Silence: The Voice and Vision of Elie Wiesel* (New York: Holocaust Library/Schocken Books, 1985).

ESSAYS

Raul Hilberg

Bitburg as Symbol

Four decades after the end of the Second World War, the people of West Germany were thriving with comforts and luxuries, but their lives had no luster. At one time, a German politician looked at the youth of his country and said:

> Our youth, primarily, but also all the others among us, do not have it as good as other peoples. Our country has nothing that glitters. Probably a long time will pass before anything in this state will glitter. That is rooted in the war; it is rooted in the "Thousand Years" and many other things besides, but that is the way it is, and it is very difficult for a people to live satisfied merely with itself and its ordered way of life in the grey of everyday, and that which in the American Declaration of Independence is called "pursuit of happiness." All this is necessary, but it is not enough by itself. One cannot live solely with prosperity and the attainment of an ever-rising standard of living. It is important and necessary that one reaches it, but in addition a human being needs something else, something to look up to. Since that does not happen here, this people is restless.[1]

The Federal Republic has rebuilt its cities and its political parties. Its new architecture lacks the massiveness that was the style before 1945. Neither graceful nor imposing, these unostentatious structures have the appearance of pure functionalism. The government of the Federal Republic has been fashioned in the same way. Colorless and undramatic, it veers toward the center of any conceivable political spectrum. Characteristically, a public opinion poll in March 1985 revealed that on a scale of $+5$ to -5, ten prominent individuals in Germany's political leadership, including men in power as well as those in opposition, were bunched in the middle from $+1.2$ to -0.3.[2] Germany is no longer a country of political oratory. The German language is filled with English or anglicized expressions, particularly in advertisements. The German armed forces are allocated in their entirety to the overall defense of the North Atlantic Community. Germany has become a "good citizen."

The Federal Republic is densely populated with more than sixty million people inhabiting territory that is almost exactly half the size of Germany's area in 1937. Its economic power is still concentrated in its manufacturing industry, much of it where it always was, in the Rhineland. From its expanding gross national product, West Germany set aside sums of money for reparations to Israel and for indemnification of refugees and survivors. These payments are the material "amends" for the physical annihilation of a third of all the Jews in the world. There is also a diplomatic and commercial relationship with Israel, which was begun with much uneasiness, but which has been continued with sizable exchanges of goods and a considerable annual flow of German tourists to the Holy Land.

Of course, postwar German society has not been totally divorced from the Nazi era. The first chancellor, Konrad Adenauer, for all of his stature and authority, could not overshadow the phalanx of former anti-Jewish perpetrators who found employment in high positions of his administration. It has taken many years for all of these people in the ministries, the railroads, the diplomatic corps, and the military to pass from the scene. By 1985, however, a younger generation, headed by Chancellor Helmut Kohl, was definitely at the helm. In Germany, the new regime is sometimes called the government of flak helpers. Flak is the acronym for *Flugabwehrkanonen,* or anti-aircraft guns, and the helpers were adolescents near the end of World War II, too young for front-line service, but old enough to haul ammunition to anti-aircraft crews shooting at Allied bombers. For Kohl, age is an important part of his credentials. As he viewed the date on his birth certificate, he felt that he had been given a special mission. For forty years, Germany had lived in psychological isolation, and 1985 was the year in which he was going to lead the German people out of the desert.

When the Western leaders met in 1984, they celebrated the anniversary of the landings in Normandy without Kohl. Deeply stung, Kohl received small consolation from a ceremony with French president Mitterand at a Verdun cemetery of the First World War. For the Germans of the 1980s, the resurrection of 1914–18 was not the right commemoration, and the holding of hands by the two men at Verdun lent itself to caricature. Kohl needed a more powerful presence, on German soil, at a place symbolizing the *Second* World War.

The man to be invited for this purpose was the genuine head of the Western world, the president of the United States, and the site of his visit was to be a typical German military cemetery near the town of Bitburg. About two thousand fallen soldiers of the Third Reich lay buried there. Interspersed among these graves were those of forty-seven or so SS men.

The forty years since 1945 have been much shorter for the Jews. Benumbed by the unprecedented blow of Nazi Germany, Jewry had been living in a make-believe world of its own. The American Jews in particular were slow to recognize the enormity of the loss in Europe. For several decades they were still preoccupied with the final stages of their emancipation as Americans with full political, social, and economic rights. At the same time they were galvanized by the creation and wars of Israel. Although they knew that the drive for equality and the rise of Israel had been catalyzed by the catastrophe in Europe, they did not gaze back at this cauldron and they made no organized effort to recapture the memory of the European Jewish community.

Memorialization as a concerted undertaking is a fairly recent phenomenon that began in the mid-1970s and that reached its peak only a few years ago. "Holocaust"—the word itself—is relatively new. A pivotal role in this awakening has been played by survivors.

As a group, survivors are not a random sample of prewar European Jewry. The nature of ghettos and camps was such that small children as well as elderly men and women died first, and anyone incapable of labor or prone to disease was eventually doomed. The "luck" of survival, of which so much is said in memoirs, was thus not simply the consequence of sheer accident. The survivor was a person with special occupational skills, or with exceptional physical stamina, or with an ability to make rapid, logical decisions in moments of crisis. More than a few of these individuals were in their teens or early twenties in 1945, and today they are not much older than the former flak helpers in Germany. Not surprisingly, some of them have achieved material success in their new homes, and several of them know how to speak about that which makes them a living link between the extinct communities and the untouched Jews of America.

They speak, however, at some cost. Part of the problem is that one cannot effortlessly say everything. It is not easy to recount the full extent of one's helplessness and humiliation in extreme situations. More than that, it is difficult to find the proper wording to convey even the bare essentials of an Auschwitz experience to someone "who was not there." For Jews, words have been the ancient, primeval form of preserving memory. Painting is subsidiary and music is ancillary. But the words of the most articulate survivors are inadequate for *this* reality. The dictum of Adorno that it is "barbaric" to write poetry after Auschwitz may be extended to all forms of expression. It is barbaric to write footnotes, to give lectures, or to make speeches. The words usurp and destroy the event, taking its place in memory. That is why the greatest spokesman of the survivors, Elie Wiesel, writes sparingly and espouses silence. That is also why Charlotte Delbo, a poet-prisoner of Auschwitz, is a minimalist. One must be artless in describing this event, discarding adjectives and adverbs. Yet that is the highest art of all. That is *Genesis* itself.

Those who make the attempt pay a price every time. Each explanation, tale, or poem, is a compromise. But the effort has been made despite the cost "to tell it to the world." Then came Bitburg. An American president, standing amid the buried German soldiers and SS men, was to place a wreath to commemorate them all without distinction. Was this to be an act of total redemption of Nazi Germany? Had the survivors' testimony not been heard? Had the captured documents of Adolf Hitler's Reich been overlooked? Had the message failed? Under President Carter, the Congress had established a United States Holocaust Memorial Council. Elie Wiesel was serving as its chairman. President Reagan had personally received the council in the White House during his first term. Was he now negating its mission? Was he playing politics with memory?

A key element in the debate was the cluster of SS graves at Bitburg, and everything seemed ultimately to depend on the measure of their significance. The history of U.S. policy toward postwar Germany had been an attempt to whittle down the size of the Nazi problem, to diminish the ranks of those who were to be held accountable for the Nazi regime. The beginning was the rejection of "collective guilt." The next step was a judicial division of organized German society into two segments, one of which was to be left largely undisturbed, while the other was to be pursued further. The first group included the vast majority of the judges, generals, diplomats, civil servants, industrialists, and bankers, only a handful of whom stood trial for an activity deemed contrary to the old laws of war or the new law of aggression. The second group consisted of power centers that were found by the Nuremberg International Military Tribunal to have had a criminal purpose.[3] If a member of such a hierarchy had joined or remained in it voluntarily with knowledge of its character, he had committed a crime. One of these criminal organizations was the leadership corps of the Nazi Party; another was the Gestapo and Security Service; the third comprised all SS men, except draftees who were given no choice and who had committed no crimes. Eventually, the SS in particular remained in the public eye as the hard core of Nazism.

Eichmann was an SS officer, Mengele belonged to the SS, and many others, known and unknown, were part of it. SS men were at the forefront of the shootings of hundreds of thousands of Jews in occupied Eastern Europe, and SS men were implicated in the killing of millions in the camps. As of 1985, there was still a Central Office for Investigation of National Socialist Crimes in West Germany, gathering evidence against SS men and party stalwarts for prosecutions in West German courts. At the same time, there was an Office of Special Investigations in the U.S. Department of Justice, charged with instituting proceedings for denaturalization and deportation of individuals, from the Baltic area, the Ukraine, and elsewhere, who had served as willing accomplices of the German SS and Police in lethal operations against Jews, Gypsies, and others. In this manner, the notion of culpability for inexcusable offenses, no matter what the date of their commission, was still being upheld by West Germany and by the United States in tangible legal actions. With the advent of Bitburg, however, a psychological reversal was in the offing. The president's wreath seemed to cover the entire history of the Third Reich with a nebulous collective innocence.

Aggravating the situation were all of the circumstances leading to the decision. President Reagan announced at first that he would not visit a concentration camp, lest he "reawaken the memories and so forth, and the passions of the time."[4] After protests were voiced about Bitburg, he decided to go to a camp after all, but when he announced the additional visit to Bergen-Belsen, he antagonized the protesters even more, for now he was going from the mass graves of Jews to the headstones of SS men, explaining that both were victims.[5]

The survivors, and more generally the Jewish community, were of course not the only complainants. Several veterans' groups and majorities of the U.S. Senate and House of Representatives went on record against Bitburg. Opinion polls revealed that on the whole the people were divided on the issue—about half did not agree with the president. But there is no question that the issue was felt most intensely by the Jews.

For President Reagan the prospective visit to the cemetery became an increasingly onerous proposition. It was a classic political situation of confronting seemingly contradictory demands from unyielding friends. The contemporary presidency, for all the power at its command, frequently operates like a brokerage house. The White House staff, and other decision-makers of the executive branch, are sometimes candid about this method of accomplishing their ends. "They owe us one," they might be heard to say, or "We owe them one." In the case of Bitburg, however, the fine art of the balancing act must have been extraordinarily difficult, because the problem could not be resolved with dollars and cents, or with political trade-offs of one sort or another. Weighing the pros and cons, the president's advisers could defend a decision in favor of Germany. They could point to the ideological affinity of Kohl and Reagan. They could refer to the German polls, which indicated that three-quarters of the German population favored the visit, and to an overwhelming vote in the Bundestag against any cancellation.[6] At a time of weakening support of U.S. policies around the world, they could verify the reliability of Germany as a NATO partner, and they could cite, among other things, the deployment of Pershing and cruise missiles on German soil. Could American Jewry muster such "credits"? There were certainly Jewish conservatives who supported the president's goals, but as an electorate the Jews of America were still voting overwhelmingly for Democratic candidates. And Israel, strong friend that it was, depended heavily on U.S. assistance. Given this equation, no one could assert that the president's attitude toward Jewish causes had not been generous in any case.

Moreover, Reagan "had given his word" to Kohl. He may have done so with insufficient preparation or knowledge, but now his "credibility" was involved. Unless there was an overwhelming reason— something the Germans had not told him that he should have known—he would have to take the walk. In the Jewish community, the search for some incriminating evidence had begun, but the quest was hampered by lack of organization and resources. While the television cameras were trained on the graves of SS Panzer grenadiers, feeble attempts were made to learn something about one or the other of these men. Might someone have served in the *Einsatzgruppen* that killed Jews in the east? Could one or the other have participated in razing a French village? Was there a possibility that one of the SS men helped in the shooting of unarmed American prisoners of war? The Germans were annoyed. The cemetery was not a Nazi institution in appearance. It had no swastikas, and the SS designations on the stones were carved in ordinary script, not the ⚡⚡ of Hitler's time. Yet the constant attention lavished on the SS graves at Bitburg was disintegrating the principal point the Kohl regime had been trying to make. How could one de-nazify a cemetery? In the end, an attempt was made to do just that. A great many of the soldiers and SS men in Bitburg had been killed late in 1944 or early in 1945, when German manpower was depleted and many youngsters were appearing at the front. It was consequently not difficult to hand President Reagan the name of one adolescent who had been killed a week before his sixteenth birthday. The president, seizing this datum, repeated it in a speech.[7]

The deepest psychological conflict between the Germans and the Jews had become a contest of public relations in which only simple, visible cues could matter. Few newspapers and fewer television programs could cope with the complexity of the issue. No one approached the question of the German army. Here was a cemetery in which most of the fallen had been soldiers. Was it "contaminated" only because of the relative handful of SS men buried alongside these men? Would the controversy have been prevented altogether if the choice had been a "pure" military burial ground? The Germans had certainly spent years trying to conjure up an image of the Wehrmacht, which was the name of the armed forces during the Third Reich, as a military organization like other armed forces fighting for its homeland. The Wehrmacht, after all, was the successor of the prewar Reichswehr and the precursor of the postwar Bundeswehr. It was a link in a long chain of generations that belong to the same culture and share its traditions. Dismantled in 1945, the German army was reborn in the early 1950s, when the personnel files of World War II German officers, located with captured German document collections in the Federal Records Center at Alexandria, Virginia, were returned to Germany. The new Bundeswehr remembered its old battles and wore its old decorations. The dead of Bitburg are some of its old comrades. But what can be said to contrast Germany's military veterans of the Second World War with the SS?

In truth, the separation of the military from the SS in terms of the soldierly professionalism of the one and the ideological fanaticism of the other has always been strained. The German army played a heavy role in Adolf Hitler's Germany, and it cannot be detached from the Nazi regime, because it was an integral part of it. Americans have not been well informed and the press has not been explicit about such topics as the fate of Soviet prisoners of war in the transit camps (Dulags) and main camps (Stalags) of the German military. By the end of the war, well over two million Red Army men in German army custody were dead of starvation and exposure.[8] By the same token, the general public is not aware of the multiple functions performed by uniformed members of the German armed forces in the destruction of the Jews. The list of these activities is long, as even a brief recapitulation will show:

1. The German army in the east established many Jewish ghettos.
2. The German army gave logistic support to the *Einsatzgruppen*

of Heydrich's Reich Security Main Office. Intelligence units helped locate Jews for shooting.

3. Military governments in Belgium, France, Serbia, and Greece issued anti-Jewish regulations in the economic sphere, including "Aryanizations" of Jewish property and taxes in the form of "fines."

4. Armament officers administered contracts with German firms employing Jewish slave labor. The German army itself made use of such labor in its own installations.

5. Transport officers in France, Greece, Italy, and elsewhere were involved in the dispatch of trains to death camps.

6. German troops stood by to deal with Jewish resistance. An artillery unit fought in the Warsaw ghetto battle. A battalion of security troops was alerted for the suppression of the revolt in the Sobibor death camp. The military was available to frustrate any large-scale breakouts from Auschwitz.

7. The German army transferred Jewish Soviet prisoners of war to the SS to be shot. It engaged in killings of its own, shooting the Jewish men in Serbia and wiping out a population of 10,000 Jews in the Glebokie region of Poland.[9]

That the German military could not be regarded as innocent in its entirety was implicitly recognized from the beginning, when Field Marshal Keitel and Colonel General Jodl were hanged in Nuremberg, and when other German generals stood trial before U.S. military tribunals. The judicial proceedings, however, served also as a purification rite, in that they facilitated the orderly retirement or reemployment of all those professionals who were not indicted. Examples are General Hans von Grävenitz, in charge of prisoners of war, who lived peacefully in Stuttgart after the war; General Fritz Rossum, commander of the military district of Warsaw during the mass deportations in 1942 and the subsequent Warsaw ghetto battle in 1943, who lived in Konstanz; and General Otto Kohl, transport officer in Paris, where he volunteered his services to the SS for the rapid deportation of the French Jews, and postwar resident of Munich. General Max Pemsel, who had been the chief of staff of the military command in Serbia when the Jewish men were shot there by the army, and who was not ready for retirement in 1945, rose to high rank in the new Bundeswehr.[10] If generals could fare this well, what need be said about the much larger numbers of implicated majors and sergeants not listed in any Who's Who?

Hardly anyone in the Federal Republic of Germany had associated the Wehrmacht with the Jewish catastrophe. The emphasis had always been placed on the blamelessness of soldiers, and now this point was reiterated. When Alois Mertes, representative of Bitburg in the Bundestag and minister of state in the Foreign Office, sat next to U.S. Senator Charles Mathias at a conference, he passed him a note, which said in effect: "The Senate resolution on Bitburg should not have ignored German soldiers who were not Nazis—Germans such as Richard von Weizsäcker, Helmut Schmidt, Franz Josef Strauss, Walter Scheel, Alois Mertes."[11]

The German army was not the only reversible symbol at Bitburg. An effort was made to transform the Second World War, to make it look like the First. The strategy was a mirror image of the Mitterand-Kohl meeting at Verdun in 1984, where the French government had substituted the First World War for the Second. The French, of course, had good reasons for centering attention on the older battle-field, if only because there they could console not only Kohl but also themselves. France had suffered five times as many casualties in 1914–18 as in 1939–45, and their dead in the Second World War included Vichy troops who had battled the British in Syria, Alsatians drafted into the German army, and ideological French collaborators in formations fighting on the German side to the bitter end. Bitburg presented more subtle problems. Not only were tripods for television cameras banned, lest an SS grave be glimpsed by viewers, but an air of timelessness was to be introduced, a blending of the wars, a walk across the ages. At the side of an American president in his mid-seventies stood an American general who was even older. During the wordless ceremony, a German bugler played "Ich hatt' einen Kameraden" (I had a comrade), a song that predated the Nazi regime. An American television audience could see nothing wrong in this scene, and Germans could be reminded of an earlier history, the period before 1933, to which no shame was attached, or for which at least no exclusive responsibility had to be taken.[12]

The complexities of history are buried in books and journals. Collective memories are highly selective and often embrace only a partial past in the form of nostalgia. How much time will pass before a future generation in Germany will have difficulty distinguishing between the two wars that occurred twenty years apart in the first half of the century? Did President Reagan already have such a moment of confusion?

At a news conference on March 21, 1985, the president said that "The German people have very few alive that remember even the war, and certainly none that were adults and participating in any way."[13]

He himself had been in his thirties during World War II, yet he pushed the whole war back a couple of decades because of another issue with which he had to deal just before his trip: the seventieth anniversary of the Armenian disaster, in the course of which at least 600,000 Armenian men, women, and children are estimated to have died at the hands of the Ottoman Turks behind the lines of the Turkish-Russian front in the First World War.[14] Armenians have not forgotten this event and periodically they ask others not to forget it. Once, in 1983, President Reagan's reaction to a reminder at a press conference was that, after all, the Ottomans of 1915 were long dead. When the seventieth anniversary was close at hand in the early spring of 1985, he was under strong pressure from the Armenians for official recognition of the disaster, and from the Turkish government for an abstention from such a step. The harried president was now facing two similar crises simultaneously, and, having been told that the Ottoman Turks were genocidal like the German Nazis, he thought of the same argument for the Germans that he had made for the Turks.[15]

In Bitburg there were to be no winners. Even before the visit of the president, Chancellor Kohl was aware of Jewish sensitivity. He cultivated American Jewish organizations[16] and planned an establishment of a remembrance committee composed of German appointees and members of the U.S. Holocaust Memorial Council.[17] But for the Germans, the lesson of the wilting garland from America was not lost. The ceremony had not lifted any burdens, and the past was coming back.[18]

After Bitburg, a number of complaints were heard in the streets of Germany about the power of the American Jews, who had managed to reduce the visit to eight minutes. The Jews of America, however, were perturbed, because the president had gone to the cemetery in the first place. Neither abandoned nor victorious, they had to ask themselves once more whether drawing in was to be preferred to reaching out.

President Reagan lost too. Caught in the middle of a situation his staff had not prepared him for, he confronted a dilemma from which he could not extricate himself. He went with anguish and possible doubts, losing his surefootedness and sacrificing his image as a man who acted out of conviction. During a press conference on June 18, 1985, he was asked whether Bitburg and other reverses were signs that his luck was running out. In his answer, he spoke of Bitburg at length, describing a reward he had received in Germany. It was given to him, he said, when he made a speech before "10,000 young teenage Germans and at the end of that heard 10,000 young Germans sing our National Anthem in our language."[19]

NOTES

1. Carlo Schmid, "Dieser Staat ist ohne Glanz," *Süddeutsche Zeitung*, May 9, 1968.

2. The poll was reported in *Der Spiegel*, April 22, 1985. Chancellor Kohl's rating was +0.6.

3. A portion of the Nuremberg judgment is included in the "Documents" section of this book.

4. Text of news conference held on March 21, 1985, *New York Times*, March 22, 1985.

5. "Responses of the President to Queries on German Visit," *New York Times*, April 19, 1985.

6. *Newsweek*, May 6, 1985. The vote was 398 to 24.

7. Transcript of the president's speech of May 5, 1985, *New York Times*, May 6, 1985.

8. On the treatment of Soviet prisoners of war, see Christian F. Streit, *Keine Kameraden* (Stuttgart: Deutsche Verlags-Anstalt, 1978). In a speech at Bergen-Belsen on April 21, 1985, Chancellor Kohl mentioned the dead Soviet prisoners, but without any reference to the German army. Text of address in German Information Center, *Statements and Speeches*, vol. VII, no. 11, April 22, 1985.

9. See Raul Hilberg, *The Destruction of the European Jews*, rev. ed., 3 vols. (Holmes & Meier, 1985).

10. See the list of World War II German generals, with ranks, commands, and cities of postwar residence, in the loose-leaf edition of Wolf Keilig's *Das Deutsche Heer 1939–1945* (Bad Neuheim, Podzun, 1956–60).

11. Statement by Senator Charles Mathias, *Congressional Record*, 99th Cong., 1st sess., June 20, 1985, p. S. 8485. Mertes and Mathias were seated alphabetically at the conference. The entry in the *Congressional Record*, made after the death of Mertes, was appended to German Information Center, *Statements and Speeches*, vol. VII, no. 21, July 1, 1985.

12. In fact, the legacy of the old days was not devoid of problems. The most controversial book in postwar Germany was not any treatment of the Nazi regime, but a heavy monograph about World War I: Fritz Fischer's *Der Griff nach der Weltmacht* (The grab for world power), translated into English and published in America under the more sedate title *Germany's Aims in the First World War* (New York: Norton, 1967). Fischer discovered records of the German Foreign Office of 1914, showing some German eagerness for war at that time. The Weimar period is similarily problematical. In 1922, Chancellor Josef Wirth summarized his "eastern program" in a conversation with Count Brockdorff-Rantzau, saying "Poland has to be finished off." Herbert Helbig, *Die Träger der Rapallo-Politik* (Göttingen: Vandenhoeck & Ruprecht, 1958), pp. 118–20. Gordon H. Mueller, "Rapallo Reexamined: A New Look at Germany's Military Collaboration with Russia in 1922," *Military Affairs*, October 1976, pp. 109–17. Rapallo was in several respects a precursor of the secret German-Soviet protocol of August 1939.

13. Text of news conference, *New York Times*, March 22, 1985.

14. [Arnold Josef Toynbee, ed.], *The Treatment of Armenians in the Ottoman Empire 1915–16, Documents Presented to Viscount Grey of Falladon, Secretary of State for Foreign Affairs: by Viscount Bryce* (London: H.M. Stationery Office, 1916), particularly pp. 664–66.

15. When the president was asked at a news conference with specialized press on October 18, 1983, whether the American government had a stand on the Turkish genocide of Armenians, he said: "I can't help but believe that there' s virtually no one alive today who was living in the era of that terrible trouble." The White House/Office of Media Relations and Planning, press release of October 18, 1983. The Armenian remembrance day is April 24, and in April 1985 the Congress considered a resolution to recognize the Armenian disaster. The resolution was opposed by the executive branch, and the efforts of Republican Governor George Doukmejian of California to change the president's mind were unsuccessful. William Endicott, "Doukmejian Pleads for Reagan Change of Heart on Armenians," *Los Angeles Times*, April 24, 1985. Richard Paddock, "Ignore Turks' Pressure on Genocide, Doukmejian Asks," *Los Angeles Times*, April 28, 1985. Barry Zorthian of the Armenian Assembly of America declared: "This is another Bitburg." Eduardo Lachica, "Reagan Opposition to Armenian Bill Starts a Second Genocide Controversy," *Wall Street Journal*, April 29, 1985. A diplomat in the Turkish embassy offered the opinion that "This effort to align themselves with American Jewry is sheer opportunism by the Armenians." Megan Rosenfeld, " 'The Forgotten Survivors': Armenians Commemorate the 1915 Killings with their First National Gathering," *Washington Post*, April 27, 1985.

16. See the speech by Mertes before the American Jewish Committee, May 2, 1985, *Statements and Speeches*, vol. VII, no. 14, May 2, 1985, and the speech by German Ambassador Günther van Well before Board of Governors, B'nai B'rith International, May 21, 1985, ibid., no. 18, May 21, 1985.

17. See the *New York Times*, June 25, 1985.

18. Domestic speeches were made almost daily, often enough with refined evasions or problematical acknowledgments of the burdensome past. Federal President Richard von Weizsäcker addressed the Bundestag on May 8, 1985, making the following points: The genocide of the Jews was "in the hands of a few people." It was concealed from the public, but no German could have been unsuspecting of Jewish suffering for long. "Whoever opened his eyes and ears and sought information could not fail to notice that Jews were being deported." Too many people, he said, did not ask. Text in *Statements and Speeches*, vol. VII, no. 16, May 9, 1985. Richard von Weizsäcker's own father was the second highest official in the Foreign Office when European-wide deportations began. After the war, the elder Weizsäcker was tried before a U.S. military tribunal and sentenced to prison for having signed crucial papers paving the way for the transport of Jews from France to Auschwitz. During the trial, Richard found "a good word" to say for his father, and assisted the defense team in the formulation of a legal argument to absolve the old diplomat of guilt in the destruction of the Jews. See Leonidas E. Hill, ed., *Die Weizsäcker-Papiere 1933–1950* (Frankfurt/M: Ullstein, and Vienna: Propyläen, 1974), pp. 421, 446–49, 452. The *Papiere* are Ernst von Weizsäcker's diary.

19. Text of the president's news conference, *New York Times*, June 19, 1985.

> What is past is not dead; it is not
> even past. We cut ourselves off from
> it; we pretend to be strangers.
>
> —CHRISTA WOLF, *A Model Childhood*

Saul Friedländer

Some German Struggles with Memory

Minor events may take on a major symbolic significance: such was the "Bitburg affair."

Bitburg came to symbolize all the dilemmas of forgetting and remembering, for Germany and its victims, for the victorious allies and the vanquished enemy, for those who lived through the war and those born after 1945: the second generation and, by now, the third. For Germans and Jews, more than anybody else.

This short piece will deal with West Germany only,* and trace *some* of its struggles with memory.

In a 1983 issue of the German periodical *Aesthetik und Kommunikation*, entitled "Germans, Leftists, Jews," one of the editors, Eberhard Knödler-Bunte, wrote: "What moved me [to write a 'confession'] is the impotent but decisive desire to break out of the entanglement of guilt . . . and the knowledge that it won't work."[1] These lines poignantly express what for some Germans seems to be an intractable predicament: the Nazi past is too massive to be forgotten, and too repellent to be integrated into the "normal" narrative of memory. For the last forty years, Germans belonging to at least two generations have been caught between the impossibility of remembering and the impossibility of forgetting.

---

* The identification of "fascism" (Nazism in Marxist terminology) with capitalism allowed the East German regime to find an easy way of shifting the burden of the past onto the Federal Republic. This strategy worked only up to a point, and some of the most forceful reminders of that past come from East Germany, from the late sixties on: the voices of Christa Wolf, Jurek Becker, Heiner Mueller, and others. But the East German scene would call for an analysis by itself, which we cannot undertake here.

There may be different ideas about what should be remembered or forgotten. It seems to me that three elements of that past clearly dominate the landscape of memory: the nature of the crimes committed; the methods used to perpetrate those crimes; the growing awareness among the Germans of that time of the criminal nature of the Nazi regime together with the fact that the majority of the population supported it into the very last months. May 8, 1945, was not the toppling of a tyranny but the defeat of a nation that fought to the bitter end.

This last point, often unmentioned, may well constitute the heart of the matter, as far as May 8 and Bitburg are concerned. Heinrich Böll clearly perceived it when he wrote: "The fact that Nazi power was not overthrown from within but had to be broken from without . . . is one of the reasons that could explain why these twelve years [of the Nazi Reich] are more or less erased from memory."[2] In this short essay, I shall very briefly outline some of the general aspects of the German struggle with memory, and suggest that, up to now at least, the predicament does not seem resolved yet.

The main part of my essay will be devoted to an analysis of four significant statements made during the first months of 1985. They illustrate forcefully some present-day attitudes toward the past. Finally, I shall also venture a few remarks about wider aspects of the contemporary German scene, not unrelated to our central issue.

I do not wish, however, to give the impression that the Nazi past remains a problem for the majority of present-day Germans. It does not. Sometimes the ignorance of the young about the Hitler years, revealed, for instance, in the famous Bossman inquiry of 1977,[3] appears almost incredible. Yet, for a part of the population, if only a small one, this past is an unresolved matter, an unsettled issue. Were it entirely irrelevant, Cardinal Joseph Höffner, in his sermon of May 8 at the Cologne cathedral, would not have felt the need to declare: "We should not, again and again, exhume past guilt and mutually committed injustices, in constant self-torment."[4]

Because of its limited scope, this essay should simply be considered as a general attempt to show Bitburg's significance within a wider cultural setting.[5]

1

From the "Zero Hour" of defeat, part of the German intellectual elite began its struggle with the immediate past. But the bulk of the population, during the "Trümmerzeit" (the "time of ruins"), and through the economic miracle and beyond, appeared unable to explore the Nazi past in any significant way. Günter Grass invents a nightclub in *The Tin Drum* where people need onion-cutting ceremonies to help them shed a few tears . . .

For the majority, official expressions of repentance and initiatives of reparation seemed to be a sufficient if ritual *Ersatz* for memory.[6] A famous psychoanalytic study has spoken of "the inability to mourn."[7] But silence as the result of a tacit agreement, in a society where within families and even larger groups most members knew about the collaboration of other members, seems a sufficient explanation of this kind of paralysis.[8]

This voluntary silence, useful as it may have been for the reconstruction of German society, became a major target of the rebellion of the "sons" during the sixties, which lasted well into the seventies. Accusations leveled against the parents, especially for their silence, were possibly compounded by the delayed effects of the Eichmann trial of 1961 and the Auschwitz trial a few years later. The convergence of this specifically German unrest with other student protests in the West undoubtedly sharpened the desire of younger intellectuals to discover the truth about a Nazism they identified with the generation of their parents.

However, this "rebellion" also created fresh mythologies and displacements and established new barriers between the second generation and the crimes of National Socialism. By considering the Bundesrepublik as a camouflaged continuation of the social structures that made Nazism possible, by considering the new German political system as a basically unchanged and continuous fascist phenomenon—and basic social structures were indeed unchanged, so that many ex-Nazis found rewarding positions within the new democratic system—by overgeneralizing, in fact, the concept of fascism, the "rebels" lost their ability to perceive essential differences between present and past. Later on, by shifting their moral outrage from their parents' deeds to America's policies in Vietnam or Israel's policies vis-à-vis the Palestinians, a sizable proportion of the young intellectual Left found itself as effectively immunized against any confrontation with Nazism as the smug old bourgeois Philistines had been, whom they so vehemently attacked.[9]

This, however, is only part of the picture as it unfolds in the sixties and seventies. For, in present-day society, collective memory is very intimately linked to the writing of history.

German historiography of the late forties and fifties had been uneasy about Nazism. Not that Nazism wasn't considered as a *German Catastrophe* (to quote the title of a book by the grand old man among

German historians, Friedrich Meinecke) with roots in the national past. But, somehow, the worst crimes of Nazism—in particular, the extermination of the Jews—were left untouched. In the case of Gerhard Ritter, almost the entire national past itself was exempted, because for Ritter Nazism was a kind of accident, the origins of which could be found, at the earliest, in 1933.[10]

Much changed toward the close of the fifties with K. D. Bracher's work on *The End of the Weimar Republic*: a new generation of German historians entered the field, and approaches came to the fore that put greater emphasis on the sociostructural conditions of the rise of Nazism, on the role of bureaucracy, and on the interplay of various internal factors that gave the movement its dynamics. Most of the major aspects of Nazi ideology and policies of the regime were soon well researched. The anti-Jewish policies of the Nazis were also dealt with either within wider studies (the Buchheim/Krausnick volume on *The Anatomy of the SS State* being the best example) or in important monographs. This particular subject, however, found its best historians in other countries.[11]

Some other "difficult" topics, such as the criminal activities of the Wehrmacht itself, mostly in relation to Russian prisoners, had to wait for the late seventies (see, e. g., Christian F. Streit, *Keine Kameraden*). Even the soothing aspects of life in the Third Reich (the normality of daily life for the average German; the "Resistenz," that is, the passive noncommitment of many citizens in the face of the regime; the devious yet identifiable continuation of scientific activities within all disciplines, even psychiatry or sociology) did not receive close attention till that time.

Today the image of the Nazi era presented by German and foreign historians, in becoming so diversified and complex, is perhaps somewhat blurred: the sheer multitude of specialized studies on the minutest aspects of this epoch tends to erase the sharp outlines of certain central issues, be they conceptual or ethical. Therefore, whether one wishes it or not, the very momentum of historiography may serve to neutralize the past.

Literature too plays a role in forming the collective memory. Its confrontation with Nazism started with the defeat (and even before, in exile). In Germany, it should have started—yet did not—during the Nazi period itself, not publicly of course, but secretively. Walter Jens once made the remark that very little "drawer literature" was written during the Nazi period.[12] This is not a minor point but a telling symptom of one of the core problems mentioned at the beginning of this essay: the adhesion to, or at least passive acquiescence in, the regime by the vast majority of Germans, including part of the intellectual elite.

Literary confrontations with the past reached a high point between the end of the fifties and the beginning of the seventies: the names of Heinrich Böll, Alfred Andersch, Alexander Kluge, Martin Walser, Günter Grass, Siegfried Lenz, and Uwe Johnson are well known, as are those of Rolf Hochhuth and Peter Weiss.[13] Despite an obvious desire on the part of these authors to face up to the past, the results reflect the same difficulty that all literature and art—German or non-German—has encountered when trying to deal with Nazism. In fact, some of the best literary works of that period, such as Günter Grass's "Danzig Trilogy" (*The Tin Drum, Cat and Mouse, Dog Years*), are impressive because of outstanding literary qualities that have little to do with the handling of the Nazi past.

The difficulties may well be insuperable. As Theodor Adorno, among others, suggested many years ago, literature may be unable to deal with a phenomenon like Hitler's Germany.[14] If we stay in the realm of the novel or drama, for instance, the massive use of authentic documentary material (as in Alexander Kluge's or Peter Weiss's works) has its limits, while mere fictionalization can often be unconvincing. This literature faces problems of aestheticization or the need for an indirect approach that may be symbolically meaningful yet produces a soothing effect. Sometimes minor incidents set against the background of a quietly unfolding provincial life are all that remain of a terror-laden era, as in Siegfried Lenz's *Deutschstunde* (*The German Lesson*). The low-key approach to the past in Lenz's novel could explain its immense popular success. Such an image of the past was acceptable.

Triggered by the Speer Memoirs, the notorious "Hitler Wave" of the seventies, with its series of best-selling Hitler biographies (from Werner Maser's to Joachim Fest's), may have signified, at the level of popular reception, more an ambiguous attraction and possible nostalgia than a true desire to remember and to come to terms with the past. So too the "New German Cinema," one of the most creative developments on the West German cultural scene, has avoided any major confrontation with the Nazi past. Four exceptions come to mind: Peter Lilienthal's *David*, which may be a real exception; Volker Schlöndorff's *Tin Drum* (of which one could say what was just said of its source, Günter Grass's novel), Rainer Werner Fassbinder's *Lili Marleen*, and Hans Jürgen Syberberg's *Hitler, a Film from Germany*. These last two movies clearly demonstrate what to my mind is a general "Western" way of recapturing the Nazi past. They use all the devices offered by the screen to juxtapose Kitsch sentimentality, grand opera effects, and apocalyptic visions of ultimate destruction. This may be a good mode of showing some of the fascination of Nazism, but it is not an unambiguous one.[15]

Some of the most successful documentary films about Nazism, like Joachim Fest's *Hitler, eine Karriere*, were highly selective in the themes they dealt with. Neither Alain Resnais's *Night and Fog* nor Erwin Leiser's *Mein Kampf* nor Claude Lanzmann's *Shoah* came from Germany. Nor for that matter did "Holocaust," but that may be all to the good.[16]

The telecasting in 1979 of "Holocaust" was considered by many, owing to the massive numbers of viewers it attracted in the Federal Republic and the strong emotional responses it evoked, a turning point in Germany's confrontation with Nazi crimes.[17] Such shock-like confrontations, however, seem to have become, for the majority of the population, a set mechanism, which began with the performance of the Anne Frank story in theaters throughout the Bundesrepublik during the late fifties, continued with the trials of the sixties, and found its most dramatic expression in the "Holocaust" series. This same confrontation repeated itself in a somewhat different form during the commemorations of 1983 and 1985. These "crises" attest to a constant seesaw between learning and forgetting, between becoming briefly aware of the past and turning one's back on it. A near automatic process.

In short, regularly retrieved, then forgotten once more by the vast majority of Germans, the Nazi past seems only partly confronted at the elite level. Four exemplary 1985 texts will throw more light on these struggles with memory.

2

During the first months of 1985, the following major figures, among many others, took different stands on the commemoration of the fortieth anniversary of Germany's defeat: President Richard von Weizsäcker; veteran liberal historian Golo Mann; Rudolph Augstein, editor-in-chief of *Der Spiegel*; and Cologne Cardinal Joseph Höffner.

Their attitudes do not represent the whole range of present-day German positions concerning the past. But the divergences they show seem to me to offer significant indications about major contemporary (and possibly unchanging) strategies of the struggle with memory. The starting point of our analysis will be the same for all four: the necessity or the needlessness of commemorating the fortieth anniversary of Germany's surrender.

In his Bundestag speech of May 8, 1985, President von Weizsäcker was unambiguous about the necessity for this commemoration: "The 8th of May was a day of liberation. It liberated all of us from the inhumanity and tyranny of the National Socialist regime. . . . there is every reason for us to perceive May 8, 1945, as the end of an aberration in German history, an end bringing seeds of hope for a better future."[18]

Cardinal Höffner too commended the eighth of May commemoration, reminding his listeners of Moses' words to his people, after forty years in the desert (Deut. 32:7): "Think of the days of the past, learn from the past."[19]

Not so Golo Mann.* In an article published in the German newspaper *Die Zeit*, under the title "Commemorations That Reopen Wounds," he declared that such observances were not only superfluous but downright harmful:

> In my opinion, it would have been better if [8 May] had remained unmentioned in Germany. . . . The word-churning machines . . . need material, including historical material, and the historian cannot object to this. But it would be better if one searched in a more distant and harmless past for the color and experience it can offer, instead of opening old wounds and quarreling about guilt and blamelessness, right and wrong, good and bad, concerning events that occurred fifty years ago.[20]

As for Rudolph Augstein, his massive article published in the weekly magazine *Der Spiegel* at the very beginning of 1985 expressed an attitude toward the forthcoming commemorations that was not only negative but indeed sarcastic. "Only a fool," wrote Augstein, "could have thought of celebrating the liberation from the Nazi terror [Die Befreiung vom Naziterror zu feiern, das kann nur einem Tölpel eingefallen sein]. We did not liberate ourselves, and a considerable part of Europe has not been liberated at all." Augstein's article ends with the following words: "Let them celebrate because they won the war. We can just watch and need not participate, as was the case in Normandy."[21]

The arguments developed in these four tests show even deeper cleavages. Richard von Weizsäcker does not avoid a detailed enumeration of Nazi crimes, and he stresses, with great sincerity and courage, the central place of the destruction of the Jewish people in Nazi ideology and practice. For the Western reader and certainly for the Jewish reader, Weizsäcker's address is an exemplary admission of the utter criminality of the Nazi state.

---

*Golo Mann, a son of Thomas Mann, is a well-known historian whose *History of Germany in the Nineteenth and Twentieth Century* is a best seller. Ideologically, Golo Mann could be identified as a conservative.

The problem of knowledge and passive acquiescence is also mentioned with as much openness as is possible. The words: "The 8th of May . . . liberated *all of us* from the . . . tyranny of the National Socialist regime" (italics added) could give the impression that a clear distinction was being established between the regime and the population, but the crucial lines come later on. In relation to the fate of the Jews, von Weizsäcker declares:

> The perpetration of the crime was in the hands of a few people, . . . but . . . who could remain unsuspecting after the burning of the synagogues, the plundering, the stigmatization with the Star of David, the deprivation of rights, the ceaseless violation of human dignity? Whoever opened his eyes and ears and sought information could not fail to notice that Jews were being deported. . . . When the unspeakable truth of the holocaust then became known at the end of the war, all too many of us claimed that they had not known anything about it or even suspected anything.

There is no evasion here, either of the crimes, or of the partial knowledge, or, by implication, of the passivity of most Germans. The position taken by the Cardinal of Cologne is somewhat different.

Joseph Höffner, too, enumerates Nazi crimes in the very first part of his sermon. He presents the evolution of events in the following sequence: the crimes were committed because the true values of religion were abandoned; many Catholics kept themselves away from the Nazi idolatry, but some were led astray; many Germans became criminals, "also from our ranks."

Up to that point, the development of Höffner's arguments aims at confrontation with the past, although the general thrust of the text is that among the Germans who were led astray, some Catholics were led astray too, and became criminals. The problem of passive acquiescence of the vast majority is omitted.

Then, however, comes what seems to me to be the most significant difference between von Weizsäcker's and Höffner's positions. Both President von Weizsäcker and Cardinal Höffner use the symbolism of the forty-year period in the desert, of forty years as a turning point. But the president of the Federal Republic declares: "In our country a new generation has grown up to assume political responsibility. Our young people are not responsible for what happened over forty years ago. But they are responsible for the historical consequences." And the president ends his address with the words: "On this 8th of May, let us face up as well as we can to the truth."

Von Weizsäcker's attitude is resolutely open-ended as far as the facing of the past is concerned. Cardinal Höffner declares, in a way, "Enough." He leaves National Socialism behind in the midst of his sermon, resolutely turning toward the present and the future. His section on the Nazi past ends with the words already partially quoted at the beginning of this essay. They read in full: "We should not, again and again, exhume past guilt and mutually committed injustices, in constant self-torment. We should not constantly weigh guilt against guilt and use it as a weapon, one against the other. All guilt is abolished in the mercy of Jesus Christ, who taught us the prayer: 'Forgive us our sins, as we forgive those who sin against us.'" The line dividing the present and the future from the past is drawn as clearly as can be.

The short essay by Golo Mann and the much longer one by Rudolf Augstein are historical-political analyses of the significance of the eighth of May, not commemorative addresses. Their aim and emphasis are obviously different from those of the two previous texts. Nevertheless, the theme of the problematic past appears clearly enough. (It should be added, to avoid any misunderstanding, that Golo Mann, as historian, and Rudolf Augstein, as editor-in-chief of *Der Spiegel*, have, over the decades, helped to question the Nazi past and so to keep it in mind. *Der Spiegel* was, possibly with *Die Zeit*, the most influential large-circulation publication that fostered whatever wider awareness there may be in Germany of the significance of the Nazi era.)

Golo Mann's article starts with a comparison between the defeat of Nazi Germany and that of Napoleonic France. Would anybody in France have had the idea of commemorating Waterloo thirty or forty years later? Indeed, Golo Mann does not avoid pointing out, later in his essay, the intrinsic difference between Napoleonic France and Hitler's Germany, owing to the criminality of the Hitler regime. But within his rather lengthy historical comparison, this specific aspect takes only one short paragraph. Moreover, in that paragraph, one is reminded that the destruction afflicted by the Nazis on the peoples of the East was also meant by them to be meted out on their own people, as defeat approached. The suffering and massive losses among German populations expelled from the East, as well as the harsh conditions imposed on Germany by the victorious Allies take a prominent place in a demonstration that, nonetheless, calls for a definitive recognition of the borders with Poland as they presently exist and for further economic and political development of a European entity.

Golo Mann's article ends by asking whether we should continue to commemorate the anniversaries of various Nazi misdeeds or—as in the passage quoted earlier—whether it would not be better to look to a more distant past for inspiration and wisdom. I shall come back to Golo Mann's article after presenting Rudolf Augstein's arguments, since both texts seem to me related.

In the Augstein article the whole of the Nazi period becomes almost irrelevant. What had to be destroyed by the coalition that finally formed against Germany during the war was less the *Hitler* than the *Bismarck* Reich, a kind of monstrous, self-prolonging entity. It had survived the defeat of World War I and had ultimately to be broken. Thus, argues Augstein, World War II would have come about anyway, Hitler or no Hitler. Augstein's perspective is reminiscent of Geoffrey Barraclough's articles of 1972 in the *New York Review of Books*, directed against the liberal view of German history, with its emphasis on the specificity of the period between 1933 and 1945.[22]

But one fact remained to be explained: the Nazi atrocities in their monstrousness. Augstein writes: "Whether the anti-Hitler allies committed fewer crimes than Hitler is not at all certain. The one who initiated such crimes against humanity was, in any case, Stalin, in 1928. Hitler's crimes were not directed so much against his own compatriots as against foreign countries and against the numerically much stronger foreign Jews; within the Reich there were only 500,000 of them."[23]

Augstein devotes an important part of his article to Roosevelt's Jewish secretary of the treasury, Henry Morgenthau. He describes Morgenthau's plans to subjugate a defeated Germany and decides that Hitler missed in him a good follower ("Offensichtlich hatte der Führer hier einen guten Gefolgsmann verpasst").[24] A footnote informs us that in 1941, "when nobody knew anything yet about Hitler's gas chambers," Theodore Nathan Kaufman, the president of the American Peace Society, advocated the general sterilization of the German population in order to bring about its disappearance. And Augstein, like Golo Mann, does not fail to emphasize the terror and massive death that accompanied the expulsion of the Germans from the Eastern territories after the war.

In short, the image one receives from Augstein's article is the following: (a) World War II had little to do with Hitler and was the necessary outcome of Bismarck's creation of an excessively powerful German Reich; (b) the Nazi crimes were not specific to the Nazis and were probably equalled by those committed by the Allies, mostly the Russians; (c) Jews, always considered the prime and quintessential victims of the Nazi regime, had some criminal ideas of their own about the fate to be meted out to the defeated Germans—indeed, one may wonder whether there was any real difference, at least on the level of intention, between Hitler on the one hand and Morgenthau, Kaufman, and company on the other.

I don't think that the Morgenthau-Kaufman argument was meant to be an essential point per se in the Augstein demonstration. What Rudolf Augstein wanted to stress, and so did Golo Mann, was the *nonspecificity of the Hitler era and of the Third Reich*. The comparison with Napoleonic France in Golo Mann's text, the prime importance given to the Bismarck Reich in Augstein's piece, the equivalence of suffering, crimes, and criminal ideas on all sides, create an overall picture in which the Nazi past can hardly claim a unique place. It is placed within a catalogue of other unpalatable phenomena of modern history. If we remember that both Golo Mann and Rudolf Augstein responded negatively to the idea of commemorating May 8, if we add to it Cardinal Höffner's plea for putting an end to broodings on past guilt, if we take note of the fact that in these three texts the problem of passive acquiescence does not even appear, we reach the conclusion that President Richard von Weizsäcker's attitude toward the past is a far from common or typical one, even at the elite level.

An indirect confirmation of this impression could be found in the law voted by the Bundestag on June 13, 1985 (after considerable discussions and delays and only after the addition of the words we shall quote). It makes an offense of the denial that persecution was suffered "at the hands of the Nazi regime, *or at the hands of another system of violent and arbitrary domination* [einer anderen Gewalt und Willkürherrschaft]" (italics added). Meant here, obviously, is the persecution suffered by the Jews, but also that suffered by the Germans in the East during the expulsions of the postwar period. This balancing act is the legal equivalent of the comparison between crimes committed by the Nazis and those inflicted on the Germans by the Allies (especially the Russians). Helmut Kohl's Bitburg initiative must be understood within this general context.

3

During the spring of 1985, a five-part television series, "The War of the Bombers," showed the systematic destruction of undefended cities by the Allied air force, with the firebombing of Dresden as a "fearful finale." The message conveyed was, again, that the Allies, like the Nazis, blindly destroyed defenseless civilian populations.

According to a poll taken by *Infas* (a West German polling organization) immediately after the airing of "The War of the Bombers," "fifty-four percent of those questioned were weary of television and newspaper documentaries about Nazis and World War II and felt any more would be superfluous." Yet according to James Markham, who reports these statistics, the poll also indicates that "sixty-one percent of those younger than 25 said they wanted to know more about the Nazi era."[25]

If the 1985 poll is correct, it illustrates the repetition of a phenomenon already apparent in the sixties: each German generation since the end of the war feels at some point a weariness regarding the Nazi past. The positions taken by Cardinal Höffner, by Golo Mann, or by Rudolf Augstein may well be signs of that weariness, or even of the impatience of many Germans belonging to the first and second generations. The question remains, however, if, by a kind of automatic process, the generation of the "grandsons," those who want to know more according to the Infas poll, will not prod the "sons" to uncover the truth about the "fathers," as in Ruth Rehmann's autobiographical quest, *Der Mann auf der Kanzel* (The man on the pulpit).[26]

In fact, the situation is far more complex than I have sketched. The weariness of the first and second generations may be apparent. Yet only in these generations is the confrontation with the past, the constant "return of the repressed," most intense and moving. To Ruth Rehmann's novel I could add a whole series of recently published autobiographies by second-generation writers like Peter Härtling, Christoph Meckel, and Sigfrid Gauch, all attempting to explore the deeds of their fathers. There is authenticity and strength in this kind of literature. Moreover, the sheer number of books annually published about the period we are dealing with, the constant flow of articles, the television programs, the scientific meetings and public discussions, show that whatever repression or reelaboration there may be, the weight of the Nazi era on the contemporary German imagination remains massive, within the limits mentioned.[27]

Many more questions arise that can only be alluded to here. What is the meaning of the quest for a new "national identity," so strongly expressed on the Left over the last few years? How should one interpret the renewed love for the soil, the village, the provincial life, not only as such, but within a sort of rediscovery of the "homeland" at its most basic level?[28] The extraordinary success of the television series "Heimat" ("Homeland") confirmed some of those longings. This fifteen-hour series tells the story of several generations living in the small village of Schabach, in the Hunsrück. It touches upon the Nazi era, to be sure, but lets it go by with a few hints of faraway terror, which casts but a fleeting shadow on the quiet flow of everyday life.[29]

Are not these themes linked to the rise of a new longing for the mystical and archaic? Myth is back. In an interview granted to *Der Spiegel* in 1983, the East German playwright Heiner Müller quipped that "Germany was still playing the Nibelungen."[30] One may speak of a spreading neo-romanticism, among painters too (Anselm Kiefer). All this has little direct political significance; but how does it impinge on the process of memory, on the elaboration of the past we are dealing with here? It is too early to say.

The extermination of the Jews is at the very core of the German struggles with memory: it was the ultimate in Nazi criminality and remains its fundamental expression. In formal reflections on the past, this theme, even when unmentioned, is never far from the surface; during the autumn of 1985 it reappeared with intensity as the result of a decision taken by the director of the Frankfurt City Theater to stage Rainer Werner Fassbinder's play *Trash, City and Death*.[31]

The offensive figure of "the rich Jew" dominates the play and (in the play) a postwar city: its shadiest deals, its shadiest morals, its shadiest politics. For some the play brings back all the demons of the past; for others, the past is distant enough to make possible the negative portrayal of a Jew.

On the opening night, October 31, 1985, the play was stopped by demonstrations; later on, it was decided that the play would not be performed. The controversy has reopened some wounds that will not be easily healed.

In 1968 the writer Horst Krüger was wondering if the Nazi era was still a matter of interest.[32] Here we are, almost twenty years later, at the end of 1985, after Bitburg, after President von Weizsäcker's speech of May 8, with Rainer Werner Fassbinder's play . . . Coming to terms with the past does not mean forgetting it; on the contrary. Could it be that in present-day Germany, the inability to come to terms with the Nazi past stems from the inability of really remembering it?

NOTES

1. Eberhard Knödler-Bunte, "Verlängerung des Schweigens," *Aesthetik und Kommunikation* 51 (June 1983): 37. Knödler-Bunte's text created considerable controversy. For this whole problem, see Eike Geisel, "Deutsche, Linke, Juden. Familienzusammenführung," *Die Tageszeitung*, 7 July 1983; *Aesthetik und Kommunikation* 52 & 53 (September and December 1983). See in particular Jessica Benjamin and Anson Rabinbach, "Germans, Leftists, Jews," *New German Critique* 31 (Winter 1984).

2. Heinrich Böll, "Enfance exemplaire," *Les Temps Modernes* 396–97 (July/August 1979): 241.

3. Dieter Bossmann, *Was ich über Adolf Hitler gehört habe* (Frankfurt, 1977). Here are some answers about what Hitler did to the Jews: "Those who

were against him, he called Nazis; he put the Nazis into gas chambers" (thir-teen-year-old); "I think he also killed some Jews" (thirteen-year-old); "He murdered some 50,000 Jews" (fifteen-year-old); "Hitler was himself a Jew" (sixteen-year-old), etc.

4. "Sermon of Cardinal Joseph Höffner at the Ecumenical Service in the Köln Cathedral, 8 May 1985, broadcast by West German Radio WDR [Ansprache des Kardinals Joseph Höffner im Oekumenischen Gottesdienst im Dom zu Koeln am 8. Mai 1985, Westdeutscher Rundfunk]."

5. In this essay, I avoid referring to the results of public opinion polls on attitudes towards the Nazi past, as I don't believe that "the discourse of memory" can be investigated with such methods. However, for those inter-ested in the fluctuations of German public opinion concerning Nazism as expressed in polls, see Institut für Demoskopie, Allensbach, *Demokratie-Ver-ankerung in der Bundesrepublik Deutschland. Eine empirische Untersuchung zum 30-jährigen Bestehen der Bundesrepublik* (Allensbach, 1980).

6. The official expressions of repentance were not always well received, even in 1945. The October 1945 Stuttgart "Declaration of Guilt" of the Evan-gelical Church, for instance, aroused considerable opposition within the ranks of the church itself.

At the level of official publications, schoolbooks etc., there seems to be a clear difference between the intense preoccupation with Nazism from 1946 to the early fifties, and the growing repression of the past during the fifties and early sixties. Helmut Dubiel and Günther Frankenberg, "Entsorgung der Vergangenheit," *Die Zeit*, 18 March 1983.

7. This is the title of a famous study by two German psychoanalysts attempting to explain the paralysis in terms of depth-psychology: Alexander and Margarete Mitscherlich, *Die Unfähigkeit zu trauern*, 1967.

8. This sociological argument was presented by Hermann Lübbe (who, all in all, considers this development in a positive way): Hermann Lübbe, "Es ist nichts vergessen, aber einiges ausgeheilt," *Frankfurter Allgemeine Zeitung*, 24 January 1983. For a sharp answer to Lübbe, see Dubiel and Frankenberg (note 6 above), as well as Hans-Ulrich Wehler, "30. Januar 1933—Ein halbes Jahrhundert danach" in "Aus Politik und Zeitgeschichte—Beilage zu *Das Par-lament*," no. 415, 1983.

9. Part of the German Left became aware of these displacements and camouflages during the early eighties. Some of the discussions were started in *New German Critique* in 1980 and 1981 and then were pursued more fully with the publication of the 1983 issues of *Aesthetik und Kommunikation* (note 1 above).

10. The literature on German historiography concerning National So-cialism is immense. For good general surveys, see Pierre Ayçoberry, *La Ques-tion Nazie. Les Interprétations du National-Socialisme 1922–1975* (Paris, 1979); Klaus Hildebrand, *Das Dritte Reich* (Munich, 1979); Wolfgang J. Mommsen, "Gegenwärtige Tendenzen in der Geschichtsschreibung der Bundesrepublik," *Geschichte und Gesellschaft* 8 (1981). For the historiography more directly related to the extermination of the Jews, see Otto Dov Kulka, "Die Deutsche Geschichtsschreibung über den Nationalsozialismus und die 'Endlösung'; Tendenzen und Entwicklungsphasen 1924–1984," *Historische Zeitschrift* 239 (December 1984); Saul Friedländer, "From Antisemitism to Extermination: A Historiographical Study of Nazi Policies towards the Jews and an Essay in Interpretation," *Yad Vashem Studies* XVI (Jerusalem, 1984).

11. Leon Poliakov, in France; Gerald Reitlinger, in Great Britain; Raul Hilberg and Lucy Dawidowicz, in the United States. It was only in 1983 that a historical congress dealing specifically with the Nazi decision to exterminate the Jews was held in Stuttgart. The papers and discussions are published in Eberhard Jäckel und Jürgen Rohwer, eds., *Der Mord an den Juden im Zweiten Weltkrieg* (Stuttgart, 1985).

12. Walter Jens, "Deutsche Literatur seit Kriegsende," *Zwanzig. Jahrbuch. Freie Akademie der Kuenste in Hamburg,* 1968, p. 211. We know of a good number of extremely impressive clandestine diaries, such as those of Ulrich von Hassell or of Friedrich Reck-Maleczewen, but few of their authors were writers. One could mention Gottfried Benn as one of the exceptions; that, in itself, would be problematic . . .

13. Among the studies on National Socialism in German literature, see André Reszler, *Le National-Socialisme dans le Roman allemand contemporain (1933–1958)* (Lausanne, 1966); Franz Futterknecht, *Das Dritte Reich im deutschen Roman der Nachkriegszeit* (Bonn, 1976); Hamida Bosmajian, *Metaphors of Evil: Contemporary German Literature and the Shadow of Nazism* (Iowa City, 1979), as well as countless articles.

14. Theodor W. Adorno, "Kulturkritik und Gesellschaft," in *Soziologische Forschung in unsere Zeit* (Munich, 1951), translated as "Cultural Criticism and Society," in Samuel and Shierry Weber, trans., *Prisms* (Cambridge, Mass., 1981), pp. 17–34; Reinhard Baumgart, "Unmenschlichkeit beschreiben," *Merkur* XIX:1 (January 1965); Peter Schneider, "Politische Dichtung. Ihre Grenzen und Möglichkeiten," *Der Monat* 207 (December 1965).

15. For an analysis of this kind of "new discourse" on Nazism, see my *Reflections of Nazism: An Essay on Kitsch and Death* (New York, 1984).

16. I am well aware of the many interesting documentaries or TV series on various aspects of the Nazi past produced in Germany. Among the most recent ones: Eberhard Fechner's TV film on Majdanek (though relegated to the relatively unimportant channel 3 of West German television) and Paul Mommertz's TV film on the Wannsee Conference, both produced in 1984; and the major 1985 six-part TV series on "The Germans in the Second World War," which certainly is as honest as can be. This being said, none of the *internationally renowned* movies or TV series trying to recapture the full horror of Nazism was, to my knowledge, produced in Germany.

17. The reception and impact of "Holocaust" in Germany is a complex problem itself. For the best discussions on this question, see the series of articles published in *New German Critique* 19 (Winter 1980), as well as the articles in a special "Dossier" of *Die Zeit*, 19 January 1979.

18. The full text of this speech is published in the "Documents" section of this volume.

19. See note 4 above.

20. Golo Mann, "Gedenktage, die Wunden aufreissen," *Die Zeit,* 15 February 1985.

21. Rudolph Augstein, "Auf die schiefe Ebene zur Republik," *Der Spiegel* 2, 1985, p. 32. The reference to Normandy alludes to the fact that Chancellor Kohl was not invited to participate in the commemoration of the fortieth anniversary of the Allied landing.

22. Geoffrey Barraclough, "Mandarins and Nazis: Part I," *New York Review of Books,* 19 October 1972, 37–43; "The Liberals and German History: Part II," *New York Review of Books,* 2 November 1972, 32–38; and "A New

View of German History: Part III," *New York Review of Books*, 16 November 1972, 25–31.

23. Augstein, p. 32.

24. Ibid., p. 31.

25. James M. Markham, "West German TV Specials Spark Debate on Reconciliation with Nazi Era," *New York Times*, 24 April 1985.

26. Ruth Rehmann, *Der Mann auf der Kanzel. Fragen an einen Vater* (Munich, 1979).

27. For instance, the Marxist literary journal *Sammlung* reviewed in its 1979 issues, nos. 2 & 3, some forty new *literary* works on the Nazi era (published between 1977 and 1979 in West and East Germany), approximately thirty-five of which were written by German authors.

28. Both themes and the link between them have been analyzed in the most brilliant way in Wolfgang Pohrt, *Endstation, Ueber die Wiedergeburt der Nation* (Berlin, 1983). Wolfgang Pohrt and Eike Geisel may well be the two most effective polemical essayists on the contemporary West German scene; although very much on the Left, they have no patience for some of the new tendencies of the German Left alluded to in this paper.

29. On "Heimat" and other German movies or TV series (Wolfgang Petersen's *Das Boot*, for example), see Markham's analysis in the *New York Times* (note 25 above), and, on the possible significance of "Heimat" in the reelaboration of the Nazi period, see my own "8. Mai, der sperrige Gedenktag: Bewältigung oder nur Verdrängung?" *Die Zeit* 7, 8 February 1985.

30. "Deutschland spielt noch immer die Nibelungen," interview with Heiner Müller, *Der Spiegel*, 9 May 1983.

31. Rainer Werner Fassbinder's play was written in 1975, on the basis of Gerhard Zwerenz's novel *Die Erde ist unbewohnbar wie der Mond* (The earth is as uninhabitable as the moon). It was turned into a movie under the direction of the Swiss writer Daniel Schmid ("The Shadow of Angels") but never performed on the stage, notwithstanding eight attempts to do so. The whole issue may have already created more controversy than Bitburg. For two excellent analyses of the main problems involved, see Joachim Fest, "Spiel mit der Angst," *Frankfurter Allgemeine Zeitung*, 29 October 1985, and Ulrich Greiner, "Der Jude von Frankfurt," *Die Zeit*, 1 November 1985.

32. Horst Krüger, "Vorbei, beinah vorbei . . . Ist die Nazizeit eigentlich noch ein Thema für Zeitgenossen?" *Die Zeit*, 16 February 1968.

Jürgen Habermas

Defusing the Past:
A Politico-Cultural Tract

In January 1983, on the occasion of the fiftieth anniversary of the Nazi seizure of power, Hermann Lübbe delivered a lecture that, even then, received a great deal of attention.[1] But it is only from the perspective of May 8, 1985, that one can properly appreciate the symptomatic character of his theses. Lübbe attributes the increasingly intense debates surrounding the period of National Socialist domination (despite our growing distance from that time) to a break in the development of the postwar Federal Republic. He claims that during the initial period of reconstruction, there was a massive process of consolidation and exoneration, which took place thanks to the discretion and willingness to reconcile shown by the generous opponents of the Nazis toward the troubled people of Germany. It was not until the late 1960s, according to Lübbe, that barely healed wounds were violently reopened by a rebellious younger generation and a few intransigent leftists. They brought the National Socialist past into the contemporary political consciousness, put an end to an era of protective and discreet behavior, and initiated a critique that has since threatened the stability of our Republic. Chancellor Kohl probably has this account or a similar "story" in mind when he solemnly asserts again and again that he has learned from history. For it was he who, with foresight, envisaged May 8 as the date on which the long overdue return to the normality of the 1950s could be staged in a highly symbolic fashion. Even the new and burdensome consciousness of this inherited past was to be alleviated by his government according to the time-honored neo-conservative recipe of "defusing the past," which was what Lübbe's therapy had been called at the time.

The Veteran Solution

The intact relations between, say, the university rector who had returned from exile or had proven himself in the Resistance and his "ex-Nazi colleagues who keep a low profile, as they must," are characterized, according to Lübbe, by a "nonsymmetrical discretion" on the part of those involved. It was just this sort of "discretion" that Kohl started to practice on the graves of Verdun. This occasion was clearly only a dry run: for in their requirements for asymmetry, the war guilt of 1939 could not possibly be matched by the war guilt of 1914 (even in light of more recent knowledge). From another point of view, the handshake of Verdun was nevertheless not a bad model for the German-American encounter still to come. On the fortieth anniversary a highly visible encounter of veterans was to seal the return to normality. As with Richthofen[2] and his colleagues long ago, chivalrous war enemies were to demonstrate once again their mutual respect in order to bestow on the present the aura of a past that had a settled look. The concentration camp Dachau, naturally, did not fit in with this plan—not as a concentration camp and especially not as one that had immediately been filled with communists and social democrats.

Ultimately all that survives of this plan for normalization is the German-American handshake between veteran generals amid the SS graves of Bitburg. Given everything that preceded it, this public spectacle of irrationality seems so bizzare that its rational aspect easily escapes us. Kohl was able to drag the American president in front of the cemetery cameras with a clear conscience. After all, he was only insisting on a symbolic recompense for having steamrollered the stationing of missiles, which also had a symbolic character. Their stationing, in fact, was a symbolic reaffirmation of the loyalty of the alliance more than a response to the interests of the German populace. As soon as one begins to replace purposive political rationality with a heavy-handed symbolism of destiny, one handshake follows the next. *Manus manum lavat.*

Thus, the Bitburg handshake was meant to consolidate both the move away from any destabilizing effort to achieve mastery of the past (*Vergangenheitsbewältigung*) and the affirmation of an existing fraternity of arms. Kohl wanted a return to German continuities, and in that he was well understood. Only popular agreement with Kohl's intentions explains the self-exposing reactions to these events, which happened to defeat those very intentions.

Why then did the defusing of the past by means of *the veteran strategy*—as it would have to be called in bureaucratese—fail? Ostensibly because there were no graves of American soldiers on German soil, and because the military cemetery in Bitburg had been covered with snow when it was inspected. But the SS markings on a number of the graves, and the feelings of those who remembered them, only exposed what would have come out anyway on some other occasion. History caught up with and made fools out of those who thought to escape it through a neo-conservative interpretation. This occurrence demonstrates that the population of a modern society is less and less able to recognize itself as a whole in the "show business" of its official representatives. Although we did have for once the reassuring experience that a collective regression cannot be staged by administrative fiat alone, the contours of the mentality that came to light in the process are quite disturbing.

Forced Reconciliation[3]

During his visit to Israel the chancellor continued cheerfully to maintain his innocence, having been fifteen years old at the end of the war. However, by the time of his first appearance at Bergen-Belsen he had learned that reconciliation cannot be crassly demanded—especially not by someone who is himself looking for and promoting forgetfulness. In any case, it was a transparent arrangement of forced reconciliation that soon brought the embarrassing circumstances to light. President Reagan had stumbled into a trap. A curious world surveyed the damage, which remained irreparable regardless of whether the gesture of reconciliation exacted would finally be granted or denied. Here in Germany a state of mind spread that at one and the same time expressed and disavowed this paradoxical setting of traps. It would be best, advised the *Frankfurter Allgemeine Zeitung*, if the president were to make the required offering "of his own accord." And a few days later: "We Germans cannot demand pardon. But it is surprising that the greatest achievement of Christianity, namely the commandment to forgive no matter how difficult it might be . . . seemed to play no role whatsoever."

In certain circles the desire to reestablish German continuities thrust aside all misgivings. Once again the thesis of collective guilt served as an invariable excuse for everyone from the waiter to the Cardinal. It was as if Karl Jaspers had never made the trenchant distinction, almost four decades earlier, between a guilt for which there is only individual responsibility, and a communal liability for crimes that could not have been committed without collective silence. Today no one still subscribes to the thesis of collective guilt. Those who nevertheless continue to argue against it are setting up a false assumption, which intends only to distract from the issue at hand, namely, the problem of what position we should take toward both the good and the bad aspects of our own past. How are we to relate to tradition and to that history with which our own identity as well as that of our children and grandchildren is inextricably entangled? Probably not like Martin Bangemann,[4] who compares the Nazi period to the devastation of a hurricane and (in a curious inversion of Walter Benjamin's concept of "history of nature") assimilates history to nature. Nor like Alfred Dregger [CDU Floor Leader in the West German parliament], for whom the entire German population was dominated by a brown-shirted dictatorship. But there are more subtle forms of such defensive displacement. One hears the claim, for example, that, after all, it was only "one part" of the population that had oppressed another part. There is talk of "events" that "dirtied" the German name or of crimes committed "in the name of Germany." The laundering and disburdening are obvious: one touches one's own past with one's fingertips and makes it into the past of the others.

Even more insistent is the desire, which can be observed among older people, to free one's experience of that earlier time from a setting that, retrospectively, has given everything a different significance. This longing for a seemingly unadulterated version of what is one's own is, after all, well served by television, which (despite Sebastian Haffner's[5] participation) keeps providing reminiscences shorn of their context: memories of daily life, sleazy nightclub entertainments, adventure and battle, all of which remain almost pristine, completely untroubled by the mollifying and protective TV commentary. The same need, toward which the TV series on the Germans in World War II is directed, comes to the fore in reactions to the reactions to Bitburg. Dregger feels that the memory of his fallen brother has been insulted. Others insist that "the dead young men of the Waffen SS in Bitburg may not be denied their honor." The foreign press, not only the American but also the Spanish and the English press, is unrestrainedly reproached for a stance that places itself "outside of the political context." There is a desire to escape, finally, from the straightjacket of a life history revised after the fact, and so to be allowed once again to sing all the verses of the *Deutschlandlied*.[6] In this context anyone who distinguishes between different types of military service "promotes the spirit of discord."

Freedom from Totalitarianism

Promoting the spirit of discord is certainly at issue here, but in a different sense. What better way to promote the return to German continuities than the *old fronts*? Ever since the days of the German imperial *Kaiserreich*, the idea of a united front against leftists, communists, Jews, and intellectuals has never quite lost its power over the mind in the spiritual household of the Germans. Twice, however, this front sustained serious damage—once from Hitler's pact with Stalin, and then from the destruction of the Jews. Still, the syndrome of anticommunist sentiments has proved to be a reliable constant in the intellectual life of our Republic. When "clever" Heiner Geissler[7] reduces the significance of May 8 to the formula that forty years ago the brown dictatorship was replaced by a red one, he is attempting to make the antitotalitarian opposition to Hitler into something totalitarian. The SPD (German Socialist Party) and those in its sphere associate themselves neither with the Bitburg veterans nor with the forced and embarrassing ceremony on the grounds—teeming with "bodyguards"—of Bergen-Belsen. They are not sufficiently selective. They open themselves to the duty of recalling *all* the victims of the Nazi regime—including twenty million dead Russian soldiers, who were not, by any means, all killed in battle. This insistence must have disturbed the outspoken one-sidedness of official attempts at reconciliation and put in question the meaning of the entire staged event.

The government had announced "Freedom or Totalitarianism" as the slogan of the day for May 8. For the chancellor at Bitburg, "totalitarian domination" also served as a term of disguise and transition. It saved him from having to call National Socialism by its name; the ambiguous meaning of "totalitarian" enabled him to remind the American president that both he and we were opponents of communism. This too is one of the implications of Dregger's letter to the American senators: "On the last day of the war my battalion and I defended the city of Marklissa in Silesia against attacks by the Red Army." For anyone who failed to grasp the meaning of these lines, the *FAZ* explained them: forty years ago there was in fact only one victor. Seen clearly, the Western powers had actually lost the war along

with the Germans; on the eighth of May they would do well to remember "this inheritance of defeat in victory."

Always Already Better Allies

Recently Stefan Heym[8] recalled the depositions of German prisoners of war that he, as an American sergeant, had taken on the
western front shortly before the end of the war. He describes how
these officers complained about the fact that the Americans had not
after all given the war a happy ending by teaming up with the Germans
against the Russians! One of those who was of this opinion at the time
serves today as Joachim Fest's[9] star witness. Fest considers 1945 as
"the greatest defeat of that very same democratic principle which the
democracies had entered the war to maintain and expand."[10] In the
context of Bitburg Fest's article reads—like Dregger's letter and a lot
of other material—as if it were an expression of boyish disappointment
that the Americans were still refusing to grant their staunchest ally a
retroactive invitation to a fraternity of arms that should have been
formed during the Second World War. Fest writes: "In February of
1943, according to a report by Ernst Jünger, the word 'Stalingrad'
often appeared written in chalk on the walls of Paris. 'Who knows,'
the poet asked himself, 'maybe they (the French) are also being defeated there.' " The poet here invoked as an authority for so wishful
an interpretation of May 8 never renounced his anti-Semitism of the
Weimar era and, during an interview before receiving the Goethe.
Prize of the city of Frankfurt, reaffirmed his distance from all political
orders, democratic or dictatorial. I mention this point only because
between Joachim Fest and myself there is no argument about the facts
to which he refers or about the rejection of bureaucratic socialism. In
dispute are the degree and the type of German continuities that we
should aim for. In Germany, the kind of anticommunism that has
recently justified the tendentious selectivity of our reconciliation efforts has always been linked to the darkest *ressentiment.*

We are not living in just any country. At deeper levels this anticommunism is linked to those residues of anti-Semitic feelings which the
men with their little briefcases in the dining cars between Frankfurt
and Munich have given vent to in recent weeks with renewed un-
selfconsciousness. Ten days after Fest's lead article, another piece on
the same subject appeared, written by a fellow editor. In the meantime, however, the United States had discovered the SS graves: "President Reagan had the right instinct. . . . But a massive journalistic machine in his country is keeping up the persecution to the nth degree

and is thankful for every occasion to exhume the distorted image of the ugly German once again and thereby reopen old wounds."[11]

No Spiritual-Moral Leadership

If, faced with this pile of political shards, one wants to struggle to produce an optimistic reading, one could say that the "veteran solution" failed because of the fundamental internal insincerity of the idea on which it was based. But there is also a more substantive lesson to be learned. The obscene undertaking had already failed from the moment that open public discussion about the changes in the Bitburg program exposed the *unavoidable* opportunism of such official actions, and thereby revealed, at the same time, the incongruity between this event and the administrative means by which it was handled. Politicians—who no longer speak from the center of the political and public sphere but rather act as functionaries of a managerial idea that keeps them in power—founder when confronted with issues that concern the identity and self-understanding of the populace as a whole. Given his intellectual makeup, the present chancellor is hardly suited for tasks of this sort. But the problem is, to repeat, not the people. The task of promoting social integration and self-awareness is no longer, today, the responsibility of the political system. For good reasons we no longer have a Kaiser or a Hindenburg. The public sphere should therefore refuse to tolerate such claims to spiritual-moral leadership among top elected officials. It must be said, however, that, thanks to his politically marginal position, the president of the Federal Republic has more of an opportunity to express respect for homosexuals, Gypsies, and Russians—without considering votes. Together with moving personal memories (those of Riehl-Heyse and Erhard Eppler[12]), the address to the parliament by its president, Richard von Weizsäcker[13] (its character almost reminiscent of Heinemann[14]), strikes me as one of the few political speeches that does justice to the demands made on us by twelve years of Nazi rule and the forty years since.[15]

Translated by Thomas Levin

TRANSLATOR'S NOTES

This essay is a translation of "Die Entsorgung der Vergangenheit: Ein kulturpolitisches Pamphlet," *Die Zeit*, no. 21, May 24, 1985.

1. Hermann Lübbe, "Es ist nichts vergessen, aber einiges ausgeheilt," *Frankfurter Allgemeine Zeitung*, January 24, 1983.

2. Manfred Freiherr von Richthofen (1892–1918), the most successful German fighter pilot in World War I, who downed more than eighty planes before he was himself hit by a Canadian flyer and buried with full military honors by the British.

3. Habermas here "cites" the title of Theodor W. Adorno's essay "Erpresste Versöhnung," (translated as "Reconciliation under Duress," in *Aesthetics and Politics*, 1980). The various allusions to the work of his former teacher begin with the title "Defusing the Past," which echoes Adorno's "Coming to Terms with the Past," included in the "Essays" section of this volume.

4. West Germany's minister for economics and the current head of the Free Democratic Party (Freie Demokratische Partie), the third major party in the German parliament; also a member of the European parliament.

5. Pen name for Raimund Pretzel, a German writer who emigrated to England in 1938, where he worked for the *Observer*; author of numerous books including, *Germany: Jekyll and Hyde*, trans. Wilfred David (1941); *Failure of a Revolution: Germany 1918–19*, trans. Georg Rapp (1973); *The Meaning of Hitler*, trans. Ewald Osers (1979); and *The Rise and Fall of Prussia*, trans. Ewald Osers (1980).

6. The German national anthem, set to a theme composed by Haydn. It again became the official national anthem in 1922 and was abandoned after World War II. Since 1952, when it was reinstated, only the third stanza is sung, the first two stanzas—which begin "Deutschland, Deutschland, über alles"—being omitted.

7. CDU Minister for Youth, Family, and Health in the West German parliament since 1982, and former general secretary of the party.

8. Famous German writer and novelist; author of essays, novels, and numerous books including, in English, *The Wandering Jew* (1984); presently resides in East Berlin after a checkered political history that included editing a German paper in New York in the late 1930s and joining the American army in 1943.

9. Journalist, coeditor of the *Frankfurter Allgemeine Zeitung* (since 1973) and director of its section on Culture; author of *The Face of the Third Reich: Portraits of the Nazi Leadership*, trans. Michael Bullock (1970) and the conservative biography *Hitler*, trans. Richard and Clara Winston (1973).

10. Joachim Fest, "Sieg und Niederlage" (Victory and defeat), *FAZ*, April 20, 1985.

11. Fritz Ullrich Fack, "Ein Scherbenhaufen," *Frankfurter Allgemeine Zeitung* 99, April 29, 1985, p. 1.

12. Erhard Eppler: Member of the SPD party in the West German parliament. Former minister for economic cooperation.

13. The text of this speech is included in the "Documents" section of this volume.

14. Gustav W. Heinemann, liberal German politician in the SPD party; long-time opponent of rearmament and advocate of civil rights; president of the Republic from 1969 to 1974.

15. Habermas concludes his essay with the following postscript: "Following his above-mentioned talk, Hermann Lübbe responded to a persistent critic (Carola Stern) by claiming, more or less, that while *she* was making public claims to an ethically more qualified relationship to National Socialism, he,

Lübbe, considered it an affront even to engage in such ethical competition. This bodes ill. I can anticipate such a reproach of 'ethical arrogance' or 'claims of intellectual leadership' being addressed to me and can only protect myself by referring to my previous work on such issues. There is no question that professors of philosophy—like scientists and intellectuals in general—have no privileged access to reality. Only Heidegger made such a claim. If they take a stand on practical questions, they do so either as experts (which I am not) or by virtue of their right to participate in a discussion among citizens."

Henry Rousso

The Reactions in France:
The Sounds of Silence

In France, President Reagan's visit to Bitburg provoked divided and contradictory feelings. Between the indignation of some and the indifference of others lay a wide range of reactions. France is in fact an ideal observation point from which to analyze the impact of the Bitburg affair. First of all, the French were able to feel directly involved in the controversy after the revelation that some of the SS soldiers buried at Bitburg might have participated in the massacre of Oradour-sur-Glane, the high point of French martyrdom during the Nazi occupation. Subsequently, the government found itself politically torn, caught between two impossibilities: either condemning officially the initiative of its two principal allies, the United States and the Federal Republic of Germany, or approving of the initiative at the risk of throwing salt on still open domestic wounds. Could President Mitterrand, a former member of the Resistance, and the Left in its entirety give the impression of rejecting the heritage of the struggle against Nazism? Finally, and above all, the French have always had an extremely complex relationship to the memory of the "black years" (*années noires*), the years of the war, the defeat, and the German occupation. This period is still identified with the detested Vichy government and with a civil war that tore apart families and consciences for a long time. Forty years later, everything that recalls this damned era inevitably provokes violent intellectual, political, and moral polemics. This situation has been particularly evident over the last fifteen years, when the representations of World War II have undergone a profound transformation.

In order to understand the French reactions it is necessary to take into account the current political situation as well as the country's agitated and neurotic relation to its past. Within this context two questions are important: did the emotions raised by Bitburg really correspond to the degree of the event's seriousness and to the traditional reflexes of the French in similar circumstances? What role did the memory of the genocide of the Jews and the problem of anti-Semitism play in this affair?

The Wounds of Memory

Even if it was a surprise, the Bitburg initiative was for the French merely a mishap in the long-term development of their memory of the last war. During a first period lasting from the 1950s to the end of the 1960s, the great majority of French people tried to repress a number of inconvenient memories, particularly the existence in occupied France of an ideological strain close to Nazism. Thanks to the exceptional charisma of General de Gaulle—"the first member of the Resistance"—many identified with the image of those who refused to lower their heads, close their eyes, and lend an ear to the soothing discourse of Marshal Pétain. Throughout the early years of the Fifth Republic, while de Gaulle and a generation of practical men who had participated in the Resistance were in power, Pétain and Vichy and the collaboration were taboo subjects. According to certain popular versions of history, only a handful of traitors had sided with the Nazis while the rest of the country had fiercely resisted the invader, just like a little Gaul named Astérix,* who was created at this very time.

In 1970–71 everything was turned upside down. This reassuring and simplistic vision collapsed. The student revolt of May 1968 began to question the legitimacy of the Gaullist memory involved with the "spirit of resistance," and the death of General de Gaulle deprived the French of the figurehead of their retrospective heroism. In 1971 Max Ophuls, André Harris, and Alain de Sédouy made a film composed of documents and testimony, which brought to light for the first time all the repressed aspects of the occupation period: the fear, the cowardice, the quite significant support of some of Petain's ideas by part of the population, the existence of an outspoken anti-Semitism, and the limited extent of participation in Resistance activities. The shock produced by *The Sorrow and the Pity (Le Chagrin et la pitié)* was so violent that the film was banned from French television until 1981!

*A popular French cartoon character.—TRANS.

Throughout the 1970s France was immersed in a "retro-mode," during which the occupation era was very popular in both movies and books. Above all, this return of the repressed was fed by the reawakening of the memory of the genocide.

Beginning with de Gaulle's 1969 embargo on the sale of French arms to Israel, and then increasingly with the Franco-Arab reconciliation during the period 1973–81, the Jewish community in France emerged from its traditional reserve. Feeling itself suddenly torn between its natural loyalty to the Jewish state and its deep patriotic attachment to France, the community began to search for its historical roots. In the process it revived the debate on French anti-Semitism during the years from 1930 to 1940.

Exacerbating the community's unease was the ambiguous political position of the French government toward Israel, which provoked an increase in anti-Zionism at many levels of the population including the Left. This anti-Zionism was, moreover, often very close to that historical anti-Semitism. Between 1978 and 1981 Jewish memory was jolted by numerous electroshocks. In 1978 a major weekly paper interviewed the former Vichy Commissioner for Jewish Matters, Darquier de Pellepoix, the man responsible on the French side for the deportation of tens of thousands of Jews.[1] The same year an academic, Robert Faurisson, along with some of his American and German colleagues, publicly denounced the "Holocaust lie," denying the existence of the gas chambers. The broadcast in 1979 of the American television series "Holocaust" further raised tensions, which then peaked in 1980: on October 3 an attack at the rue Copernic in Paris left four people dead, murdered as they left the synagogue. Small neo-Nazi groups that had recently surfaced were immediately blamed. From that moment on, the anti-Semitism of the Vichy period returned to the center of all the debates, films, and books on World War II, reviving a violent, if long-dormant, controversy.

But even apart from the issue of anti-Semitism, in a country inclined to ideological disputes, the memory of the war has always served as the preferred weapon with which to attack a political opponent. At one point or another, all of France's leaders (except, of course, de Gaulle) have had this question posed to them accusingly: "What were you doing between 1940 and 1944?" During the presidential election of May 1981, the final debates before the election of François Mitterrand dealt less with the economic or social positions of each of the candidates than with Mitterand's past, since he had been accused— falsely—of "working with Vichy." Equally prominent in the debates was the issue of the actions of one of the ministers in Raymond Barre's last administration, Maurice Papon, whom the press accused of having participated in the deportation of French Jews and who was then charged with "crimes against humanity."

The memory of the war thus plays a large role in the French mentality, ranking among the chief causes of domestic ideological division.[2] From this standpoint, the Bitburg affair simply aggravated a still unhealed wound of memory.

Some Very Divergent Reactions

Far from reacting only with hostility or approval, French public opinion, the press, and political circles displayed very different attitudes according to their respective preoccupations. From these responses, there emerges a typology that reflects the ambiguities of collective memory and the dissonance between past and present.

Ideological Hostility

In the political arena, only the French Communist Party openly demonstrated opposition to Reagan's gesture. Neither the Socialist Party—which is the only support of the government—nor the opposition on the Right made an official statement for or against it, although some political figures reacted on a personal basis.

It is important to understand that, unlike Gaullism, which thrived on the heritage of the Resistance but was, in turn, sustained by its twenty-three years in power, the French Communist Party has found acceptance only by virtue of its record of actions against the Nazi occupation forces. This chapter in the party's history (ignoring shady times like 1939–41, following the German-Soviet nonaggression pact) is the touchstone of its past and present legitimacy and indeed is the only distinction that can successfully offset the always topical accusations of fealty to the Communist Party of the USSR.

On April 24, 1985, the Communist delegates twice asked the National Assembly whether the government intended "to disapprove of such events which equated the Waffen SS, their victims and the members of the Resistance."[3] A delegate from Haute-Vienne—the region in which the martyr city of Oradour-sur-Glane is located—struck a very emotional chord in his address to the government. He recalled explicitly the massacre of 642 people shot or burned alive in Oradour on June 10, 1944, by a detachment of the "Das Reich" division of the Waffen SS—an act that remained for the French the symbol of the barbarism of the Nazi occupation. This address was delivered even before anyone had learned that among the soldiers of the Waffen SS buried in Bitburg were some who may have quite possibly taken part in this massacre.[4] To drive the point home, while Reagan was paying his respects to the German graves, the Soviet ambassador to France, Youri Vorontsov, placed a spray of flowers on the memorial to the martyrs of Oradour-sur-Glane, honoring "the eternal memory of French patriots and Soviet patriots."[5]

On May 2, again at the National Assembly, the Communists renewed their attack by referring to the position of Mrs. Thatcher, the principal ally of the American government, who had not hesitated to declare publicly that she shared the indignation of her British constituents. A rather unlikely model for the Communists! When they demanded a suspension of the session of the assembly—a symbolic gesture in the best parliamentary tradition—they were supported neither by the opposition on the Right nor by the Socialist majority.[6]

In fact, the Bitburg affair was a good political opportunity for the Communist Party. By denouncing President Reagan's conflation of the victims of the Nazis and the Nazis themselves, the party gained the support of numerous organizations of former Resistance members and deportees, Communists and non-Communists alike, and found itself in agreement with the majority of French public opinion. But in the same move, the Communists were also able to condemn American politics in Europe, despite the fact that their statements on this subject are usually dismissed as extreme. They were able to show that the visit to Bitburg masked the political stakes of the summit meeting of the seven industrialized countries that had convened on May 4 in Bonn. Even better, Bitburg offered a good opportunity to conflate yesterday's enemy—Nazism—and today's enemy—American "imperialism":

> Forty years later the lessons of the 1945 victory are of burning importance: peace is the most precious good. Freedom and independence are the sacred rights of every people. . . .There is a large movement afoot, led by the President of the United States, to efface these lessons of history. By absolving the torturers at the expense of their victims, by developing a delirious propaganda campaign against the Soviet ally of yesterday who is now designated today's enemy, Reagan wants to restore—in West Germany above all—the good conscience and the influence of the forces of hate and aggression. Reagan thereby also wants to justify the acceleration of the arms race and insane projects to militarize space as well as to prepare attitudes for war. The Bonn summit meeting was one stage of this dangerous enterprise.[7]

Despite the obvious demagoguery of the statement, these arguments unquestionably had some influence on public opinion, even though the Communist Party had been completely discredited since its departure from the government in 1984. This situation gives some idea of the extent of the effect produced by Reagan's gesture: the very amorality of his visit and the involuntary (?) homage paid to the SS, far from serving the Western cause, improved for a while the public image of the Soviets and their allies, presenting them as the sole defenders of anti-Nazism.

Concerned Hostility

The indignation of the Communists, which was not fake, was of a political nature. The groups of former Resistance members and deportees, along with the Jewish community in France, reacted in a more spontaneous manner, torn between anger, surprise, and, indeed, incredulity that the United States and its president could so offend their memory.

The National Federation of Deportees, Internees, Members of the Resistance, and Patriots (FNDIRP) reacted very quickly. Commenting on Helmut Kohl and Ronald Reagan's decision and, even more, on the latter's assimilation of the authentic victims of Nazism to the Waffen SS in Bitburg, the executive office of the FNDIRP declared:

> Such lack of understanding of what constituted a horrifying reality is worrisome. In this month of April we are commemorating the 40th anniversary of the liberation of the concentration camps liberated by the Allied armies—among them the American army. The FNDIRP stresses again that the necessary reconciliation between the French people and the German people cannot occur through forgetting or denying the crimes of Nazism.[8]

The FNDIRP thus protested, along with many other organizations, against the risks of a "banalization" of the Nazi crimes, unwilling to believe in the sincerity of the American president: "The slightest gesture by a head of state is calculated. This one is no different."[9] Other organizations of the Left such as the Movement against Racism and Anti-Semitism and for Peace (MRAP) called for public demonstrations against the Bitburg visit.

The reactions of the Jewish community were very similar to their responses on previous occasions. Whether on the Right or on the Left, French Jews, those who had lived through the war as well as those born since, refused to accept the thought that the necessities of Western politics could pay so little heed to the memory of their dead.

Simone Veil, a figure of great stature in the liberal opposition and a former deportee, leveled some extremely severe criticisms on behalf of the very European unity that Reagan's gesture was supposed to reinforce: "The conflation cleverly maintained during the course of this visit may be serious for the future of Europe. . . . A true democracy can only be based on the unreserved denunciation of an abominable system. . . . Shaking hands among the graves is merely play-acting when one's heart is not in it."[10] Henri Bulawko, the president of the Association of Former Jewish Deportees from France, did not believe in Reagan's sincerity either: "His gesture cannot be considered innocent. Hesitating between the American Jewish voters and the German 'allies,' he goes back on his decision, searching for an impossible compromise by trying to 'please' everyone. There is something profoundly shocking in this, coming as it does from a head of state who speaks for the most powerful country in the world."[11]

Nevertheless, although the entire Jewish community had displayed its disapproval, the most spectacular gesture did not come from this establishment, which occasionally muted its attacks. Indeed, it was the youth—representing a generation that had experienced neither the war nor the genocide—who took the most concrete initiative. With the support of the writer Marek Halter and the lawyer Serge Klarsfeld, the Union of Jewish Students in France organized a Bitburg protest march that brought together hundreds of people. This action was further supported by a young antiracist organization, "SOS-Racism,"[12] and by intellectuals and organizations of immigrant Arabs, who expressed their views through their journal *Sans Frontière* (Without a border). The following petition was signed by both academics and members of the AMF, the Association of Moroccans in France:

> There are wounds and acts which can never be effaced from the collective memory. The Nazi horror is one of them. Everything which allows and facilitates its forgetting is an outrage to the memory of the victims of the Holocaust. Such forgetting also poses a danger to the living, to all those who might be afraid because of their ethnic background, their religious faith, or their political opinions: the awakening of the horrible beast and the development of racism and intolerance. . . . The recent victims of anti-Arab racism demand of us this show of solidarity with all the Jewish communities throughout the world, stunned by Ronald Reagan's visit to the Bitburg cemetery.[13]

Even though such rapprochements had become frequent in the last few months, this reaction was the most unusual and without doubt the most significant of the demonstrations of hostility to the Bitburg affair. Indeed, the unexpected alliance between Jews and Arabs to defend the memory of the victims of Nazism had an infinitely larger impact than the more traditional reactions of the organizations of former members of the Resistance or the official responses of the Jewish community.

Intellectual and Moral Criticisms

Part of the French press, while taking up the arguments developed by the Communists or by the Jewish community, insisted instead on the "error" or indeed the "political mistake" of the Bitburg ceremony. From the very beginning *Le Monde* emphasized the perverse effect produced by this gesture, which uselessly revived old passions without contributing to any sort of rapprochement. Alfred Grosser, an expert in German politics, noted that while the fundamental intention of the American president could not be criticized, the choice of Bitburg had been a serious mistake:

> I would have preferred that Ronald Reagan, François Mitterand and Helmut Kohl had met at the concentration camp in Dachau. By doing so they would have proclaimed to the entire world that Hitler's regime had been barbaric but that the camps had been created for Germans. Hundreds of thousands of non-Jewish Germans had been made martyrs before the arrival of the first foreign deportees. Indeed May 8, 1945, marks a common victory over Nazism in which many Germans took part while, between 1940 and 1944, French people were helping Hitler.[14]

Libération—a newspaper widely read in intellectual and political circles and no longer affiliated with a moribund "leftism"—adopted a distanced and ironic stance, which is captured in one of its headlines: "Reagan: 'F' in History."[15] Without openly condemning the American initiative, *Libération* stressed the ignorance of European political and historical matters on the part of both the American president and his advisers, and, at the same time, mocked their hesitations and their about-face. Presenting the affair as a farce starring the heavy-handed "cowboy" Reagan, *Libération* was careful not to take an overtly hostile position, as if the blunder were too obvious to deserve anathematization. But, in fact, this irony could just as well indicate the lack of interest among twenty-five- to thirty-five-year-olds in all these old veterans' quarrels.

Favorable Reactions

Favorable reactions came from part of the Right and the extreme right, expressed in the name of a "Realpolitik" and solidarity with the

Western bloc as well as in the interest of forgetting and forgiving. This theme had been developed by the French Right, particularly among the non-Gaullists, since the Cold War: the struggle against Communism required that one not emphasize too systematically the crimes of the Nazis and their French accomplices in order to concentrate the attack on Soviet totalitarianism.

For the *Quotidien de Paris*, Reagan's gesture was a political necessity, given the imperative "of anchoring West Germany to the Free World" and because the history of Germany was not "reducible to a dozen years of barbarism."[16] General Bigeard, a former star of the colonial wars, stated that "the Free World should stop these little squabbles and stick together in the face of the real danger which is posed by the Soviet Union."[17] Jean Dutourd, editorial writer for *France-Soir*, as usual reached heights of provocative stupidity by claiming that, "had it not been for the fools," he "would have written off Hitler," and furthermore, that Reagan had chosen the Bitburg cemetery "completely innocently."[18]

Because there could be no question of implicating the United States and West Germany, and because of the large scale of the Soviet Union's commemoration of the fortieth anniversary of the end of the war, those on the Right—with only a few exceptions such as Simone Veil—refused to take into account the moral and historical dimension of the affair, preferring instead to develop cynical political arguments. Even the extreme right tempered its satisfaction in seeing an American president taking up positions that it had supported for a long time. Thus, the newspaper *Rivarol*—which had been the refuge of former French fascists in the 1950s and remains the mouthpiece of anti-Semitic tendencies today—did not make any triumphant proclamations, remaining content to comment in its own way on Reagan's gesture: "Counseled by his advisers, Ronald Reagan is clearly aware of Moscow's game. As a result, he decided that it was not up to the American (or foreign) Jews to decide whether or not the Germans were to be considered as allies and loyal friends or forever treated as infamous 'Nazis.' "[19] In fact, ever since the extreme Right gained some parliamentary legitimacy thanks to the election of Jean-Marie Le Pen (the leader of the National Front) to the European Parliament, it has been trying not to outdo others on touchy subjects such as the reminder of its past sympathies with Nazism. It is almost as if *Rivarol* were sorry that President Reagan had decided not to visit a concentration camp, "contrary to his initial intention which was so justly founded."[20] Strangely enough, some of the positions of the Right agreed with the analyses made by the Communists. The Bitburg affair eclipsed the summit at Bonn—but this time because of "provocation by the Soviet propaganda agencies."[21]

The Silence of the Government despite
the Current of Public Opinion

In this chorus of discordant voices, the French government remained remarkably reserved. Twice, responding to the Communist delegates in the National Assembly, it acted in a manner that without doubt did not reflect the deeper feelings of a large majority of the Socialist ministers and delegates. While Roland Dumas, in his capacity as minister for external affairs, declared that "it is not customary for the government to pass a verdict on the travels of a foreign head of state in another foreign country," as a citizen he felt that "there are certain major human traumas where one must avoid reopening the wounds."[22] Only once did a minister affirm to the parliament that the government "shared the strong feelings" of the public sector.[23] But its pain was evidently very well contained. . . .

Nevertheless, a poll taken one month after the events revealed that the majority of the French did not agree with Reagan's gesture. In response to the statement that "the American president was right to go and pay his respects at the Bitburg cemetery," the reactions were quite clear: 8 percent said that they "agreed completely," 22 percent "more or less agreed," 13 percent were "not really in agreement," and 29 percent were "not at all in agreement." At the same time 64 percent of the French public felt that the struggle against Nazism in West Germany had not been carried out completely and that the danger of its eventual resurrection had not been entirely foreclosed. Both the Right and the Left were practically in agreement on this point. In any case—and this is a remarkable fact—West Germany's image was not damaged and remained excellent. Among the major Western countries, the Federal Republic of Germany is the one to which the French feel the closest.[24] This investigation shows that the French people were not duped by the Bitburg gesture: by distinguishing their country's already thirty-year-old commitment to Western reconciliation—particularly between France and Germany—from a possible renaissance of Nazism, they demonstrated that in order to seal the friendship between former enemies there was no need to go and salute the remains of former SS soldiers.

The Moral of the Story/The Morality of History

Reactions to the Bitburg affair in France raise some fundamental questions. First of all, even if the visit to the German cemetery was condemned afterwards, the mobilization against it was weak, except in some highly motivated circles such as the Communists or the Jewish community. Official reactions were rare, and commentary took up much less space in the press than a simple recounting of the facts—when usually the opposite obtains under such circumstances! The revelation that some of the SS at Bitburg could have participated in the massacre of Oradour did not provoke a great wave of indignation, which is surprising. And these anomalies can hardly be explained by invoking some sort of indifference toward forty-year-old memories: less than a month later France would be profoundly shaken by very violent polemics that broke out in response to a television film called "Des 'terroristes' à la retraite" ("Terrorists" in retirement), recounting the story of a group of Resistance fighters composed of foreigners—primarily Jews—and known by the name of the "Manouchian Group." For weeks the unrest attained heights rarely seen in France, mobilizing all of the press and all the political parties, one of which, the Communist Party, was accused—wrongly—of having handed over these foreign Resistance fighters to the Gestapo. What accounts, then, for the relative moderation of the response to the Bitburg affair, which was, after all, no less serious and of much greater symbolic import?

The silence of the French government and the reserved attitude of the opposition (based on one of the only points of consensus that exist between the two, namely the conduct of foreign policy), were major factors behind this moderation. During the entire affair the French government had been embarrassed for many reasons. It could not criticize the decision of the president since it undoubtedly preferred to save its ammunition for more vital subjects such as those discussed in Bonn, i.e., its hostility to "Star Wars" or the high level of American interest rates. Given these circumstances, to criticize the Bitburg affair was a more complicated matter for France than for Mrs. Thatcher. Above all, the French government did not want to offend Chancellor Helmut Kohl, who was already annoyed at not being able to participate symbolically in the commemorations of June 6, 1984. Starting with the historic handshake between Kohl and Mitterand at Verdun on September 22, 1984, the plan had been to celebrate the anniversary of the end of the war "in a spirit of reconciliation and peace," and to avoid all signs of hostility toward the German people.

This prudent silence was unusual for a government whose political tendency has been, in other circumstances, to denounce the risks of forgetting and of banalizing Nazism. Equally unusual was the attitude of the opposition on the Right, particularly the Gaullists, some of whom might have felt that the memory of their battles of yesteryear had been offended. Since the opposition never misses a chance to harass the Socialists, the absence of criticism of the government's silence helped to weaken the impact of the affair in France. In the end, the politicians pretended to ignore the feelings of one part of the French public and treated the affair as involving only the United States and West Germany, that is to say, as a "foreign affair."

Second, it is remarkable that the debates on anti-Semitism, which are always in the foreground in such affairs, did not take their usual course. The initiative to react concretely—that is, the Bitburg protest march—came from young people rather than from the generations that had lived through the genocide. In its official statements the Jewish community hardly voiced its objections, embarrassed as it was by the fact that doing so would mean criticizing an American president. Furthermore, the commentaries were very careful to distinguish between, on the one hand, the necessity for Jews and others never to forget anything of the Nazi crimes and, on the other hand, the importance of not harassing either Israel's principal ally or today's West Germany.

Above all, the history lesson took on a different color in the contemporary social context of France. The issue of racism, the growing and menacing hostility toward immigrants, most of them of Arab origin, is today a problem objectively more acute than the renaissance of anti-Semitism. The challenge of the coming years lies in the capacity of the French—those born in France as well as those who have chosen to live there—to form a community in solidarity. In this light, the mobilization of young Jews and young immigrants against the potential meanings of the Bitburg gesture certainly was just as important for the antiracist movement in general as it was for French Jews. This ephemeral union took place in an atmosphere of widespread indifference and in the margins of the traditional and—why not say it—stereotyped discourse of former Resistance members and deportees. Furthermore, it showed that transmitting the memory of the horrors of the past required articulation in terms of a contemporary situation. It was not only young Jews—as sensitive as their parents to any attack on the memory of the genocide—who marched in the Bitburg protest. They were joined by young French people aware that the contemporaneity of Nazism resides just as much in the renaissance of a racism in France as it does in the always potential risk of a resurgence of anti-Semitism. In the last few years, many survivors of the Nazi horror have had to face the difficulty of conveying their unspeakable experience. Such gestures of reciprocal solidarity may have given them hope that communication is not totally impossible, even if these gestures did not always conform to their desire to denounce above all the anti-Semitic nature of the Hitler regime.

By its very nature the gesture of the protest marchers pointed to some contradictions within the traditional expression of the memory of the genocide: one cannot simultaneously analyze Nazism as a regime based *exclusively* on anti-Semitism (an approach that could be organized in terms of history or even better in terms of memory or ideology) and also ask that it serve as the scarecrow against *all* forms of racism and totalitarian tyranny. Even if the genocide of the Jews by the Nazis constituted a unique phenomenon in the history of humanity, the moral of this history has meaning only if it concerns other communities. One may summarize the matter in one line: rejection of all forms of exclusion of the other. This is the message delivered by the participants of Arab origin in the protest march.[25]

Bitburg is a good example of the political illusion of thinking it is possible to manipulate memory deliberately and with impunity. The results of such a misconception are entirely perverse. Reagan's attempt to effect a reconciliation between nations almost provoked the opposite by recalling everything that might divide the countries victimized by Nazism from a Germany searching legitimately to establish a clean slate. The appeal to forget led, in this case, to a brutal revival of still painful memories. A project undertaken in the name of the necessary solidarity of the Western Bloc ended up providing the Soviets and their allies, notably the French Communist Party, with strong arguments. Any symbolic gesture that tries to modify the perception of the past cannot ignore that this perception obeys an extremely complex and multi-faceted causality. To want to control that perception requires great sensitivity to history: in this case the history of Europe, on the one hand, and Jewish memory and that of the anti-Nazi Resistance on the other. Because President Reagan ignored this necessity, he found himself caught in his own trap, apparently convinced that looking straight ahead with head held high exempted him from looking back. "Reality takes form only in memory," wrote Marcel Proust. Could Reagan be a shining example of this "unreality" of the real, Reagan, the pragmatist full of good sense?

Or was Bitburg only a provocation intended to divide Europe? If so, the maneuver certainly failed and would explain the silence of the French government. In any case, and fortunately, this silence could not deaden some dissonant voices. They were an echo of a past that is still alive, or they were an alarm bell against an anxious future.

Translated by Thomas Levin

NOTES

1. *L'Express*, October 28, 1978.

2. On this subject, see "Les guerres franco-françaises," (The Franco-French wars), a special issue of *Vingtième siècle. Revue d'histoire* 5 (January 1985), Presses de la Fondation nationale des sciences politiques.

3. *Journal officiel, débats parlementaires, assemblée nationale* (Official journal of parliamentary debates at the National Assembly), Session of April 24, 1985: Appeal by the Communist delegate Roland Mazoin.

4. This only became known after revelations by the *New York Times*, April 29, 1985.

5. *Le Monde*, May 7, 1985, and *L'Humanité*, May 6, 1985.

6. *Journal officiel, débats parlementaires, assemblée nationale*, Session of May 2, 1985.

7. Statement by the political office of the French Communist Party, in *L'Humanité*, May 7, 1985.

8. *Le Patriote résistant*, Journal of the FNDIRP, no. 547, May 1985. While closely tied to the Communists, the FNDIRP is one of the most important organizations of former members of the Resistance, consisting of 32,000 members from every ideological order including the Gaullists.

9. *Le Patriote résistant* 548, June 1985.

10. Statement made to the European section of the Jewish World Congress on May 19, 1985.

11. *Droit de vivre* 511, May 1985.

12. "SOS-Racism" was created in 1983 by sons and daughters of immigrant workers of the "second generation." The organization and its activities constitute the most visible sign of a potential resistance in France to renascent racism.

13. *Libération*, May 4 & 5, 1985.

14. Statement in the *Quotidien de Paris*, April 28, 1985.

15. *Libération*, April 21, 1985.

16. *Le Quotidien de Paris*, May 4 & 5, 1985.

17. Statement made to the *Quotidien de Paris*, April 28, 1985.

18. *France-Soir*, May 2, 1985. The "fools" are of course the former members of the Resistance, the Jewish victims, the antiracists—in short, all those who do not seek refuge in appeasing vows of silence. It should be noted that Dutourd has always pretended to have participated in the Resistance, a claim that renders his statements even more incomprehensible to any average intelligence.

19. *Rivarol*, April 28, 1985.

20. Ibid.

21. An editorial by R.P. Bruckberger, also a former member of the Resistance, in *Le Figaro*, May 6, 1985.

22. Discussion on the French television channel TF1 on May 5, 1985.

23. Statement by Catherine Lalumière, the secretary of state for external affairs, in response to a question by one of the Communist delegates, at the National Assembly on May 2, 1985.

24. Opinion poll taken between June 11 and 17 and published in *Le Monde*, June 28, 1985.

25. See *Le Monde*, May 7, 1985.

William Bole

Bitburg: The American Scene

Around the same time that major American newspapers were repeatedly citing opposition by "Jewish and veterans" groups to President Reagan's planned visit to Bitburg cemetery in West Germany, an advertisement appeared in the *New York Times* that offered a different picture. Calling on the president to change his plans, the advertisement included the names of no Jews or veterans' officials, but 143 leaders of most of the major Christian denominations in the country.

The newspaper appeal on April 28, 1985, came at a timely point in the public dispute over Bitburg. Murmurs about Jewish responsibility for instigating the painful controversy had begun to surface,[1] as the president and conservative commentators placed blame on "the media."[2] Meanwhile, the major news media, even after it became clear that not only Jews and veterans were upset, usually went no further than to point out criticism by Jews, veterans, "and others."

In fact, the "others" were a highly unusual outpouring of most of the major religious, ethnic, and racial groups in American society. In telegrams to the president, press statements, letters to the editors, and even public rallies, a virtual "rainbow" coalition of black, Hispanic, white ethnic, Asian American, and religious organizations emerged in a drive to head off the visit of an American president to a cemetery where 49 Waffen SS soldiers were among those buried. From Philadelphia, for instance, came a telegram to the president signed by an unusual, if not odd, collection of groups and individuals: The Board of Rabbis of Greater Philadelphia, the Philadelphia Yearly Meeting of the Religious Society of Friends (Quakers), the Urban League of Philadelphia, the Roman Catholic Archdiocese and Holy Child Sisters, pastors of black Baptist and Presbyterian churches, the Episcopal Hospital, the Irish American Unity Council, and the Order of Friars Minor, among others.

These and other groups might have spoken out as they did even if the only point of contention had been Mr. Reagan's determination to lay a wreath in honor of German war dead at Bitburg. But what ensured that this would turn into a full-blown national debate was the Reagan administration's awkward handling of the affair. The president's initial refusal to visit a concentration camp because it would open up "old wounds," and his remark that SS soldiers buried at the military cemetery were "victims [of Nazism] just as surely as the victims in the concentration camps,"[3] stirred additional anger and widened the scope of the debate. A show of unity and reconciliation between the United States and postwar Germany may have been the intent of Mr. Reagan's plans but the effect was something else, in the eyes of his critics: a downplaying of the significance of the Holocaust and a muddied understanding of the crimes of the SS, the elite Nazi guard that ran the concentration camps. In a particularly sharp response, a spokesman for the 9.3-million-member United Methodist Church underscored the difference between "systematic attempts by the Hitler regime to annihilate a people because of race" and the "normal deaths incurred in the game of war." Insensivity to this distinction, the church official said, is a "tragic illustration of racism."[4]

While united in their opposition to the visit, the various groups were hardly uniform in their reasons for speaking out. They came to the debate with different perspectives and interests, reflecting their own recollections and experiences of World War II. Common to many of them, however, were formal ties that they had developed with American Jewish groups, ties that contributed to a feeling that Jews should not be left standing alone on an issue so central to their concerns. All this created the atmosphere needed for the U.S. Senate to formally call on the president to reassess his plans,[5] an action taken even though the general public—as shown in national opinion polls—was much less united on, and interested in, the issue.

Like few events since World War II, the Bitburg visit on May 5, 1985, was, and continues to be, an important part of the discussion about the contemporary meaning of the Holocaust. Most of the discussion of Bitburg has centered on the visit itself and the administration's handling of it. How different groups and the public reacted during the three weeks of intensive debate leading up to the visit is a separate matter, which has received less attention. Yet the responses shed light on how Americans think of the Holocaust and how—or whether—that event is considered important today. According to opinion polls, leaders of various institutions displayed much more concern about preserving the memory of the Holocaust than did the general public.

Aside from Jews, for whom keeping alive the memory of the Holocaust is a permanent endeavor, those who felt the most direct stake in what happened at Bitburg were American veterans. From their point of view, Mr. Reagan could honor those buried at Bitburg only by dishonoring Americans who fought and died against them. The American Legion, largest of the veterans' groups, reminded the president that Waffen troops (who formed the combat arm of the SS) were responsible for the summary executions of more than seventy-five unarmed American prisoners at Malmedy, just thirty miles from Bitburg. "Are these the same SS troops buried beneath the stones of Bitburg?"

Following the lead of the 2.7-million-member Legion and the Jewish War Veterans, other major veterans' groups such as American Ex-Prisoners of War, Catholic War Veterans, and the American Veterans Committee joined in the criticism. The Committee, an organization of World War II veterans, emphasized that the dead at Bitburg fell during the 1944 Battle of the Bulge, a German offensive that took 19,000 American lives. Other veterans recalled that the city of Bitburg was a Battle of the Bulge staging area used by the SS's Sixth Panzer Army, which led the attack under the command of SS General Joseph "Sepp" Dietrich, later convicted of war crimes at Nuremberg for the Malmedy massacre. "Those buried at Bitburg included S.S. active Nazis and not just conscripts," said the Committee, disputing Mr. Reagan's comments that the SS included many young men drafted against their will, "and the Battle of the Bulge was closely linked to the Nazi plan of total domination of Europe and furtherance of its genocidal purposes against innocent peoples."

Staying out of the battle over Bitburg, however, was the nation's second largest veterans' group, Veterans of Foreign Wars, which waited until late in the dispute to send off a telegram simply extending to the president its best wishes for a successful trip abroad. For the 2.2-million-member VFW, the question came down to whether it should go against a foreign-policy decision by the commander-in-chief of the armed forces.[6] This was less a matter of concern to the American Legion than it was to the VFW, the most politically active of the veterans' organizations. Unlike the Legion, the VFW operates a political action committee that gives money to political candidates, one of whom, in 1984, was Ronald Reagan.

Not only Jews and veterans felt a direct, personal interest in the images projected by the visit; leaders of major ethnic groups, in particular, looked upon it as a slight against the memory of their suffering of forty years before. Michael Preisler, spokesman for the Polish American Congress and a Roman Catholic survivor of Auschwitz, illustrated the potential of this dispute to touch people of various backgrounds when he wrote to the president:

> Nowhere else did the Hitlerites unleash the insane fury of their bestial rage and hatred as in Poland. They drenched Polish soil with the blood of innocent people.
> We mourn the death of six million Polish citizens, most of whom were mercilessly butchered by the type of primitive barbarians who lie in the graves of the cemetery you will visit. Their goal was to forever destroy everything Polish, be it Christian or Jewish. In the genocide of Europe's Jews, at least half were Poles.
> Measured by those who died, Polish Jews and Polish Christians perished almost equally. Measured by percentage, Poland lost more of her population to the Nazis than any other country. As Christians, we feel compelled to forgive them. As their victims, we find it inconceivable to honor them.

Even Americans with less direct experiences of Nazi Germany felt they had a distinct role to play in the debate over Bitburg. Japanese American leaders spoke on Bitburg in light of their own plight in the United States around the time that Jews faced extermination in Europe. "As Americans we often forget that the death camps are the extreme result of ethnic and religious prejudice, hate, and ignorance from which no nation is immune," the Midwest District of the Japanese American Citizens League told the president in a telegram. "Japanese Americans are all too aware of the fragility of our own legal protections. While the imprisonment of 120,000 Japanese American citizens and resident aliens by the United States government during World War II was fundamentally different from the Nazi program of genocide, it demonstrates how easily the concepts of due process and equal rights can be brushed aside."

The Japanese American appeal illustrated another dimension of the response to Bitburg—that is, the tangible expression of years of intergroup dialogue with Jews. "We have many friends and neighbors of the Jewish faith. Some are survivors of the very death camps that you originally neglected to add to your itinerary. They can never forget. Your actions are an affront to them and, even more so, an affront to the six million victims."

These were serious concerns aroused by the visit. But an important explanation for the mobilization by ethnic organizations— heard most clearly when they came together for joint statements enunciating common concerns—actually had less to do with Bitburg than with the

American "ethnic" movement generally. These groups—among them the American Jewish Committee, Sons of Italy, Ukrainian National Association, United Hellenic American Congress, and the Mexican American Legal Defense Fund—were able to reach such a high level of cooperation because they had worked together on issues in the past. Before Bitburg came along, they had already built a coalition rooted in a sense of common purpose and interests, which stemmed in large part from the 1970s movement toward a renewed appreciation of ethnicity.

Through this movement (a principal facilitator of which is the American Jewish Committee), the organizations addressed common concerns such as negative images of ethnic people in the media. Many of those speaking out on Bitburg had received help from the Jewish community when they were on the front lines with their own issues. With Hispanics, for instance, Jews have argued for open immigration policies and national legislation granting temporary legal status to undocumented Salvadoran refugees. Jewish groups have called for reparations for Japanese Americans interned during World War II, and spoken out against spates of anti-Asian violence. They have also intervened with the Israeli government on behalf of Greek Americans concerned about the treatment of Eastern Orthodox Christians in the Jewish State.

Officials of these groups acknowledge that this kind of cooperation is based on the idea of political "reciprocity," and that the help given to Jews by other ethnic groups when the Bitburg dispute arose was a part of that reciprocity.[7] Yet it is unlikely that any narrowly political alliance alone could have resulted in the types of reactions that came from ethnic communities. To the extent that this response was influenced by friendships between Jews and others, it was due less to any political debts owed than to genuine relationships that had developed; these relationships made it easier for various groups of Americans to understand what Jews were going through.

Such relationships played an even larger part in the positions taken by the leaderships of mainline Christian denominations. These church bodies did not have the same personal and historical reasons for speaking out as did, say, veterans and Polish Americans. But they had enjoyed twenty years of interfaith dialogue that also produced formal commitments never to repeat past Christian mistakes of anti-Semitism and silence in the face of Jewish suffering. They sought to put that commitment and understanding in practice when the issue of Bitburg arose, particularly in light of frequent conflicts with Jewish groups over other issues, such as U.S. policy toward the Middle East.

"Unlike other times, it was not a case in which Jews had to solicit

Christian names," recalled Rabbi A. James Rudin, director of interfaith relations for the American Jewish Committee. "They called us.
They said this was what we want to do. My phone was ringing off the
hook." As one explanation for the response, Dr. Rudin pointed to
Holocaust education programs sponsored by such groups as the National Council of Churches, which he said helped lay the groundwork
for Christian awareness of what was at stake in the Bitburg dispute.[8]
Two weeks after the wreath-laying ceremony, the Rev. Arie Brouwer,
general secretary of the church council, was asked if his stance didn't
conflict with the Christian value of forgiveness. "It is not for us or
President Reagan to forgive the Nazis of their sins," he replied. "This
is something the Jews have to work out."[9]

Illustrating the initiative taken by mainline Christians was the
April 28 "open letter" to the president in the *New York Times*. "I was
aware of statements by non-Jewish groups, but they did not seem to
be getting picked up by the media. . . . It was imperative that the
Jewish community not be seen as standing alone on this," Sister Carol
Rittner, who initiated the newspaper appeal, explained later on. Sister
Rittner, who teaches courses on the Holocaust at Mercy College in
Detroit, recalled fearing that the Bitburg debate might turn ugly.
There was the potential, she said, for people to blame the controversy
on Jews and "say the Jews are throwing their weight around."[10] This
was no unsubstantiated fear. A *Washington Post*/ABC News poll taken
on April 22 found that 60 percent of Americans thought Jewish leaders were "making too big a deal out of Reagan's visit." In a *New York
Times*/CBS News poll taken on the day after the visit, a smaller percentage—about 38 percent, including 18 percent of those who opposed the visit—agreed that "Jewish leaders in the United States protested too much over his visit." Adding to this was the fear by some
Jews that the dispute was pitting "Jewish" concerns against American
security and interests abroad.

Helping to divert some of the attention away from criticism were
the 143 Christian leaders—among them national leaders of the Roman
Catholic, Baptist, Presbyterian, United Methodist, African Methodist
Episcopal, and Reformed churches, as well as heads of theological
seminaries and local councils of churches. In the *Times* advertisement,
they called on the president to cancel his planned ceremony with
Helmut Kohl, and symbolize reconciliation by, instead, going to the
home of postwar German leader Konrad Adenauer, or Flossenberg
concentration camp, where Lutheran theologian Dietrich Bonhoeffer was hanged for his part in a plot to assassinate Hitler.

The very fact that churches, and not just Jews, were speaking out
affirmed that the Holocaust was not just a "Jewish" issue. In the view

of Christian critics, the White House and Chancellor Kohl had in effect marginalized concerns about the Holocaust and cast Jews in the role of a special-interest group, by giving the impression they could not honor German-American friendship and at the same time remember the six million Jewish victims. This, according to one Christian study group on the Holocaust, was an affront to many Germans who have sought reconciliation with other nations by facing up to the shame of the past, rather than by denying it.[11]

Liberal church denominations had another interest in Bitburg that had less to do with who is buried there than with reports that the city's air base is the site of one of the largest concentrations of American nuclear weapons anywhere.[12] The mainline church leaderships are, for the most part, vocal critics of administration foreign and nuclear policies. In their view, the wreath-laying ceremony had less to do with reconciliation than with advancing hard, ideological goals—in particular, the stationing of American missiles on European soil and allied support for other administration programs. To liberal church representatives, it was bad enough to be willing to sacrifice, or distort, the memory of the Holocaust, but to do so on the altar of national security was even worse.

Yet, amid the church criticism, some mainline religious representatives felt uncomfortable with the positions taken by their denominational executives. The influential *United Methodist Reporter* faulted national church agencies for contributing toward a wave of anti-German sentiment with their statements. While taking no stand on the visit itself, the *Reporter* said in an editorial that the president's visit had released a lingering hostility toward the German people, which reflects "a stubborn unwillingness among countless persons to follow Christ's admonition to forgive and forget." Although Christians should speak out against any action that gives the appearance of insensitivity toward the memory of Jewish suffering, the newspaper said, there was also a need to "deplore the words and actions of all those who would try to afflict present-day Germans with guilt for actions for which they bear no responsibility."

In the weeks following the twenty-minute ceremony at Bitburg, the moral questions came under further examination in intellectual Christian magazines. In an editorial titled "When you say 'Never again,' mean it," *Christianity and Crisis*, which has a readership of liberal Protestants and Catholics, took aim at the speech delivered by Mr. Reagan at Bergen-Belsen, the death-camp site that he decided to go to only after a furor developed over his refusal to visit Dachau. The magazine said:

Speaking at this place on this occasion, the president uttered not a single phrase suggesting that any but one man and his "hated regime" were responsible for the Holocaust, for Anne Frank's suffering and death, for those piles of bodies of Jews (and gypsies and homosexuals and Catholic and Protestant and Communist resisters and mentally ill persons). That is an absurd and dangerous distortion. All Germans had occasion to know Hitler's hatred of the Jews before they voted him into office, and ... he succeeded in making the whole nation a tool of his hatred.[13]

For its post-Bitburg analysis, the *Christian Century* turned its pages over to a Jewish writer, Mark Krupnick. Mr. Krupnick lamented the implicit portrayal of the Bitburg debate as a conflict between those espousing the Christian concept of forgiveness and those still bent on revenge.[14] This article, as well as one published by the *Century* before the visit, could be seen as part of a continuing act of penance by the magazine. At the time that Hitler was advancing toward his "final solution," the ecumenical Protestant weekly cited Jewish radical activity as an explanation for the persecution of the Jews. While many newspapers were supporting the 1939 Wagner-Rogers bill to admit 20,000 German Jewish children into the United States, the *Century* preferred not to "exacerbate America's Jewish problem."[15] In the post-Holocaust era, however, the journal has been a model for attention by Christians to the lessons of the Holocaust.

One Christian journal often noted for its outspokenness in behalf of the Jews during World War II is *Commonweal*, a lay-edited liberal Catholic magazine. In an editorial titled "Bitburg and the Century of Ash," *Commonweal* passed up an opportunity to single the president out for criticism, and examined, instead, what the desire to visit Bitburg revealed about Americans in general.

As Americans, we have little stomach for prolonged, enduring suffering. When President Reagan chose not to go to Dachau as part of his initial itinerary, he was seeking, in the name of reconciliation with a German ally, to evade what Saul Friedländer has called the most extreme upheaval of our time, the "indelible reference point of Western imagination." There is no question as to the president's abhorrence of the Holocaust. Yet what has become apparent in his recent actions and unguarded phrases is what we secretly sense of ourselves. Like Mr. Reagan, we have a deep desire to be spared, to be rid of the unpleasant present and past. We go to great lengths to assure our personal contentment and it constitutionally guaranteed pursuit.[16]

Commonweal noted that West German chancellor Helmut Kohl

had won favor from the United States by installing cruise missiles and supporting research into Star Wars, the space-based weapons proposal. "Yet none of this can take away from the fact that the Jewish cemetery in Bitburg is today tended by non-Jews. *There are no Jews left in Bitburg.* Surely, Elie Wiesel was correct when he insisted before the president that the issue was not one of politics, but good and evil."

When asked why no conservative evangelical and fundamentalist leaders had joined in the *New York Times* advertisement, Sister Rittner said it was because they weren't among her contacts. Yet even if they were, it is unlikely that they would have come on board. Asked to sign a similar appeal, all but one of a group of well-known television evangelists and conservative Christian leaders turned down the request. A coalition of Jewish groups had requested them to back a statement that appeared as a *New York Times* advertisement a week after the mainline Christian appeal.

Two of those contacted—evangelist Billy Graham and Pat Robertson, head of the Christian Broadcasting Network—gave assurances that they had privately made contact with the White House to urge that the president cancel his visit.[17] In the end, the only conservative Christian leader joining in the appeal was the Rev. Jerry Falwell, the leader of the Moral Majority political organization, who had been trying to cultivate closer ties to Jewish groups.

The lack of response by evangelicals required some explanations from Rabbi Yechiel Eckstein, who had been trying to convince wary Jewish leaders that these conservative Christians—some of whom had emerged as vocal supporters of Israel—wanted to enter into a genuine relationship with the Jewish community. Eckstein said that no "structure" of ties existed between evangelical Christians and Jews, as had been established between Jews and liberal Christians. While the liberal churches, after more than twenty years of interreligious dialogue, were sensitive to questions relating to the Holocaust, evangelicals "have not been exposed to this kind of dialogue." Their silence on Bitburg only underscored the need to work toward a "true relationship between the two groups, and not a narrow political alliance based on certain issues." (In making this point, Rabbi Eckstein was alluding to support by some Jews for an alliance with evangelicals based solely on common political support for Israel.) But at one point Eckstein too ran out of explanations. "This [Bitburg] was not a hard or risky political issue. They should have come out with statements of their own, without solicitation, on a moral issue like this," he said. "I don't have an excuse."

More willing to speak out on Bitburg—and in favor of the visit—

were leaders of the secular Right. William F. Buckley concluded in his widely syndicated column that "Reagan did the right thing. And he performed spendidly. And he is owed apologies he will never get." Despite warnings by some critics, he said, the visit resulted in no wave of anti-Semitism. Appearing on Public Broadcasting's "MacNeil/Lehrer Report," Richard Viguerie complained that the debate over Bitburg was focusing too much on the Holocaust and too little on modern-day atrocities committed by the Soviet Union. In an interview following the visit, Mr. Viguerie, editor of *Conservative Digest* and known as the direct-mail marketing whiz of the New Right, praised Mr. Reagan for helping "heal the wounds of West Germany, a key ally of the United States in the fight against Communism." He said:

> We need to be more worried about holocausts of everybody, not just of one group. I'd like to see more emphasis placed on those dying today. We're not making light, minimizing what happened (to Jews in Nazi Germany). But we also recognize that if we're not careful we can all participate in a holocaust of 1985, courtesy of the Soviet Union.
>
> What's the difference between Communism and Nazism, except that Communism is more effective. They kill more people than the Nazis did. I don't understand the hypocritical feeling that we must keep the torch burning so everyone remembers the Nazis, but [we] don't see the same groups doing anything about the terrors of Communism, which is much more threatening now.[18]

Within the Jewish community, the reactions heated an already lively debate over relationships between Jews and other groups. Much of this debate—along with general news media attention—centered on the fledgling alliance between Jews and evangelicals, two groups that have traditionally viewed each other with suspicion but that found common ground on the issue of Israel. During 1985, influential Jewish neoconservatives had been arguing that Jews ought to rethink their traditional relationships with blacks, Hispanics, and liberals, on grounds that they were moving in directions ever more hostile to Jewish concerns, including the state of Israel. Instead, they asserted, Jewish interests lay in cultivating their newer alliance with conservative Christians and the movement known as the Christian New Right, which had become an important source of support for Israel. To forge these ties, according to the analysis, Jews had to drop their traditional opposition to such things as prayer and Bible reading in public schools. This should be done, said noted neoconservative Irving Kristol, for the sake of "political expediency" and as a quid pro quo for evangelical support for Israel.[19]

The neoconservative designs for a profound alteration of Jewish political identity opened the way for questions about whether alliances based on such politically expedient grounds could lead to genuine relationships between groups. (And the Bitburg issue showed how little the single-issue alliance between evangelicals and Jews had produced in the way of mutual understanding.) But, even putting aside these concerns, the neoconservative forecast of rapidly shifting Jewish interests collapsed—at least temporarily—under the cloud of Bitburg. Leaders of the conservative movement and Christian Right expressed little sympathy for what Jews were going through, while the Jews' traditional allies turned out in large numbers to protest the visit.

Interestingly, however, a poll taken three months after the visit found that people who describe themselves as conservatives were slightly more likely to oppose the visit than self-described liberals. The reason for this, according to an analysis by the American Jewish Committee, which commissioned the Roper survey, was that liberals saw the visit as a "contribution to international amity and the healing of old wounds." Conservatives, on the other hand, were influenced more by nationalist feelings against conferring honor on those who fought against the United States. What this seemed to show was that the average American liberal and conservative thought about Bitburg in terms different from those of their more ideological and partisan political leaders.

More significant, however, was the overall response in public opinion polls. In the same survey, the Roper Organization found that, three months after the visit, only 32 percent of the public had an opinion on whether the president should have gone to Bitburg—a small segment considering the heatedness of the debate among institutional leaders. Two polls taken closer to the time of the visit found more interest, but also registered deeply divided opinion on whether the president should go—again, in contrast to the united stand taken by leaders of various institutions. In the *Washington Post*/ABC poll, taken two weeks before the visit, a majority of those surveyed—52 percent—expressed the view that Mr. Reagan should cancel his visit; 44 percent agreed with the statement that the president should "go ahead with his plans."

The gap closed, however, around the time of the actual visit. In a poll taken on the day after the ceremony, the *New York Times* and CBS found an American public equally divided over Bitburg: 41 percent said he should have gone, and 41 percent said he shouldn't have. In a news article, the *Times* attributed the diminished opposition to the actual visit, along with the president's decision to make a stop at Bergen-Belsen.

These two surveys also shed some light on attitudes toward the

Holocaust. For most Americans, the Nazi campaign of genocide against the Jews was evidently not a major factor in their opinions on Bitburg. Even among those who opposed the visit, according to the *Times*/CBS poll, only 9 percent cited SS atrocities against the Jews as their reason. Furthermore, in the *Post*/ABC poll, only a third of those surveyed agreed with the argument (attributed in the survey question to "American Jewish leaders and others") that Mr. Reagan's visit to Bitburg would "dishonor the Holocaust victims."[20] If anyone was being dishonored, in the eyes of the public, it was the American veteran. Forty-five percent agreed with the statement that if Mr. Reagan went to Bitburg, "he [would] in effect be dishonoring American soldiers who fought against the Germans in World War II." Gauging reactions to the broader debate, this survey also found considerable support for Mr. Reagan's remarks that German soldiers buried at Bitburg were victims as surely as the victims in the concentration camps were; 47 percent agreed with the description, while 45 percent disagreed, and the rest had no opinion.

But the clearest indication of how Americans think about the Holocaust came in the poll taken by Roper for the American Jewish Committee. This survey found widespread uneasiness with continued public discussion of the Holocaust. Forty percent of those surveyed expressed the view that Jews should "stop focusing" on the Holocaust, while a larger segment—46 percent—welcomed being "reminded" of the Holocaust annually. "There would appear to be a widespread desire to invoke a kind of statute of limitations on being reminded of the Holocaust," the Committee's Milton Himmelfarb said in an October 1985 internal memorandum reporting the survey's findings. When asked, further, if there should be continued efforts to find Nazi war criminals, about half of those surveyed agreed it would be better to "put it behind us"; 41 percent still supported the efforts. So, while divided over the visit itself, the public seemed more comfortable with what the critics described as the overall message behind Bitburg—that the time had come to put aside old wounds. Paradoxically, this feeling surfaced just as formal Holocaust-education programs—epitomized by the creation of the U.S. Holocaust Memorial Council—were taking root in the U.S. The responses by the general public brought into sharp focus the challenges facing the Memorial Council and others seeking to promote understanding of the lessons of the Holocaust.

Beyond this, the Bitburg debate offered a rare glimpse into the diversity of American institutional life and private voluntary organizations. Most people probably didn't know that so many institutions for so many different ethnic and religious communities exist, let alone that they know each other and work together. From the Japanese and Polish Americans who related the Holocaust to their own experiences, to the careful scrutiny many gave to the events of Bitburg against the backdrop of the Nazi genocide, these American groups illustrated how the Holocaust acts indeed as an "indelible reference point" for Western imagination and moral analysis. Yet Bitburg also showed that if attention to this great reference point runs wide, it does not run deep. At the grass roots, little connection was made between Bitburg and the Holocaust, and the feeling that there should be less talk about the Holocaust was strong. One explanation for this difference is that while community leaders came to appreciate the significance of the Holocaust after many years of dialogue and cooperation with Jews, their constituents shared few such experiences. Perhaps another is that ordinary citizens and families wanted less attention given to other people's suffering because they face their own daily struggles for survival, and are more likely than the elites of society to see themselves as victims. In any event, average people, moral leaders, and nations were all handed a historic opportunity to show how they have come to terms with the destruction of European Jewry. It was an opportunity pressing no less heavily on American Jews themselves—who, as one Jewish observer pointed out, had barely begun to face up to their loss, let alone put themselves in a position to "forgive" the Nazis.[21] Like the Jews, the rest of the public showed that it has much to work out and come to grips with before the matter can, in good conscience, be put "behind us."

NOTES

1. *Quick*, a popular West German magazine, attracted international attention in April 1985, when it blamed the uproar on the "influence of the Jews."

2. Mr. Reagan said American journalists "have gotten ahold of something, and like a dog worrying a bone, they're going to keep chewing on it." Interviewed by ABC News, *National Review* publisher William Rusher termed Bitburg a minor incident exaggerated by the news media.

3. See excerpts from White House press conference in *New York Times*, April 19, 1985.

4. Remarks by the Rev. Robert W. Huston, general secretary of the church's Commission on Christian Unity and Interreligious Concerns, in an April 24 news release by United Methodist Communications in Nashville, Tennessee.

5. Fifty-three U.S. senators co-sponsored a non-binding resolution urging the president to reconsider his trip to Bitburg (see *New York Times*, April 17, 1985). For a similar measure passed by a 390–26 margin in the House of Representatives, see *Times* on May 1, 1985.

6. In a telephone interview with the author, conducted in November 1985, VFW Washington spokesman Ronald Duchin cited this concern as a reason for the group's position.

7. Joseph Giordano, of the American Jewish Committee's Center on Ethnicity, explained the cooperation in terms of "reciprocity" in a November 1985 interview with the author.

8. Remarks made by Dr. Rudin, after the visit, in a May 1985 interview with the author.

9. Remarks to reporters at a gathering on trends in religion sponsored by the Washington Journalism Center in May 1985.

10. Interview in May 1985 with the author.

11. Statement on April 30, 1985, by the National Conference of Christians and Jews' Christian Study Group on Judaism and Jewish People.

12. Bitburg's military role was cited in an editorial in the May 17, 1985, edition of *Commonweal*.

13. *Christianity and Crisis*, May 27, 1985.

14. Reprinted in the "Press Commentaries" section of this volume.

15. *Christian Century* articles cited in *Beyond Belief: The American Press and the Coming of the Holocaust, 1933–1945*, by Deborah E. Lipstadt (New York: The Free Press, 1985).

16. *Commonweal*, May 17, 1985.

17. Interview with Rabbi Yechiel Eckstein conducted by the author in May 1985. While little is known about any private intervention by Mr. Robertson, a Jewish confidant of Billy Graham, Rabbi Marc Tannenbaum of the American Jewish Committee, later reported that the evangelist was deeply distressed by the Bitburg affair and had personally asked the president and Nancy Reagan not to go. The committee's Washington representative, Hyman Bookbinder, also said afterwards that Graham's interview is believed to have contributed to Mr. Reagan's decision to visit the home of postwar German leader Konrad Adenauer.

18. Interview with the author in May 1985.

19. *Commentary*, July 1984.

20. Fifty-one percent said the visit would not be dishonoring to the victims, and 16 percent said they were not sure. A slight majority (51 percent) agreed, instead, with Mr. Reagan's view that the visit would "observe postwar U.S. friendship with West Germany."

21. See Krupnick's article in "Press Commentaries" section of this volume.

One must have a good memory
to be able to keep the promises one
has given.

—Nietzsche, *Menschliches,*
Allzumenschliches

A. Roy Eckardt

The Christian World
Goes to Bitburg

President Richard von Weizsäcker of the Federal Republic of Germany praised President Ronald Reagan of the United States for his "courage" in persisting in his promise to take part in a memorial visit at the cemetery of Bitburg. And West German Chancellor Helmut Kohl thanked Mr. Reagan for sending "a very powerful message" in determining to go on with the visit.[1] But whose brand of courage was the American president manifesting? And what kind of message did he in fact send?

One salient means of grappling with these questions is recourse to the history of Christendom in its relation to the Jewish people and Judaism. The subject before us is anything but a restrictedly "Jewish issue"; it is a Christian and a world-moral issue.

I

A large number of contemporary scholars advance the finding that the Christian church's traditional anti-Jewish teaching conjoined with the Christian world to help make inevitable the Holocaust of the Jews of Europe. The finding has even become something of a truism. Be it noted that many of these historiographers are themselves Christians.[2]

The causative phenomenon here identified suggests a certain perspective for comprehending and assessing President Reagan's resolution to go to Bitburg.

There is no question of Mr. Reagan's sympathy toward the victims of the Holocaust, his commitment to the prevention of another such terrible event, and his strong support of the State of Israel. It would be wholly unfair to number him among the many leaders of the Christian world who have failed to understand the moral implications of the Holocaust or remanded it merely to the history of the Jews. Nevertheless, it was as supreme representative of a land largely composed of Christians that the president traveled to that other, even more explicitly Christian land, the one that had consumed itself in Nazism. The American people are heirs of a religious tradition that has for centuries taught contempt for Jews, yet vast numbers of Americans are sympathetic to Jews, to Judaism, and to the State of Israel. The American problem is one of ambivalence. The president's refusal to cancel the Bitburg visit, despite the hue and cry against it, reflected this ambivalence. In addition, as pointed out by the Rev. Robert Huston of the United Methodist Church, such errors of judgment provide implicit support for anti-Semitism. Again, and of the highest significance, how ironically concordant it is that Mr. Reagan should be presiding over the very nation that, as David S. Wyman and others have reminded us, was in the 1930s and 1940s responsible for "the abandonment of the Jews" to what would be for most of them certain death.[3] By resolving to honor, among others, fallen members of the Waffen SS who may have carried out the murders of Jews, President Reagan and his advisors were recapitulating symbolically both the hostilities of the long Christian tradition and the more recent American abandonment of the Jewish people.

The president's action reincarnated the historic Christian acceptance of, and alliance with, the enemies of Jews. Bitburg was and will remain an event of celebration for all Nazis and neo-Nazis. It was to be expected that as soon as they heard the news of Mr. Reagan's visit, numbers of Waffen SS veterans in Germany would rejoice in the assurance that they had been "rehabilitated." One of them said: "The Zionists stop at nothing. But the President is an honest man. He made his decision, and he sticks to it."[4] The visit could thus also reembody the long-familiar utilization and prostitution of the Christian teaching of forgiveness in the service of anti-Semitism.

In such ways as these the Christian world, past and present, was standing at the side of the American president as he journeyed to Bitburg.

II

We shall be referring to the morality and hopefulness in the opposition by Christians to the memorial visit. The fact remains that this body of protest is of little if any immediate ethical or practical help in addressing the relation of Bitburg to Christian teachings and traditional behavior. Such protests simply pose highly moot questions: Were the objectors honoring integral Christian teachings or were they somehow managing to escape and surmount those teachings? More profoundly, just which teachings are to be identified as intrinsically Christian? The applicable and compelling datum, accordingly, is the failure of the Bitburg visit substantially to jeopardize Ronald Reagan's long-run high approval rating among the American populace.[5]

Of still greater moral significance is the split that invariably obtains between Christians and Jews—it surfaced once again at Bitburg[6]—respecting the praxis of "forgiveness." In light of highly divergent historical experiences as between Christians and Jews, the fact that the "forgiveness of one's enemies" plays a more conspicuous verbal and at least professed role in Christian circles than it does in Jewish circles opens the fateful question of the presence of Christian ideology (= rationalization at the collective level) or what is often denominated false consciousness. The reason for saying this is that on purely objective moral grounds, Christians, as past and present victimizers of Jews,[7] ought to be infinitely wary of propagating the idea of forgiveness for anti-Semitism, especially for wholesale murder of Jews. Whenever the victimizers of our world preach to the victims such ideals as love and forgiveness, we do well to adopt a "hermeneutic of suspicion" (Paul Ricoeur). The element of self-serving on the part of the victimizers enters in as an extremely destructive eventuality, as against any analogous situations among the victims.

A. C. J. Phillips, chaplain of St. John's College, Oxford, used the occasion of Mr. Reagan's Bitburg cemetery visit to call upon the Jewish community to forgive the perpetrators of the Holocaust. Phillips concluded his summons with the unbelievable statement: "In remembering the Holocaust, Jews hope to prevent its recurrence; by declining to forgive, I fear that they unwittingly invite it."[8]

Here was a typical instance of the capture of Christian faith by an ideological taint and false consciousness. The truth that as a Christian clergyman, *Stellvertreter* of the church catholic, Anthony Phillips carries upon his hands (as do many of the rest of us) the blood of the Christian ages ought at least to have compelled him to refrain from such imperialistic moralizing directed to the Jewish people respecting how they ought to have responded to Ronald Reagan's act.

Even though I write as a Christian, I believe that condemnations of the Bitburg memorial visit from within the Jewish community embody a much higher level of morality than do Christian preachments upon the virtues of love and forgiveness. For there can be neither love nor forgiveness without repentance and righteousness on the part of the guilty: this is a main pillar of the biblical witness (see, e.g., Matt. 5:23–24), so often negated by the ideological drives and pious sentimentalities that beset the Christian community.

III

Let us return to our epigraph from Friedrich Nietzsche. The Christian memory is an afflicted memory. Christians of America bear a dual psycho-moral burden: the more recent culpability of their country's abandonment of the Jewish people, and the much more archetypal and more deeply repressed, never-ending destructiveness of their religious community vis-à-vis Jews. Because the American nation's abandonment of the Jews only a generation ago has never been gathered up, internalized, and grappled with in a life-and-death way as an abidingly accusing fact of life for the American collective conscience, our representatives can go about dispensing the cheap grace of forgiveness for those German Nazis who committed murder. Cheap grace is the kind that is "sold on the market like cheapjack's wares." The forgiveness of sin is distributed at cut prices.[9] In quite sincere fashion Ronald Reagan could act to shower the German people with these pretensions of grace while turning his back upon the horrendous record of the United States respecting the Jews in the Nazi time.[10] And Mr. Reagan could go even further. Shortly before departing for Bitburg, he declared to a group of foreign journalists: "All of those in that cemetery have long since met the Supreme Judge of right and wrong, and whatever punishment was needed has been rendered by one who is above us all.[11]

The "good memory" that induced President Reagan to "keep the promise" he gave Chancellor Kohl to visit Bitburg bore no relationship to any imaginable existential memory of the Holocaust. For the latter memory would have compelled him and his advisor to do something entirely different: to honor instead Elie Wiesel's counsel, "Your place, Mr. President, is with the victims." No, Mr. Reagan's "good memory" arose out of his participation in the collective unconscious of Christendom: a company comprising the crusading legions, theologians, and ecclesiastics of the imperialist Christian church, the historic calumniators and destroyers of Jews and Judaism.[12] Friedrich Nietzsche rejected the Christian virtues of love, pity, and forgiveness. The affinities between Nietzsche and Nazism are well known. Yet, irony of ironies, Bitburg has pointed up the element of moral convincingness in Nietzsche's antipathy to the Christian virtues. For once human forgiveness gets transubstantiated into ammunition for the devil's own cause; i.e., anti-Semitism, the perniciousness that perennially lurks within the Christian ethic, comes to reveal itself in finally destructive form.

Thus, while Nietzsche's aphorism upon the essentiality of memory in the keeping of promises applies strikingly to Ronald Reagan's promise to go to Bitburg, it does not do so at the level of conscious memory. For at the conscious level Mr. Reagan comes across as the well-intentioned though ignorant grandfather,[13] whose awareness of the recent history of Germany is, with that of countless other Americans, either selected or deficient or distorted, or all three. (At one point Mr. Reagan presented the astounding historical datum that very few Germans living today were old enough to remember the Nazi times.) But in the murky world of the unconscious, everything is different; our president was largely acting out the collective memory of 1900 years of Christian history. In Mr. Reagan's particular case, and with Bitburg especially upon our minds, the evil could be actualized and compounded by his special obsession—identical to the one that inspired the Vatican to make its peace with the Hitlerites—the obsessive fear of Bolshevism. Most portentous of the visit to Bitburg was Ronald Reagan's declaration shortly before becoming president: "The Soviet Union is behind everything that is going on in the world." At this juncture, the unconscious and the conscious domains tend to be mutually supportive.

The ongoing character of collective Christian culpability for the Holocaust is demonstrated in the truth that the Christian crime goes on. Any who today support the central Christian doctrines of supersessionism and triumphalism vis-à-vis Judaism and the Jewish people thereby act to keep alive the *Anschauung* that helped make inevitable the death camps of Europe. In keeping with this truth, the head of a nation made up mostly of Christians had in fact only one choice that could be deemed righteous: to stay away from the Bitburg cemetery.

But President Reagan and his advisors also aggravated the psycho-moral plight of persecutors and perpetrators within Germany, those "countless ones who were in some fashion accessory, as well as the standard-bearers of the perverted racist world view." Among these people,

> their beloved objects—the Nazi ideology and the delusion of chosenness—continue to survive. No loss has occurred; at worst they were "robbed" by the enemy. The libido has not been required to relinquish its objects. This means that no loss, no demise has taken place—and thus, in turn, that no mourning work could be or needs to be performed. Substitutes were not acceptable. By incessant rationalization

and the use of other multiple, convoluted, out-of-the-way defense strategies, a liberating result was achieved that led to a rehabilitation of the old Nazi *Weltanschauung*. Perpetrators became innocent victims. They felt doubly confirmed in their paranoia, for the war was lost—"as we all know"—due to treachery and sabotage, while the victorious Allies were incited and led by "World Jewry."[14]

To this frightening condition—as described by a psychoanalyst in the Germany of today—our president has now added his own contribution. Instead of fostering the reconciliation that he claimed for his act, Mr. Reagan helped to compound human alienation.

The inability to mourn (*die Unfähigheit zu trauern*)[15] is dialectically-existentially linked with the inability to repent (*die Unfähigkeit zu bereuen*).

The future may do its best to obscure or obliterate these truths. But this will not prevent them from crashing down upon the human sphere. History, symbol, and morality are all inseparable.

The etiology of the Bitburg event is, in sum, closely tied to the ethos of vast numbers of church people. Inevitably but revealingly, one such individual found the president's action "to be the most Christian act of his administration." Untold numbers of church people will keep on preaching and supporting a self-righteous, "high morality" of forgiveness for enemies of Jews because they have never repented of their own enmities toward Jews. They have instead been able to justify their own anti-Semitisms on the ground of the Jewish "sin" of "rejecting" the Christian claim. Thus is Jewish suffering transmuted into deserved suffering. Here is the fundamental reason we Christians can turn our backs upon Jewish suffering. Because Christians fail to see the log in their own eye, they are prevented from seeing a log of comparable size in the eye of foes of the Jewish people. Were they themselves Christianly penitent, they would not be so ready to parcel out for the enemies of Jews the cheap grace of forgiveness, any more than would the president whom they had elected. Redemption for acts of cheap grace takes place only when it is made to cost dearly. Mr. Reagan's appearance at Bitburg revealed once more the modern transformation of the original Christian gospel into an ideology of "forgive and forget"—a comfortingly pleasant notion but no less an effectively anti-Jewish and immoral one.

IV

And yet, a deep paradox is present. Something incommensurable, something impertinent, something daring, enters in to break the depressing spell. Amidst the gloom of Bitburg a strange kind of hopefulness intrudes—and this from within the Christian community itself.[16] In point of redeeming truth, some persons of the Christian church immediately grasped and made public the morally intolerable quality of Ronald Reagan's "good memory." To the group of foreign journalists mentioned above, Mr. Reagan had argued that his visit would symbolize "the great reconciliation that has taken place" between the United States and Germany. Therefore, he insisted, it was "morally right" for him to go to Bitburg. But to a considerable number of Christians the president's visit was morally wrong. Thus, the Christian Study Group on Judaism and the Jewish People, a body of American theologians and scholars, found Reagan's "intention to put the past behind us and not to remind the German people of the crimes of the Nazi regime [to be] an affront to many in the new Germany who have been struggling again to become a member of a community of civilized nations by accepting the shame of the past and not denying it." This group further identified the Reagan decision as an offense to Jews and to other victims of the Nazi crimes. Again, some 150 American Protestants and Catholics asserted in an open letter to Mr. Reagan:

> We are shocked by the insensitivity and inaccuracy of your explanation that the German soldiers buried [in Bitburg] "were victims, just as surely as the victims in the concentration camps."
> The failure to distinguish between perpetrators and victims, between the death of combatants in battle and the slaughter of innocents in the Nazi concentration camps does injustice not only to the memory of the dead but to the most basic tenets of Jewish and Christian morality.[17]

The signatories included the president and general secretary of the National Council of Churches; Baptist, Presbyterian, Episcopalian, Lutheran, Methodist, Congregationalist, United Church of Christ, and Roman Catholic officials; heads of theological seminaries and academic institutions; noted theologians and scholars; and clergy, nuns, and lay leaders.

These persons were not only evidently unimpressed by the president's reputedly inside knowledge of the divine procedures; they also found his "moral" position to be perfidious. But how could such protests ever become possible? Other protests were made, in Germany as in America. *How could it be that certain Christians, heirs as they equally are with Ronald Reagan of the very same collective memory that ensures the denigration of Jews, should rise above all such conditioning?*

The aphorism of Nietzsche requires a corollary: One must have a replacement memory if one is to gain the courage to expunge the evil in promises previously given. These protesting Christians have come under the power of just such an antithetic memory. They remember the small Hungarian children of Auschwitz being burned alive in the presence of other Jewish children who *knew* that in the next moment they would be murdered in the same way (this for the "crime" of being Jewish). Here is a memory that sentences to perdition the collective anti-Jewish memory of the Christian church. It is this new memory that gives life and meaning to a faithful remnant of Christians who will never abandon the Jewish people. Had he wished to do so, or had he possessed the courage, Ronald Reagan could have confronted himself with this other memory. And thereby he could have used the unspeakable occasion of Bitburg in order to represent— or at least to plead for—the remorse of the American people for their part in the abandonment of the Jewish people.[18] Thus could Bitburg itself have been transfigured into a world-decisive act of authentic reconciliation—*with* the people of Germany, *with* the Jewish community, and, incredibly, even *with* possible penitents within the Waffen SS as with other Nazis, the living dead of today's Europe.

A personal observation may be allowed. Perhaps it is the writer's roots in the land of Germany that motivate part of his sorrow over acts of cheap grace directed to—more accurately, directed *against*— the German people. Only costly grace can redeem. The act of the American president and his counselors was, descriptively speaking, a snare and a perversion: this judgment must be entered by one American who perforce lives as though next to the people of Germany. The contention concerning grace is made in the very name of the persecutors and their children, who must otherwise remain lost souls.[19]

As matters stand, the name of Bitburg will ever bear the stigma of human alienation instead of human reconciliation. Nevertheless, this fact may itself be treated heuristically. President Reagan claims to be privy to the fact of divine punishment. Let us at the end venture to implement his own reasoning: One day he too may be summoned to judgment and asked how he could ever have acted to memorialize the killers. Yet the action by him and his administration must remain a relatively lesser episode within the larger, unending, and much more infamous tale. It is the entire Christian corpus that will be brought to judgment for its role in creating the victimizers. Once this takes place, the War Between the Memories will have reached its denouement.

NOTES

1. *New York Times*, May 3, 1985.
2. Among Christian sources consult, e.g., Alan Davies, ed., *Antisemitism*

and the Foundations of Christianity (New York: Paulist, 1979); A. Roy Eckardt, *Your People, My People* (Quadrangle/New York Times, 1974), chap. 2; A. Roy Eckardt and Alice L. Eckardt, "Christentum und Judentum, Die theologische und moralische Problematik der Vernichtung des europäischen Judentums," *Evangelische Theologie* 36 (1976): 406–26; idem, *Long Night's Journey into Day* (New York: Holocaust Publications, 1986); Friedrich Heer, *God's First Love,* trans. Geoffrey Shelton (New York: Weybright and Talley, 1970); Charlotte Klein, *Theologie und Anti-Judaismus* (Munich: Chr. Kaiser Verlag, 1975); Franklin H. Littell, *The Crucifixion of the Jews* (New York: Harper & Row, 1975); Rolf Rendtorff and Ekkehard Stegemann, eds., *Auschwitz—Krise der christlichen Theologie* (Munich: Chr. Kaiser Verlag, 1980); and Rosemary Radford Ruether, *Faith and Fratricide* (New York: Seabury, 1974).

3. David S. Wyman, *Paper Walls: America and the Refugee Crisis, 1938–1941* (Amherst: University of Massachusetts Press, 1969); idem, *The Abandonment of the Jews: America and the Holocaust, 1941–1945* (New York: Pantheon, 1984).

4. John Tagliabue, "SS Veterans Feel 'Rehabilitated' by Reagan Visit," *New York Times,* May 3, 1985. It was not until after 1943 that, because of a high attrition rate, SS members were conscripted; before then the units were wholly composed of volunteers.

5. On April 22, 1985, a *Washington Post*–ABC News poll found that 51 percent of respondents disapproved of the cemetery visit, 39 percent approved, and the remainder voiced no opinion. True, the poll showed an immediate drop in the president's approval rating to 54 percent (*Washington Post,* May 8, 1985). Yet the Bitburg "incident" was all too soon forgotten. President Reagan was probably right that his Bitburg visit was not "of that much concern" to most Americans. Of great relevance here is the peculiar social-psychological truth that national, majority attitudes to Mr. Reagan show over the long range little if any connection to his personal policies and behavior.

6. Consult, e.g., the exchange of correspondence reproduced in *European Judaism* (London), Spring 1985, pp. 5–17.

7. Consult, e.g., Edward H. Flannery, *The Anguish of the Jews,* rev. ed. (New York: Paulist, 1985); and Hyam Maccoby, *The Sacred Executioner* (New York: Thames and Hudson, 1982).

8. *The Times* (London), June 8, 1985.

9. Dietrich Bonhoeffer, *The Cost of Discipleship,* trans. R. H. Fuller and Irmgard Booth (London: SCM, 1959), p. 35.

10. On balance, the ongoing American record respecting its own Jewish citizens is among the best in the world. But the preeminent moral source for this achievement is a trans-Christian and constitutionally guaranteed cultural pluralism.

11. *New York Times,* April 30, 1985.

12. Such participation does not require fervent or active religiousness; the most nominal gentile lives under the power of Christian history.

13. By Ronald Reagan's good intentions at the conscious level, we mean both his self-image and his image as received by many other people. Objectively speaking, Mr. Reagan is of course not above the use of falsehood to advance his position. Thus, one young Jewish woman wrote to urge him not to go to Bitburg. In his speech at the U.S. air base there, the president said she had advised him to *go* to Bitburg (Anthony Lewis, "The One-Track Mind," *New York Times,* May 9, 1985: see "Press Commentaries.")

14. Erich Simenauer, "The Return of the Persecutor," in *Generations of the Holocaust*, ed. Martin S. Bergmann and Milton E. Jucovy (New York: Basic Books, 1982), pp. 172, 173.

15. Alexander and Margarete Mitscherlich, *Die Unfähigkeit zu trauern, Grundlagen kollektiven Verhaltens* (Munich: R. Piper Verlag, 1967).

16. One can readily interject that the vigorous protests against Mr. Reagan's visit on the part of the Congress of the United States and from many other quarters were closely affinal to, or were at least made possible by, a true Christian consciousness (contra Christian ideology). In the United States a secular ethic in behalf of justice for Jews has (good) Christian roots—which is another way of saying that it has Jewish prophetic and rabbinic roots. However, the present essay is delimited by self-identifiably Christian praxis respecting Jews.

17. Advertisement in the *New York Times*, April 28, 1985.

18. There is a limited but real sense in which entire nations may express repentance. At the fortieth anniversary of the United Nations, Prime Minister Yasuhiro Nakasone of Japan expressed profound regret, in the name of his country, for "the ultranationalism and militarism it unleashed, and the untold suffering the war inflicted upon peoples around the world and, indeed, upon its own people" (*New York Times*, Oct 24, 1985). Even Chancellor Kohl is reported to have spoken to a group of American Jewish leaders "as a German and as a Christian" in seeking forgiveness for the Holocaust (*New York Times*, October 26, 1985).

19. Consult Part III, "The Persecutors' Children," in Bergmann and Jucovy, eds., *Generations of the Holocaust*.

Alvin H. Rosenfeld

Another Revisionism: Popular Culture and the Changing Image of the Holocaust

The image of the Holocaust is a changing one, although just how it is changing, who is changing it, and what the consequences of such change may be for us and those who come after us are matters not often considered. I propose to discuss them here on the basis of the following assumptions:

1. It is not primarily from historians that most people gain whatever knowledge they may acquire of the Holocaust but rather from novelists, filmmakers, playwrights, TV program writers and producers, popular newspapers and magazines, political figures and other public personalities, and the like.

2. Thus, the "history" of the Holocaust that is available to most people is largely a product of popular culture and does not always derive from or necessarily even resemble the history of the Jews under Nazism that professional historians must strive to establish. Indeed, we might do well to see the two versions as rival enterprises and the contest between them as one between basically antithetical drives or ambitions.

3. The public at large remains readily drawn by the spectre of the Holocaust and is thus a receptive audience for stories and images of the Third Reich, yet one cannot assume that such popular fascination is tantamount to a serious interest in Jewish fate during the Nazi period.

4. Indeed, far from being an effective means of educating the public about the evils of Nazism and the tragedy of the Jews, a pro-

longed exposure to popular representations of the Holocaust may work in the opposite way—namely, to dull rather than sharpen moral sensibility. Images of mass suffering may awaken conscience, but they also have the power to perversely excite the imagination. A pornography of the Holocaust, in other words, may undercut a didactics of the Holocaust.

5. In sum, the image of the Holocaust, far from being fixed, is in the process of being transfigured, and the several stages of its transfiguration, which one can trace over the course of popular culture, may contribute to a fictional subversion of the historical sense rather than to a firm consolidation of historical knowledge. One result of such a development may be an incipient rejection of the Holocaust rather than its retention in historical memory.

This prospect and the subtle motives that underlie it have been studied recently in Saul Friedländer's book *Reflections of Nazism* and in my own *Imagining Hitler*.[1] Instead of trying to recapitulate the complex arguments of these two books, however, I will cite a few recent examples of the phenomena they were written to explain. To locate them I look to political life and to popular culture, primary sources for the dissemination of knowledge in an age dominated by the media.

I begin by recalling a code name that is no longer in the news, although only a short time back it fairly dominated it: *Bitburg*. Prior to the spring of 1985 it is doubtful that very many outside of Germany had ever heard of this small town (and inside Germany almost its only resonant association was with a local beer, "Bit Bier" produced there). Within a very short time, however, "Bitburg" came to symbolize far more than its place name and pointed to an extraordinary tension in historical awareness, moral evaluation, and German-American political relations. What came to the fore with "Bitburg" implicated a whole range of major and obviously unresolved issues, all of them rooted in the traumatic period of World War II and the still unassimilated history of Nazi crimes against the Jews and others. "Bitburg," we soon realized, set in motion a debate about some of the largest values of Western culture. The imperatives of historical memory, national responsibility, forgiveness and justice, politics and morality—all these were stirred up by "Bitburg," often in inchoate and conflicting form.

The question before us, therefore, is how so much of consequence could emerge from what, on the face of it, started out to be little more than a ceremonial gesture between the heads of two allied governments. *Newsweek*, in its usual easy way, summed up the matter as rooted in "one of the deepest moral quandaries of modern times—the tension between world Judaism's need to remember the crimes of the Holocaust and post-Nazi Germany's need to forget."[2] This formulation is too simplistic, yet it is not altogether off the mark and comes close to expressing the popular sense of what "Bitburg" was all about. For a more detailed sense of what was stirring, though, we should look closely at the words of one of the major actors in the Bitburg affair, namely Ronald Reagan. We can profit from recalling a few of the high (or low?) points on the road to Bitburg.

Recall what the president of the United States had to say at his news conference of March 21 in reply to a reporter's question about his reluctance to visit Dachau:

> Q. Mr. President, would you tell us [of] your decision not to visit a Nazi concentration camp site when you make your trip to Germany in May commemorating V-E Day?
> A. Yes. I'll tell you. I feel very strongly that this time, in commemorating the end of that great war, that instead of reawakening the memories and so forth, and the passions of the time, that maybe we should observe this day as the day when, 40 years ago, peace began and friendship, because we now find ourselves allied and friends of the countries that we once fought against, and that we, it'd be almost a celebration of the end of an era and the coming into what has now been some 40 years of peace for us. And I felt that, since the German people have very few alive that remember even the war, and certainly none of them who were adults and participating in any way, and the, they do, they have a feeling and a guilt feeling that's been imposed upon them. And I just think it's unnecessary. I think they should be recognized for the democracy that they've created and the democratic principles they now espouse.[3]

This is a remarkable statement, not least of all for its striking linguistic fractures and imprecisions. (One can lie, just as one can tell the truth, in a straightforward manner, but to express sentiments as ambivalent as Mr. Reagan's requires that language be stuttered, not spoken straight out.) Apart from the awkward mumblings, what is it about these words (and they presaged worse to come) that bothers us so?

In part, one is offended by the note of historical ignorance they register and also perplexed by it: after all, if we know that there are still large numbers of Germans alive today who fought in the war and even larger numbers who remember it (knowledge, incidentally, never denied in Germany itself), why does the president seem not to know it? And if he does know it, what moves him to declare the opposite to be the case? Why, in brief, is he intent on stripping Germany of its recent past?

The notion that "unnecessary" guilt feelings have been "imposed upon" the Germans is similarly wrongheaded and goes against the grain of common morality, which says that those who are guilty of wrongdoing should in fact feel guilty. Indeed, if they deny such feelings or suggest that they have them only because someone else insists on them, there is not a chance in the world that they will ever begin to acknowledge their misdeeds, let alone repent of or atone for them. For Mr. Reagan to relieve the consciences of the guilty by suggesting that it is unfair to reawaken memory of the war years was another startling instance of presidential rhetoric gone astray.

Most troubling about Mr. Reagan's words, though, was something else: the sense that what he was saying, as bizarre and objectionable as it seemed, might not be idiosyncratic but might actually represent the sentiments of large numbers of people. The president of the United States is not unintelligent, and he certainly is not out of touch with popular feeling and common aspirations. Much of the success of his presidency, indeed, is probably owing to Mr. Reagan's natural ability to express what is on the minds and in the hearts of his fellow countrymen and to articulate some of their basic views.

Americans on the whole have a difficulty with history, most of all someone else's history, especially if it is unpleasant. In this respect their president represents them very well indeed. One of his aides in the White House, questioned about the prospects of a visit to a concentration camp, recalled the president saying, "You know, I don't think we ought to focus on the past, I want to focus on the future, I want to put that history behind me." Another administration official explained, "The President was not hot to go to a camp. You know, he is a cheerful politician. He does not like to grovel in a grisly scene like Dachau."[4]

These are familiar sentiments today. Like the president, most people do not wish to be reminded of the brutalities of the past and would not be eager to have them linger in their memory. They would prefer to put Dachau, which *is* grisly, behind them. A forward-looking people, Americans in general endorse the notion that one should forgive and forget and get on with the business of living, even, if one can find a way, with a former enemy.

As Mr. Reagan saw it, his task at Bitburg, therefore, was to patch up old quarrels with the Germans and forgive them the old hurts they had caused, a task for which he devised a twofold solution: (1) to celebrate the achievements of the New Germany, and (2) to offer absolution to the Old Germany by blaming its sins on what he repeatedly called "one man's totalitarian dictatorship"—a dictatorship portrayed as absolute and as victimizing not only other peoples of Europe but the German people as well.

With respect to the first solution, we all recognize that there is a good deal to celebrate: German democracy in the postwar period has proven itself, and the Federal Republic stands today as a prosperous, strong, and reliable ally. For an American president to say as much is neither astonishing nor objectionable. But for him to do so as part of a planned visit to a German war cemetery situated just near the site of the Battle of the Bulge, and containing the graves of SS men, obviously was bound to raise troubling questions.

Mr. Reagan's answers to these questions greatly deepened the embarrassment of his upcoming visit to Bitburg, yet they nonetheless showed his determination to proceed with his task of historical cleansing. I quote from the president's news conference of April 18 and emphasize that only a month before, he declared that he did not want to visit a Nazi concentration camp for fear of reawakening old passions: "I think that there is nothing wrong with visiting that cemetery where those young men are victims of Nazism also, even though they were fighting in the German uniform, drafted into service to carry out the hateful wishes of the Nazis. They were victims just as surely as the victims in the concentration camps."[5] If ever a public utterance was designed to reawaken old passions, this one was, for in two simple sentences it succeeded in leveling the distinctions between those murdered in the camps and the comrades-in-arms of their murderers and at the same time in echoing a Nuremberg-style defense of the murderers, who appear in Mr. Reagan's apologetic view as reluctant agents of somebody else's aggressive will.

Curiously enough, the "somebody else" was never formally named by the president, although on several occasions he referred to "the awful evil started by one man," to "one man's totalitarian dictatorship," and the like. Undoubtedly there are aspects of Nazi Germany that we do not understand fully, but by now it *is* clear that the Nazi state was not run by "one man," that the Nazi war machine was not and could not have been driven by "one man" alone, and that the terror carried out for a dozen years in the name of the Third German Reich could not have come about had a great many people not actively and willingly followed the lead of this "one man." Nazism, in short, was a mass phenomenon, and in both large and small ways involved vast numbers of Germans over the course of the war. In attributing the evil of Nazism to Hitler alone, and, inexplicably, by never referring to him by name, Mr. Reagan was reducing history to cartoon shapes, to a celluloid image of pervasive, if ineffable, malevolent force.

At Bergen-Belsen, a camp that he belatedly added to his German itinerary (and this only as a result of public pressure), Mr. Reagan referred to "the awful evil started by one man—an evil that victimized all the world with its destruction." He continued in the same figurative vein: "For year after year, until that man and his evil were destroyed, hell yawned forth its awful contents." Such sentences, employing old and by now empty abstractions, dismiss history in its particular features and promote oblivion about its individual actors. Hitler appears in Mr. Reagan's view as a terrifying but vague embodiment of evil, and Hitler's soldiers, "the young men" in their graves, as his innocent and unwilling victims. As for the real victims—mourned by Mr. Reagan as those "Never to hope. Never to pray, never to love. Never to heal. Never to laugh. Never to cry"—they are sentimentalized out of mind. One victim and one alone is referred to by name—Anne Frank—but the passage from Anne Frank's *Diary* that Mr. Reagan quoted at Bergen-Belsen is the one always recalled by those who want to put the horrors of the past rapidly behind them ("In spite of everything I still believe that people are really good at heart"). In the relative safety of her Amsterdam attic hideaway there were moments when the young girl did experience such optimistic feeling, but it is doubtful that this passage from the *Diary* represented anything close to what she must have felt at the end, surrounded by the dead and dying of Auschwitz and later herself a victim of the deprivations and disease of Bergen-Belsen.

To say that the whole episode was the product of historical ignorance and bad planning is to say too little. It was a setback of major proportions in public education about the Holocaust, an education that relies overwhelmingly on image-making and thus is vulnerable to manipulation by revisionists of every kind. Yet the public, or at least half of it, saw the matter differently, and their reaction must have been a source of satisfaction to both Mr. Reagan and Chancellor Kohl. For however incensed American Jews, ex-GIs, and others might have been over Bitburg, a *New York Times*/CBS News Poll taken after the visit revealed that there were as many people (41 percent) who approved of Mr. Reagan's actions as there were (41 percent) who opposed them.[6]

Beyond these statistics, a sampling of readers' letters to the editors of American newspapers reveals a similar degree of opinion for and against the Bitburg visit. I do not have any fine-tuned analyses of popular perceptions to offer, but I think it is probably not unfair to take the following two letters as representative of the range of popular feeling at the time. Both letters, I should add, are taken from campus newspapers in midwestern college towns, and so might be regarded as expressing a degree of educated opinion.

The first letter, written by a history professor who had himself fought in Europe during World War II, strongly objected to the president's visit and regarded it as a callous affront. The writer calls the president to task for not making proper distinctions between the German war dead and their victims and comments as follows: "Undoubtedly there were thousands of decent, honorable men in the German Army in the Second World War. But the army they fought in was not decent and honorable, and the regime they were serving was perhaps the most horrible in human history. As for the Waffen SS, they were not victims at all; they were ruthless victimizers." The writer praises Elie Wiesel's words at the White House beseeching the president to cancel his visit to Bitburg and ends his letter on this note: "We are told that if the Bitburg affair is called off the Germans will be insulted. Too bad. I do not believe that decent Germans will be insulted. As for the others, if they do not yet realize how the rest of the world feels about the Waffen SS, it is time they found out."

The author of the second letter is a student and writes from another perspective altogether. His major concern is that preoccupation with the Holocaust is not allowing us to advance confidently into the future and is also unfairly and negatively stereotyping Germans. He regards Wiesel's words to the president as an affront, chastises "the powerful Jewish lobby" for placing undue pressure on the administration, and argues that it is time to stop harping on the Holocaust as an example of exceptional Jewish suffering. "Holocausts are a dime a dozen," he writes. "I can understand pleas for sympathy, but I refuse to be manipulated into pseudo-worship of the formerly persecuted." "Must we be sidetracked," he continues, "by a bunch of bones lying halfway around the world?" He urges the president to carry out his plans to visit Bitburg, a visit, he writes, "that is much more important than the whinings of people like Wiesel. It will signify that we are beginning to forgive the German people for their past sins, in much the same way that America has begun to seek forgiveness for Vietnam." The visit will also show, he continues, that we can refuse Jewish pleadings (understood as serving the interests of an Israeli government "which says 'gimme, gimme' when it wants and 'anti-Semitism, anti-Semitism' when it does not receive"). The letter ends by acknowledging that "the methodical murder of over six million Jews is indeed a tragedy," but that "those who killed them were undoubtedly of very warped reasoning" and hence also victims. Thus theirs is "a tragedy, too," one that the president can and should address by going to Bitburg.[7]

My intention in citing these letters is not to praise the one and damn the other (although I obviously have my preferences), but rather to see them both as illustrative of strongly mixed feelings about the Bitburg affair and, through it, about the larger issue of public memory of the Second World War and the Nazi persecution of the Jews.

There may have been a time, not long ago, when one might have assumed a degree of common understanding of the Holocaust and common feeling for its victims, but it is far from certain that any such consensus exists today. To be sure, most people express revulsion over the crimes of the Nazis and sympathy for those who fell victim to them, but it is doubtful that very many would like to think about these matters for very long. Who can blame them? A serious confrontation with the history of the Holocaust is a wrenching experience and places upon us greater demands than we can easily bear. As a consequence, we would prefer to let that past be past. It is too painful and incomprehensible, filled with nightmare images of cruelty and terror, deprivation and death, guilt and shame. To give in to the impulse to forgive and forget, therefore, is understandable, even if not especially admirable.

Against this background, "Bitburg" suggests that we may have reached a point of surfeit with respect to moral attention to the Holocaust. This point is exemplified by Mr. Reagan's performance, at which the actual character of historical events began to give way to counter-histories and other kinds of fabrication. For however much the president may have insisted before the cameras that we must never forget, his words and actions reflected an erosion of historical memory and a desire to have the past press less demandingly on contemporary consciousness. If "Bitburg" troubles us today, it is because it manifests so clearly the suddenly tenuous position of the Holocaust in popular awareness, a position that only a short while ago few people would have thought to question.

If one looks at all critically at how the Holocaust has been represented to the public, one sees that an attenuation of its place in history is not, in fact, a sudden development but has been going on for years. Some erosion can be located within professional historical writings themselves, which have not been free of fictionalizing tendencies.[8] The greater danger by far, however, is to be found in the area of popular culture—in countless novels, and stories, poems, plays, films, and television programs about the Third Reich and the Jews. In reflecting on these, one sees that the road to Bitburg was prepared long before Chancellor Kohl and President Reagan embarked on their stroll through the graves at the Bitburg military cemetery.

Consider, for instance, the figure of Hitler, by which I refer quite literally to the various shapes he has assumed in word and image and thus to his changing configuration in the popular mind. To be sure, the dominant image of the man is one of menace, and in the form of undifferentiated evil favored by Mr. Reagan. Yet such figures not only repel, they also fascinate and attract. Not infrequently they have a human side, too. So it is with Hitler, who stands before us today as the most compelling figure of destructive power our century has thus far produced. Yet he has also taken on overtones of humanity that balance his malevolent side with a sometimes comic, sometimes tragic appeal.

Review his image in film—from Leni Riefenstahl's heroic portrait (*Triumph of the Will*), through Charlie Chaplin's satiric one (*The Great Dictator*), to Hans Jürgen Syberberg's Wagnerian one (*Hitler, A Film from Germany*)—and you will find a Hitler of the most variegated shapes, not all of them repellent. Review his image in literature— from the self-serving political portrait of *Mein Kampf*, through Wyndham Lewis's apologetic portrait (*Hitler*), to George Steiner's neo-kabbalistic one (*The Portage to San Cristobal of A.H.*)—and you will find much the same thing. Hitler on television, Hitler in the oversized picture books, Hitler in the popular magazines, Hitler in science fiction, song, joke, and cartoon—this Hitler is a figure of omnipresent and infinitely plastic shape. As Gordon Craig has summed him up, "One and a half generations after his death in the bunker, Hitler was like the little man upon the stair in the old song. He wasn't there, but he wouldn't go away."[9]

Let's assume, therefore, that Hitler has become an allegorical as well as a historical figure, a presence that haunts the mind of this generation and undoubtedly will continue to do so for years to come. The question then becomes, who is it who keeps his ghost alive and in what shapes? Consider, then, this little "biography" of the man from Norman Spinrad's novel *The Iron Dream*:

> Adolf Hitler was born in Austria on April 20, 1889. As a young man he migrated to Germany and served in the German army during the Great War. After the war, he dabbled briefly in radical politics in Munich before finally emigrating to New York in 1919. While learning English, he eked out a precarious existence as a sidewalk artist and occasional translator in New York's bohemian haven, Greenwich Village. After several years of this freewheeling life, he began to pick up odd jobs as a magazine and comic illustrator. He did his first interior illustration for the science-fiction magazine *Amazing* in 1930. By 1932, he was a regular illustrator for the science-fiction magazines, and, by 1935, he had enough confidence in his English to make his debut as a science-fiction writer. He devoted the rest of his life to the science-fiction genre as a writer, illustrator, and fanzine editor. Although best known to present-day SF fans for his novels and stories, Hitler was a

popular illustrator during the Golden Age of the thirties, edited several anthologies, wrote lively reviews, and published a popular fanzine, *Storm*, for nearly ten years.

He won a posthumous Hugo at the 1955 World Science-Fiction Convention for *Lord of the Swastika*, which was completed just before his death in 1953. For many years, he had been a popular figure at SF conventions, widely known in science-fiction fandom as a wit and non-stop raconteur. Ever since the book's publication, the colorful costumes he created in *Lord of the Swastika* have been favorite themes at convention masquerades. Hitler died in 1953, but the stories and novels he left behind remain as a legacy to all science-fiction enthusiasts.[10]

Bizarre? Outrageous? Amusing? Whatever your response may be to this Hitler, he bears little resemblance to the Führer of the Third Reich. It may be, of course, that this is precisely the point that Spinrad wishes to make, but if so his parodic attempt has failed. Certainly it has not prevented others from reconceiving the figure of Hitler along equally original lines. Read Beryl Bainbridge's *Young Adolf*, and you will find him as something of a bumptious shlemiel. Read George Steiner's *The Portage to San Cristobal of A.H.* and you will see him almost as a Torah-inspired visionary. In story after story, we have had the raging Hitler, the contrite Hitler, the artistic Hitler, the tender Hitler. There are fictions that bring him back to life as a woman; others that recreate him as a Jew. Look at Joachim Fest's documentary Hitler film, and you will be hard put to find the man whose passion and program it was to murder the Jews. Look at Syberberg's phantasmagoric Hitler film (all seven hours of it) and you will see the romantic artist bent on reaching an epic moment of apocalyptic fulfillment. In the work of various comedians he has been good for a gag. To the rockers he was "the first rock star." To the pornographers, who like to recreate his private moments with Eva Braun (about which we know almost nothing), he is, as Nazism as a whole has become, a source of imagery for sadomasochistic sex.

Just what he would have looked like in the infamous "Hitler Diaries" we do not know, for they were exposed as a fraud before serialization in the periodicals had a chance to progress very far, but you can be certain that Mr. Kujau and his colleagues would have cleaned him up. As it is, others are doing that right now. Thus Austria's best-selling mass-circulation daily, the *Neue Kronen Zeitung*, recently ran excerpts from a book by Christa Schroeder, one of Hitler's private secretaries, that portray her former boss as an amiable man, who liked flowers and dogs, pretty women and vegetarian food, and was generous with presents to his employees. (The paper came under fire for presenting such a grossly apologetic view, which made Hitler appear, according to one critic, as "a blend of Robert Redford and a Boy Scout leader.")[11]

A handsome brochure recently received announces "Adolf Hitler, the unknown artist" and advertises a large format picture book ("in gold-embossed burgundy linen") containing "over 830 pictures, 94 in full color, most published for the first time." A descriptive account alludes to "adolescent memories of pre-World War I Vienna, portraits of people who passed through his life, pastoral scenes long gone, glimpses of forgotten streets of old Europe, soaring churches, still-life floral arrangements, architectural plans for the future." Why any-one would want to know this "unknown Hitler" is beyond me, but the book's forty-dollar price indicates that its publisher believes there is money to be made in marketing still one more version of Hitler, in this case, a most benign one.

And there *is* money to be made, or otherwise we would not have so much Hitler on the market. (Nazi memorabilia of all sorts gross about $50 million a year, according to one recent report.)[12] Does Hitler on the market also mean Hitler on the brain? According to one of his recent biographers, "more will be written about Adolf Hitler than about anyone else in history with the exception of Jesus Christ."[13] Such a figure, which seems to be able to satisfy at one and the same time our fantasies for power, madness, money, sex, murder, politics, pageantry, ambition, and art, obviously has appeal. It is not an appeal that will help us better understand the Nazi persecution and slaughter of the Jews, but then it is not meant to. Rather, it is meant to fascinate us with the Holocaust, to some degree even to entertain us with it, and ultimately to turn it into something else—a fad, a fiction, a source of vicarious danger and excitement, a new mythology of violent sensations.

The popularization and commercialization of Hitler, in sum—and one could also look to other figures from the Third Reich and see that they are faring similarly—is not only *unhistorical* but at bottom *antihistorical*. Over a period of time, it will inevitably subvert the his-torical sense and strip it of any moral implications it may carry. Just as the politicization of the Holocaust—as "Bitburg" shows us all too clearly— falsifies the past for its own ends, so too does the sustained fictionalization of the Holocaust reshape the actors and events of the past to suit present-day fantasies. In both cases, history, once suffered by real men and women at the hands of other real men and women, is not of primary concern.

Richard von Weizsäcker, the president of the Federal Republic of Germany, was one of the few public figures at the time of the Bitburg affair who saw fit to oppose these tendencies in a forthright manner. In a speech to the Bundestag of May 8, commemorating the fortieth anniversary of the end of the war in Europe, he spoke of the need "to look truth straight in the eye—without embellishment and without distortion." "The past had been terrible," he declared, and had to be remembered honestly. Yet in one respect even von Weizsäcker, whose intentions were noble and whose words were uncompromising in their dedication to preserving an unapologetic sense of the past, was not severe or acute enough in his attack on revisionism. "All of us," he declared, "whether guilty or not, whether old or young, must accept the past. We are all affected by its consequences and liable for it. The young and old generations must and can help each other to understand why it is vital to keep alive the memories. It is not a case of coming to terms with the past. That is not possible. It cannot be subsequently modified or made not to have happened. However, anyone who closes his eyes to the past is blind to the present."[14]

The moral impulse behind these words is wholly admirable, yet in one crucial respect they are not wholly correct: "Bitburg" and countless other tamperings with the Holocaust tell us that the past *can* be "subsequently modified," *can* be made "not to have happened." An industry of considerable size is laboring, not without effect, to change the memory of the past and even to obliterate it. The few Hitler examples I have cited are but one instance of this process. There are many more. What they all add up to is a refashioning and falsification of history, sometimes in small and subtle ways, sometimes wholesale.

The Nazi genocide of the Jews will not soon be forgotten, but how it is remembered depends overwhelmingly on what our memory chooses to recover or to refashion from the past, on what we choose to ignore and what we choose to newly invent. As a consequence, the crime that we have come to call the Holocaust is today in flux, its historical character changing under the pressures of political expediency and popular indulgence. Even without these pressures, the hideousness of the crime, while a source of endless fascination, is subject to unconscious denial. While Jews may live under the obligation to remember, for others remembrance is not a primary duty and perhaps not even a possibility. Hence the impulse behind and at least partial approval by so many of "Bitburg," and hence the agony of the Jews.

This agony brings me to conclude with some reflections on history and memory that I take from the writings of the Czech author Milan Kundera. On the one hand, he has written—hopefully, I should think—that "the struggle of man against power is the struggle of memory against forgetting."[15] That sentence seems charged with an imperative truth, one that one feels moved to endorse and to advocate. Yet Kundera is a realist more than he is anything else and knows that most people most of the time are not up to such a struggle. And so he has also left us with a contrary truth, which he formulated long before President Reagan and Chancellor Kohl ever dreamt up their moment of reconciliation at Bitburg but nonetheless one that seems to have an exact application to it and to the condition we find ourselves in after Bitburg:

> Most people willingly deceive themselves with a doubly false faith; they believe in *eternal memory* (of men, things, deeds, peoples) and in *rectification* (of deeds, errors, sins, injustice). Both are sham. The truth lies at the opposite end of the scale: everything will be forgotten and nothing will be rectified. All rectification (both vengeance and forgiveness) will be taken over by oblivion. No one will rectify wrongs; all wrongs will be forgotten.[16]

NOTES

1. Saul Friedländer, *Reflections of Nazism: An Essay on Kitsch and Death* (New York: Harper & Row, 1984), and Alvin H. Rosenfeld, *Imagining Hitler* (Bloomington: Indiana University Press, 1985).

2. *Newsweek*, April 29, 1985, p. 14.

3. *New York Times*, March 22, 1985.

4. Ibid., March 22, 1985; April 22, 1985.

5. Ibid., April 19, 1985.

6. Ibid.

7. *Indiana Daily Student*, May 1, 1985, and The Notre Dame *Observer*, April 24, 1985.

8. See Rosenfeld, *Imagining Hitler*, pp. 13–25.

9. Gordon Craig, *The Germans* (New York: G. P. Putnam's Sons, 1982), p. 80.

10. Norman Spinrad, *The Iron Dream* (New York: Avon Books, 1972), p. 9.

11. Cited in *Philadelphia Jewish Exponent*, June 28, 1985.

12. "The Hitler Business," *Life*, July 1983, pp. 83–88.

13. Robert G. L. Waite, *The Psychopathic God: Adolf Hitler* (New York: Basic Books, 1977), p. xi.

14. See "Documents" in this book.

15. Milan Kundera, *The Book of Laughter and Forgetting* (New York: Penguin Books, 1981), p. 3.

16. *The Joke* (New York: Harper & Row, 1982), p. 245.

James E. Young

Memory and Monument

In a shaded clearing at the end of a farm road near Timmendorf, West Germany, a large plaque commemorates the "Catastrophe of the SS *Cap Arcona*," a German luxury liner with 8,000 people aboard that was sunk by the RAF in the last days of World War II. From the diagrams and narrative of events inscribed on this plaque, we learn that the SS *Cap Arcona* was one of three converted cruise liners carrying thousands of *Häftlinge* (i.e., concentration camp prisoners) into the Baltic Sea, where, we are told, it was strafed and bombed by British warplanes that had apparently mistaken the ships for troop transports. According to local villagers, *Nacht und Nebel*–clad bodies washed onto the meticulously groomed beaches along Lübeck Bay for months afterwards and were immediately buried by the townspeople to prevent the spread of disease.

From the plaque, however, it is not clear whether the "catastrophe" of the SS *Cap Arcona* lay in the massacre of so many innocents by the RAF or in the horrible irony of these camp survivors' ultimate fate. For even though the attack on this ship is recorded here in detail, there is no mention of whence these *Häftlinge* had just come, or how they came to be gathered in Lübeck Bay, or where they were going. That it was a catastrophe of some sort demanding memorialization seemed clear enough. But what kind of catastrophe came into view only within the context of its memorialization: the result is a monument to 8,000 defenseless prisoners killed by the British. That many of these prisoners had survived the death marches from Auschwitz, that most were Jews, and that all were being hastily evacuated from concentration camps in northern Germany to somewhere—anywhere—away from German soil is not recalled in this memorial.[1]

At issue here, however, is not that this plaque in Timmendorf has deliberately manipulated the events surrounding "the catastrophe of the *Cap Arcona*," but that the creators of memorial texts necessarily reconstruct historical events, and so reflect as much their own understanding and experience as the actual events they would preserve. Self-interest and selective memory may indeed have played some role in the creation of the memorial plaque at Timmendorf. But, as I hope to make clear, such distortion is inevitable. The problem is not so much the conscious or unconscious manipulation of history, which is intrinsic to all memory and representation. Rather, as we have seen in the Bitburg affair, the real danger lies in an *uncritical* approach to monuments, so that a constructed and reified memory is accepted as normative history—and then acted upon as if it were pure, unmediated meaning.

President Reagan thus drew what seemed to be "natural" conclusions from the memorials to the German war dead at Bitburg. Because both Waffen S.S. and Wehrmacht soldiers lie together in a patch of land designated to commemorate Germany's war dead, the different roles they may have played in the war are subsumed in the larger, more general memory of their common fate. United now with countrymen they may have spurned during the war and with forebears from the First World War, some of whom—if Jews—would have been considered their enemies, the SS soldiers buried here have not only been absorbed into the greater continuum of all Germans who ever fell for their *Vaterland*, but have also become the universal victims of war itself. On the strength of this particular configuration of memory at Bitburg and its "self-evident" truths, both Ronald Reagan and Helmut Kohl ignored many other historical perspectives on the war, and even encouraged their loss.

The plaque at Timmendorf is not a Holocaust memorial as such. But in light of the ways in which it (like the cemetery at Bitburg) shapes memory, we can no longer afford to ignore the different understandings of events and types of memory these monuments reflect. For what was a period of "Holocaust," "*shoah*," or "*dritte Churban*" in the victims' eyes is to this day "*Hitlerzeit*," "*Weltkrieg*," or increasingly "*KZ-Zeit*" for the Germans themselves. Though these terms—like the monuments—refer generically to the same era and occasionally to the same events, they cannot be considered synonymous; for what is signified in each instance depends profoundly on the manner in which each term organizes, locates, and even explains these events for its users.

In an age that tends to probe the significance of every message and text, it is surprising how little critical attention is being devoted to the forms and meanings of remembrance engendered by memorials and museums constructed expressly to deepen the memory of the Holocaust. Like literary and historical narratives, these memorials recall the national myths, religious archetypes, and ideological paradigms along whose contours a history has been constructed—and perhaps acted upon. Their iconographic, architectonic, and textual organization, by reflecting politically and culturally determined perpectives, is bound to constrain the knowledge succeeding generations will have of this time.

So if the *raison d'être* for these monuments is "never to forget," the critical visitor might now ask what precisely it is that is not forgotten at Bitburg, Timmendorf, Bergen-Belsen, Dachau, Auschwitz, Babi Yar, Yad Vashem, or Liberty State Park in Jersey City. For *what* is remembered here necessarily depends on *how* it is remembered; and how these events are remembered depends in turn on the icons that do the remembering.

The aim of a critical inquiry into the iconography of such monuments is not merely to expose the various ideological transformations. Rather, it is primarily to examine the process itself of Holocaust memorialization: the simultaneous preservation and limiting of memory, the type of meaning that is generated, and the manner in which viewers respond to the reification of memory in such icons.

A rose bush at Dachau designates the plot of ground where thousands of prisoners were lined up and shot. One hundred crab-apple trees in the Babi Yar Park in Denver, Colorado, signify thousands of Jews cut down in a ravine outside of Kiev, Russia. A solitary concrete obelisk amid dozens of mass graves condenses Jewish memory at Bergen-Belsen. Mountains of hair, eyeglasses, and toothbrushes at Auschwitz refer metonymically to the lives that once animated them. In coming to *stand for* past realities, each of these icons displaces them and creates new ones in their stead: hence, an inescapable potential for "historical revision" in the memorialization process.

By identifying 100,000 victims massacred at Babi Yar only as "citizens of Kiev and prisoners of war," for example, the memorial there not only inflates the actual number of victims, but also forgets that almost all were killed for having been Jews.[2] By juxtaposing in a photographic montage images of Wehrmacht soldiers killed in battle, bombed German cities, and liberated Jewish *KZ-Häftlinge*, the memorial at Neuengamme recalls collectively the "victims of war" as it forgets who the specific *makers* of that war were. A nation's monuments efface as much history from memory as they inscribe in it.

Once again, however, the danger in these "forgetful monuments" lies in the viewer's mistaking the rhetoric of a monument for the nature of the events it commemorates. In contrast to literature, for example, which often calls attention to itself as a medium, these more monumental and putatively documentary representations of the Holocaust often cause a confusion between the memorial texts and the remembered events. This confusion is most striking in the case of monuments located at the sites of the original concentration camps, where a sense of authentic place tends to literalize the particular meaning assigned.

In these "memorial camps" (as I will call them), the icons of destruction seem to appropriate the very authority of the original events themselves. Operating on the same rhetorical principle as the photograph, in which representation and object appear to be one, the memorial camps at Majdanek and Auschwitz are devastating in their impact—not just for what they remember, but because they compel the visitor to accept the horrible fact that what they show is "real." In both cases, the camps have been preserved almost exactly as the Russians found them forty years ago. Guard towers, barbed wire, barracks, and crematoria—abstracted elsewhere, even mythologized—here stand palpably intact. Nothing but airy time seems to mediate between the visitor and past realities, which are not merely *re*-presented by these artifacts, but *present* in them. As literal fragments and remnants of events, these artifacts of catastrophe collapse the distinction between themselves and what they evoke. Claiming the authority of *un*reconstructed realities, the memorial camps invite us not only to mistake their reality for the actual death camps' reality, but also to confuse an implicit, monumentalized vision with unmediated history.

Like photographs without captions, however, the memorial camps remain essentially meaningless: their very significance derives from both the knowledge we bring to them and from their explanatory inscriptions. But just as the silent ruins of the camps are "completed" by inscriptions, their simple reality as ruins unfortunately works to corroborate *all* historical explanation—no matter how insidious or farfetched. Thus, the commentary that accompanies the "black wall" at Auschwitz appears to find its material testimony in the wall itself. If it is written that the killings here were primarily political, or that these barracks housed prisoners-of-war identified only as Polish, then this is what these icons "remember."

In fact, Holocaust memorials throughout the Eastern Bloc are often as *Judenrein* as the countries in which they stand. Jewish themes in these monuments are usually found only in the languages used to inscribe a memorial message. So in the center of a symbolic graveyard at Treblinka, enclosed by hundreds of protruding, jagged rocks set in concrete slabs, a stone plaque reads from top to bottom in Yiddish, Russian, English, French, German, and Polish: "Never again" (see photos). *What* it is that must not happen again is left to the visitor's imagination. On the death ramp at Auschwitz-Birkenau, surrounded on all sides by crumbling barracks, rusty electric fences, bombed-out crematoria, and ash-filled ponds, four blocklike sarcophagi mark the end of the rail line, the beginning of the "death zone." Behind them stands a tower of stone blocks, resembling a giant tombstone, bearing in its center a single triangle recalling the patch all prisoners wore on their camp clothing. In concert with the artifacts all around them, these monuments thus remember and provide evidence for the simple message inscribed on twenty stone tablets in twenty different languages, including Yiddish and Hebrew: "Four million people suffered and died here at the hands of the Nazi murderers between the years 1940 and 1945." Within the context of the remembering icons, the religious identity of these people and why they suffered is elided.[3]

The absence in Poland of iconographic reference to its murdered Jews is so pervasive that it almost becomes emblematic in itself, recalling the way in which two holes in a door jamb might signify the *mezuzah* that is no longer there. Upon inquiring at the State Museum in Kielce, for example, one learns that there is no record of the pogrom that occurred there July 4, 1946, which left forty-six returning Jewish survivors dead and hundreds injured. At first, the archivist feigns ignorance of the entire matter; but on being pressed further, she admits that there are actually many detailed photographs and eyewitness accounts—the result of an official investigation. But they have been sealed for one hundred years to allow "memory to heal itself." But why no plaque, no sign at all? It is not necessary, for there are no Jews left here anyway. "Besides," she says, "this is a political matter, and I am only an archivist."

Since many of the cemeteries in Poland were vandalized by the Nazis, the ones that have not been plowed under for soccer fields or paved over for highways are now simply ruins of ruins. In Lukow, camp survivors have gathered their community's broken and scattered tombstones and piled them—pyramidlike—into a memorial obelisk (see photos). The only sign of a Jewish presence in Lukow, which was half Jewish before the war, is now this monument *to* the Jewish cemetery. Even more striking, iconographically, are the "tombstone walls" in both the Warsaw and Krakow Jewish cemeteries: retaining walls built with the broken fragments of tombstones smashed by the Nazis. Arranged into a pastiche and set in mortar, angular chunks of Hebrew-inscribed marble and granite, variously smooth and time-eaten, now recall not only the broken Jewish communities of Warsaw and Krakow, but also the "pogrom" of headstones itself.

History, memory, and state policy intersect in even more complicated ways in Warsaw, where the Jewish ghetto uprising preceded by months the Poles' own revolt against the Nazis—both rebellions crushed by the Germans while the Red Army watched from across the Vistula. That the state has chosen to commemorate these uprisings at all may thus be as significant as the differences between the Jewish and Polish monuments. Without reference to the Jewish revolt, the memorial to the Polish uprising is modeled after the open-air memorial camps: one block of reconstructed rubble and burned-out armored personnel carriers is supported by an indoor exhibition detailing the histories of rebel brigades, battles, and strategies. Of the Jewish ghetto, on the other hand, there is nary an artifact left: torched and demolished a block at a time by the Germans, it was eventually bulldozed altogether for new apartment buildings. All memory of the rebellion and destruction is thus compressed into Nathan Rapoport's Warsaw Ghetto Monument, which stands strikingly alone in an otherwise clear—and well-maintained—memorial square (see photos).

Designed and constructed between 1947 and 1948, this thirty-six foot-high bronze statue codifies a mythically proportioned Mordecai Anielewicz, commander of the ghetto revolt, standing heroically amid flames and ruin. Muscular and bare-chested, clenching a Molotov cocktail in one hand, this archetypal worker/partisan has risen against the Nazis, not as a Jew, but as a Socialist hero. The monument is, to be sure, dedicated to "The Jewish People, its heroes and its martyrs," but for the martyrs, we must walk around to the stone bas-relief on the other side of the monument, where the Jews are remembered separately and just as archetypally. As surely as Anielewicz is a worker, the huddled and stooped figures on the reverse are archetypal Jews in exile, with only three Nazi helmets and two bayonets barely visible in the background to distinguish this expulsion from any other.[4] Eyes to the ground, all trudge resignedly and passively to their fate—except for a rabbi holding a Torah scroll in one arm, who looks up and reaches to heaven with his free hand, as if to beseech God. The result is a two-sided monument, each side to be viewed separately, each preserving an archetype as much as a historical event.[5]

In Germany, two factors mitigate against the iconographic memory of mass murder: there were no killing centers per se in Germany, and because so few non-Jewish Germans were interned in them, the death camps seem to have entered German memory only in an abstract sense. As the first concentration camp in Germany, Dachau epitomizes now the German memorialization of their "*KZ-Zeit.*" Built in 1933 for political enemies of the Reich, Dachau housed and thereby created *German* victims, many of whom were also Jews. As horrifying as the conditions were at Dachau, its gas chamber was never used, so the crematoria burned "only" the remains of those who died of shootings, beatings, or, most often, disease. Of the Dachau survivors still living in Germany, most are Christians, many of them clergymen and Social Democrats, whose own memories constitute the core of these memorial projects. There are, therefore, three religious memorials in the camp: one each for the Catholic Church, the Protestant Church, and the Jewish community.

As the name "The Trustees for the Monument of Atonement at the Concentration Camp Dachau" suggests, however, the very reasons for the memorials at Dachau differ for each group of victims. It was not to mourn the loss of a Jewish population that either of the Christian memorials was established, but rather to atone for Nazi sins against humanity. Stylized and cerebralized, all of the monuments within the grounds of the camp tend to emphasize the great gulf between past and present. From well-scrubbed barrack floors, to the swept gravel walks outside, to the crematorium (open, a sign tells us, from 9:00 to 5:00), cleanliness and order now govern the "remembrance" of filth and chaos. Given the almost antiseptic cleanliness of the grounds and of the two replicated barracks, the tasteful symbolism of the other barracks' foundations, and the excellent museum, it is not so surprising to hear visitors complain that this memorial aestheticizes the past as if to vanquish it, rather than to recall it. Where the seemingly unadorned ruins of memorial camps in the East compel visitors to take them literally as the physical artifacts of the Nazi era, the freshly painted, efficiently organized icons at Dachau openly invite *meta*physical speculation.

If the monuments in Europe are inevitably constrained by political and ideological coordinates, those in the United States are equally limited by our own experience of the Holocaust. For the young American GI's who liberated Bergen-Belsen, Dachau, and Buchenwald, a history of the Holocaust necessarily excludes the conditions in Europe before the war, the wrenching breakup of families, deportations to the ghettos and camps, and even the killing process itself. The Americans did not witness the process of destruction, but only its effects. Inasmuch as the "American experience" of the Holocaust in 1945 was thus confined to the *liberation* of the camps, it is appropriate that the recently dedicated monument (entitled "Liberation") should be located in Liberty State Park, New Jersey, within sight of our greatest ideological icon, the Statue of Liberty (see photos). In this new work by Nathan Rapoport, a young, solemn-looking GI walks forward, his eyes on the ground, cradling—almost pietà-like—a concentration camp victim. With skeletal chest showing through tattered prison-garb, his arms spread, and his eyes staring vacantly into the sky, the victim exemplifies helplessness. This monument is thus consonant with both the specific experiences of Americans in the war and with traditional self-perceptions and idealizations of our role as rescuers in war and a sanctuary for the world's "huddled masses."

Of all memorials to the Holocaust, the vast complex of monuments, shrines, archives, and exhibitions at the Yad Vashem Heroes and Martyrs Memorial Authority in Jerusalem represents the most sophisticated and multilayered memory of events. Established by Israeli parliamentary law in 1953 expressly to commemorate "the disaster and its heroism and to promote a custom of joint remembrance of the heroes and victims," Yad Vashem (literally, "a memorial and a name," from Isaiah 56:5) institutionalizes the perpetual activity of remembrance. Though diverse and complicated, Yad Vashem's icons also locate events in several distinct traditions, thus conferring specific national and historical meaning onto them.

As its full name implies, Yad Vashem's aim is to preserve the memory of the *heroes* as well as the *martyrs* of the destruction, thus countering what Israelis view as an exaggerated fascination with the Jews as victims—and victims only. This is one of the reasons why a reproduction of Rapoport's Warsaw Ghetto Monument has a home at Yad Vashem; yet instead of allowing these particular archetypes to stagnate, Zionist ideology requires that the contrast between the passive "old Jews" and the fighting "new Jews" be heightened. For in Israel there exists an acute sensitivity to the historical consequences of these competing images. Since the historians in Israel find that commonly held stereotypes of the Jews in Christian Europe may have underpinned traditional anti-Semitism, and that the Jews' own limited perception of themselves as victims may have contributed to their vulnerability, current Israeli memorial-makers ensure that alternative icons are provided for subsequent generations. Thus, the traditional vulnerability and weakness of diaspora Jewry (central tenets of Zionism) are recalled side by side with iconographic images of the new, fighting Jews, in order both to explain past events and to provide viable models for the young.

Divided into three main sections, the powerful historical exhibition at Yad Vashem also reflects a characteristically Israeli perspective.

In the first section, the rise of anti-Jewish laws and actions between 1933 and 1939 is traced through a mixture of photographs, leaflets, Nazi propaganda, and historical narrative. The harassment, deportations, and even the pogroms of *Kristallnacht* are all presented here as being consistent with the European anti-Semitic tradition. But then there is a break in the exhibition, and we must move physically from one hall—i.e., one era—to another. The next room is then devoted solely to the killing process itself between 1941 and 1945, the proportions and methods of which were so unlike anything before, that—as the lay-out suggests—it cannot be located iconographically within the context of traditional anti-Jewish persecution. And finally, unlike other memorial expositions of the Holocaust, the history traced at Yad Vashem does not end with the liberation of the camps, but continues: for as the photographs of survivors coming ashore at Haifa and Caesaria illustrate, the "end of the Holocaust" comes only with the survivors' return to—and redemption in—Eretz Israel.

As we enter the great memorial hall at Yad Vashem—a huge megalithic tomb sunk into the earth—we also pass beneath the words of the Baal Shem Tov, which distill the *raison d'être* of this memorial in Israel: "Forgetting lengthens the period of exile! In remembrance lies the secret of deliverance." In the dim light, our eyes are drawn downward to the eternal flame and to the names of the death camps inscribed on the stone floor. Invited to remember and then to contemplate remembrance in this great dark space—itself an objectification of absence—we do so within an ever-vigilant context: exile, memory, and redemption.

The Nazis had intended the destruction of the Jews to be total: they were to have been removed from history *and* memory. Any record of the Holocaust thus appears *in principle* to defeat Nazi plans. But beginning with an ordinance in 1936 forbidding German stonemasons to carve gravestones for Jews, continuing through the Nazis' methodical destruction of documents in Vilna recording past persecutions, and ending with Hitler's plans for a museum in Prague devoted to the extinct Jewish race, it grows clear that if the first step toward the destruction of a people lay in the *blotting out* of its memory, then the last step would lie in its calculated *resurrection*. Through the Prague museum and other monuments to his victory over the Jews,[6] Hitler never planned to "forget" the Jews but rather intended to supplant their memory of events with his own. Total liquidation would not have come through the Jews' physical annihilation only, or in the expunction of all reference to them afterward. But by eradicating the Jewish *type* of memory, the Nazis would also have destroyed the possibility of regeneration through memory that has marked Jewish existence.

The usual aim in any nation's monuments, however, is not solely to displace memory or to remake it in one's own image: it is also to invite the collaboration of the community in acts of remembrance. To the extent that the myths or ideals embodied in a nation's monuments are the people's own, they are given substance and weight by such reification and will appear natural and true; hence, an inescapable partnership grows between a people and its monuments. It is at precisely this point, however, that a critical approach to memorials might rescue us from a complicity that allows our *icons* of remembrance to harden into *idols* of remembrance. For memorialization occurs not merely within these icons, but between the events and icons, and then again between the icons and ourselves. By recalling this movement between events, icons, and ourselves, we accept more than a ritual responsibility for the images that lie enshrined in our monuments. It is not to Holocaust monuments as such that we turn for remembrance, but to ourselves within the reflective space they both occupy and open up. In effect, there can be no self-critical monuments, only critical viewers.

NOTES

1. For a complete account of this incident, see Günther Schwarberg, *Angriffsziel Cap Arcona* (Hamburg: Stern–Buch im Verlag Gruner, 1983).

2. According to Yehuda Bauer, the actual number of Jews killed at Babi Yar between September 29 and October 1, 1941, was probably 33,000 (*History of the Holocaust* [New York, London, Toronto, Sidney: Franklin Watts, 1982], pp. 198–99). The larger figure cited on the plaque at the memorial refers to all Kiev citizens killed by the Germans between 1941 and 1943.

3. This observation is in reference to the *icons* only. The inside of the barracks at Auschwitz–I have been converted into national pavilions, including one devoted solely to an exposition of the Jewish experience at Auschwitz, which was dedicated in 1978.

4. For further discussion of the archetypal sources for these figures, see David Roskies, *Against the Apocalypse: Responses to Catastrophe in Modern Jewish Culture* (Cambridge, Mass., and London: Harvard University Press, 1984), pp. 297–301.

5. For further insight into the commissioning and building of this monument, see the sculptor's own description of the process in Richard Yaffe, *Nathan Rapoport Sculptures and Monuments* (New York: Shengold Publishers, Inc., 1980).

6. In a further twist, it is worth noting that the granite blocks supporting

the Warsaw ghetto memorial were originally imported by Hitler for a projected monument to his victory over Polish Jewry.

For a more complete discussion of Hitler's plans for a "Central Jewish Museum" in Prague, see Linda A. Altshuler and Anna R. Cohn, "The Precious Legacy," in *The Precious Legacy: Judaic Treasures from the Czechoslovak State Collections*, ed. David Altshuler (New York: Summit Books, 1983), pp. 24–38.

Theodor W. Adorno

What Does Coming to Terms with the Past Mean?

Editor's Note: This lecture, included in Eingriffe *(Interventions), has not been previously translated into English. The basis for the translation is the text in Adorno's* Gesammelte Schriften, *vol. 10, pt. 2 (Frankfurt am Main: Suhrkamp Verlag, 1977), pp. 555–72. For remarks added when the lecture was given a second time, see the same volume, pp. 816–17.*

Adorno anticipates many issues raised by Bitburg. He places these in the broadest possible context. Themes included are: the survival of totalitarian tendencies in contemporary democracies; the anxiety about Russia; the importance of recognizing "objective" social forces so that the individual citizen or "subject" can become truly such, i.e., fully aware and politically responsible; a need to forget the past arising both from its criminal nature and from the sensitive consciousness itself; the nature of anti-Semitism; the possibility of achieving "enlightenment" through education or re-education as well as the role of psychoanalysis in this endeavor; and finally, how to advance political maturity in the new Federal Republic of Germany. The spirit of the essay and its title recall Immanuel Kant's tract of 1784: "Response to the Question: What Is Enlightenment?" ("Beantwortung der Frage: Was ist Aufklärung?"). Kant's opening sentence has become famous. "Enlightenment is humanity's exodus from its self-imposed immaturity."

Adorno's title needs clarification. "Aufarbeitung" is colloquially yet inadequately translated as "Coming to terms with." The German phrase has psychoanalytic as well as political connotations and may also allude to the way old materials are "worked up" into something new, like the fabric of a hand-me-down. The idea of reprocessing introduces a material metaphor even as Adorno deals with an intellectual or spiritual crisis: how to take the Hitler era into consciousness. Always a stylist, sensitive to any turn of phrase that might imply an easing or idealizing of the historical task at hand, Adorno uses "Aufarbeitung" to evoke (1) the personal and painful character of the consciousness that must emerge from Germany's "Zero Hour"; (2) the psychoanalytic effort to confront and "work through" the memory of offense and catastrophe; (3) the convergence, however distantly, of "Aufarbeitung" and "Aufklärung" (enlightenment, clarification); (4) a critique of the parallel notion of "mastering the past" (Vergangenheitsbewältigung), which is tainted, verbally at least, by the idea of some ultimate repression.

The question "What does coming to terms with the past mean?" must be elucidated. It is based on a phrase that has recently become highly suspect as a slogan. "Coming to terms with the past" does not imply a serious working through of the past, the breaking of its spell through an act of clear consciousness. It suggests, rather, wishing to turn the page and, if possible, wiping it from memory. The attitude that it would be proper for everything to be forgiven and forgotten by those who were wronged is expressed by the party that committed the injustice. In a scholarly controversy I once wrote that in the hangman's house one shouldn't speak of the noose; otherwise, you wind up with ressentiment. But the fact that a tendency toward an unconscious and not-so-unconscious defense against guilt combines so absurdly with thoughts of coming to terms with the past, is occasion enough for reflections about a region from which, even today, such horror emanates that one hesitates to call it by its name.

One wants to get free of the past: rightly so, since one cannot live in its shadow, and since there is no end to terror if guilt and violence are only repaid, again and again, with guilt and violence. But wrongly so, since the past one wishes to evade is still so intensely alive. National Socialism lives on, and to this day we don't know whether it is only the ghost of what was so monstrous that it didn't even die off with its own death, or whether it never died in the first place—whether the readiness for unspeakable actions survives in people, as in the social conditions that hem them in.

I don't want to go into the question of neo-Nazi organizations. I consider the continued existence of National Socialism *within* democracy potentially more threatening than the continued existence of fascist tendencies *against* democracy. Infiltration designates something objective; dubious figures make their comeback into positions of power only because present conditions favor them.

No one disputes the fact that in Germany it is not only among the so-called incorrigibles—let the term stand for the time being—

that the past has still not been mastered. Concerning this, people always refer to the so-called guilt complex, often adding that such a complex actually came into being only with the "construction" of a collective German guilt. Now it is indisputable that, in relation to the past, there is much that is neurotic: defensive gestures when one isn't attacked; massive affect in situations that do not fully warrant it; lack of affect in the face of the most serious matters; and often simply a repression of what was known or half-known. Thus, in a study of groups conducted by the Institute for Social Research,[1] we discovered many times that recollections of deportation and of mass murder were described by saving expressions or euphemistic circumlocutions, or that a vacuous sort of discourse formed around these memories—the universally accepted, almost benevolent expression "Kristallnacht," used for the pogrom of November 1938, is evidence of this tendency. A very large number of people claim not to have known what was happening then, although Jews were disappearing everywhere, and although it can hardly be assumed that those who experienced events in the East would always have kept silent about what must have been an unbearable burden for them. One may certainly suggest that a proportional relation exists between the gesture of "I didn't know anything about all that" and an indifference that is obtuse and frightened, at the very least. In any case, the confirmed enemies of National Socialism knew early on precisely what was up.

All of us today also recognize a readiness to deny or belittle what happened—however difficult it is to conceive that people are not ashamed to argue that it was surely at most only five million Jews, and not six million, who were killed. Irrational too is the widespread "settling of accounts" about guilt, as if Dresden made up for Auschwitz. There is already something inhuman in making such calculations, or in the haste to dispense with self-reflection through counter-accusations. Surely, military actions in time of war—Coventry and Rotterdam—are not comparable to the organized murder of millions of innocent people. Even their innocence, absolutely simple and plausible, is contested. The enormity of what was perpetrated is the very cause for a self-justifying attack: such things, so a lazy consciousness comforts itself, could not have occurred if the victims had not presented some kind of provocation; and this vague "some kind of" can then flourish wildly. The delusion goes even further than this glaring miscombination of fictitious guilt [of the victims] and a punishment that was only too real. At times the victors are represented as the originators of what the losers did when they themselves were still in power. As for the unspeakable acts of Hitler, those who tolerated his seizing power are made responsible, and not those who cheered him on. The idiocy of all this really does testify to a lack of psychic mastery and an unhealed wound—although the thought of wounds is more appropriate to the victims.

All this talk, by the way, of a guilt complex displays something untruthful. Psychiatry, from which the phrase is borrowed (bringing with it associations from that source), implies that such guilt feelings are pathological, inadequate to reality: "psychogenic" as analysts call it. With the help of the word "complex" the impression is created that the guilt—which so many fend off, abreact, or deflect through the craziest rationalizations—is really no guilt at all, but exists only inside them, in their psychological makeup. So a real and terrible past is rendered harmless by being transformed this way—into a mere figment of the imagination of those who are affected by it. Or is guilt itself perhaps only a complex? Should we consider it pathological to burden oneself with the past, while the healthy and realistic person is absorbed in the present and its practical concerns?

That would be to appropriate a moral from "And it's as good as if it never happened," which is written by Goethe but uttered by the devil at a decisive point in *Faust* to reveal his innermost principle: the destruction of memory. The murdered are to be cheated even out of the one thing that our powerlessness can grant them: remembrance. The fixated attitude of those who don't want to hear or know anything admittedly finds itself in agreement with a mighty historical tendency. Hermann Heimpel has spoken repeatedly of the atrophy of the consciousness of historical continuity in Germany, a symptom of that social weakening of personal autonomy [*des Ichs*] that Horkheimer and I had already sought to trace in the *Dialectic of Enlightenment*.[2] Empirical findings of the kind that the younger generation in many cases no longer recognizes who Bismarck or Kaiser Wilhelm I was, have confirmed this suspected loss of history.

The forgetting of National Socialism should be understood far more in terms of a general social situation than in terms of psychopathology. Even the psychological mechanisms that defend against painful and unpleasant memories serve highly realistic ends. This is revealed when those who are defensive point out, freely and in a practical mood, that a too vivid and lasting remembrance of those events could harm Germany's reputation abroad. (Such zeal jibes poorly with the comment by Richard Wagner, who was nationalistic enough, that to be German means to do something for its own sake— so long as it is not taken a priori as a business venture.) The effacement of memory is more the achievement of an all-too-wakeful consciousness than it is the result of its weakness in the face of the superiority of unconscious processes. In this forgetting of what is scarcely past, one senses the fury of the one who has to talk himself out of what everyone else knows, before he can talk them out of it.

Of course, the emotions and modes of behavior involved here are not plainly rational insofar as they distort the very facts to which they refer. But they are rational in the sense that they depend on social tendencies, and that anyone reacting in such a way feels at one with his time. Such a reaction is directly opposed to a successful resolution of the problem. If one doesn't trouble oneself with useless thoughts, one doesn't throw monkey wrenches into the works. It is advisable to speak along the lines of what Franz Böhm so pregnantly called "non-public opinion." Those who conform to a mood that is held in check by the official taboos—but therefore only gains in virulence—qualify simultaneously as part of an ingroup and as independent agents. After all, the German resistance movement remained without any grass-roots support during the war, and it's not as if Germany's defeat had magically conjured it up. One can rightly presume that democracy is more deeply rooted in Germany today than after the First World War: National Socialism—antifeudal and thoroughly bourgeois—politicized the masses and so, against its own interests, partly prepared the way for democratization. The Junker caste as well as the radical workers' movement has disappeared; for the first time something like a homogeneous bourgeois milieu has been produced. But the fact that democracy came to Germany too late—that is, that it didn't coincide historically with the high point of economic liberalism—and that it was introduced by the Allied victors—leaves the German people's relation to it without strong emotional connections.

It is rare that this is ever openly admitted, because for the moment things are going so well under democracy; and also because it would be contrary to the community of interests institutionalized by political alliances with the West, above all with the United States. But the rancor against "re-education" is sufficiently evident. The best to be said is that political democracy has been accepted in Germany as what Americans call a "working proposition"—something functional that up till now has allowed and even promoted prosperity. But democracy has not domesticated itself to the point that people really experience it as their cause, and so consider themselves agents [*Subjecte*] of the political process. It is felt to be one system among others, as if one could choose from a menu between communism, democracy, fascism, monarchy—yet not as something identical with people themselves, as the expression of their own maturity. Democracy is valued according to its success or failure, whereby special interests must also come into play, rather than as the union of the individual and the collective interest.

(The parliamentary system, in mass democracies, that represents the general will by "delegating" it, makes that process no easier.)

In Germany one often hears Germans themselves advancing the strange proposition that they aren't yet ready for democracy. They make an ideology of their own immaturity, not unlike youngsters who, when caught for some violent act or other, talk their way out of it by virtue of being mere teenagers. The grotesque character of this mode of argumentation reveals a flagrant contradiction. People who so unnaïvely play upon their own naïveté and political immaturity must already consider themselves, on the one hand, as political subjects whose responsibility it is to determine their own fate and to construct freely their own society. But, on the other hand, they come up against the fact that the existing circumstances [Verhältnisse] impose strict limits on such projects. Since they aren't capable of breaking through these limitations by their own powers of thought, they ascribe this inability—from which they do, in truth, suffer—to themselves or to the big shots or others. Once again, they divide themselves from within into subject and object. In any case, it characterizes the dominant ideology today that the more people are exposed to objective forces[3] over which they have no power or believe that they have none, the more they personalize this lack of power. According to the received idea that all depends on the individual, they attribute to the individual everything that actually resides in the existing circumstances. As a result, the circumstances once again remain unclarified. In the language of philosophy one would say that in the people's alienation from democracy is mirrored the alienation of society from itself.

Foremost, perhaps, among these objective forces is the developing course of international politics. It appears to offer retrospective justification for the attack that Hitler launched against the Soviet Union. When the Western world essentially defines itself as a united front in its defense against the Russian threat, then it appears as if the victors of 1945 had foolishly torn down proven bulwarks against Bolshevism, only to rebuild them a few years later. From the only too readily available phrase "that's just what Hitler always said," it is a short step to the extrapolation that he was also right about other things. None but armchair preachers could gloss over the historical fatality that the very conception that once led Chamberlain and his ilk to tolerate Hitler as a watchdog against the East has outlived Hitler's defeat. And it truly is a fatality. For the threat by the East against the outposts of Western Europe is clear, and whoever does not resist it is quite literally guilty of a repetition of Chamberlain's "appeasement."

The only thing that's forgotten—the only thing!—is that this very threat was first unleashed by the actions of Hitler who brought upon

Europe exactly what, according to the "appeasers," his expansionist war was supposedly meant to prevent. Even more than with the destiny of single individuals, the destiny of political entanglements involves a nexus of guilt. The resistance to the East has its own dynamic that brings Germany's past back to life. And not only ideologically—for sloganeering about the struggle against Bolshevism has always served as camouflage for those who have no greater esteem for freedom than the Bolsheviks did—but really so.

It was already observed in Hitler's time that the organizational power of totalitarian systems imposes something of its own essential character upon its opponents. So long as the economic differential between East and West continues to exist, fascist tactics have better chances for success with the masses than Eastern propaganda, although admittedly no rush toward fascism's *ultima ratio* is presently visible. But the same character types are susceptible to these two forms of totalitarianism. We misunderstand altogether the authoritarian personality type if we construe it as a function of a particular politico-economic ideology; the well-known oscillation before 1933 of millions of voters between the National Socialist and the Communist parties is no accident when considered in terms of social psychology. American research has established that this type of personality structure does not correlate easily with politico-economic criteria. It must be defined, rather, in terms of character traits such as thinking within the paradigm of power-powerlessness; rigidity and the inability to react; conventionality; conformist behavior; lack of self-reflection; and finally an altogether deficient capacity for experience. Authoritarian types identify with real power as such, prior to any particular content. Basically, they have only weak egos at their disposal, and thus need, as a substitute, to identify with large collectivities whose protection they seek. The fact that wherever one turns one finds characters like those depicted in the film *Wir Wunderkinder*[4] is a consequence neither of the basic depravity of the world nor of peculiar traits attributed to the German national character. Rather, it is due to the identity of those conformists—who relate before the fact to the levers of any power apparatus—as potential followers of totalitarianism.

It is an illusion, moreover, that the National Socialist regime meant nothing but fear and suffering, although it did mean this even for many of its adherents. For countless people it wasn't all that bad under fascism. Terror's sharp edge was directed only against a few relatively well-defined groups. After the crises-ridden experiences of the pre-Hitler period, people were overcome by a feeling of "everything is taken care of," and not only ideologically by means of collectively organized "fun-through-fitness" trips and flower boxes in the factories. Compared with a previous laissez-faire, Hitler's world really did shield its own members—up to a point—from the natural catastrophes of communal life to which people were abandoned. A barbaric experiment in state control of an industrialized society, it anticipated today's crisis-management in violent fashion. The much-noted "integration"—the organizational tightening of the communal net that covered everything—also guaranteed protection against the universal anxiety of falling through the interstices and disappearing. For countless people, alienation's chill seemed to be eliminated by the warmth—however manipulated and imposed—of togetherness; the "people's community" [*Volksgemeinschaft*] of the unfree and the unequal was, as a lie, also the fulfillment of an old, familiar, evil bourgeois dream.

To be sure, the system that offered those kinds of gratification carried within itself the seeds of its own downfall. The economic burgeoning of the Third Reich rested to a great extent on the rearmament for war that brought on the catastrophe. But that diminished faculty of memory of which I spoke resists considering these arguments. It stubbornly glorifies the National Socialist period, which fulfilled the collective power-fantasies of those who were powerless as individuals and, indeed, felt themselves to be somebody only by virtue of such collective might. No analysis, however illuminating, can remove the reality of this sense of fulfillment, or the instinctual energies invested in it. Even Hitler's risky gamble was not as irrational as it then appeared to average liberal thought, or as its failure appears today to historical hindsight. His plan, to exploit the temporary advantage gained through massively accelerated rearmament, was not all that foolish from the perspective of what he wanted to achieve. Whoever looks closely at the history of the Third Reich, and above all of the war, will always feel that Hitler's defeat at particular moments appears to be accidental, while only the course of events as a whole displays a sense of necessity, as the greater technological and economic potential of the rest of the world finally prevailed so as not to be eaten alive—to a degree a statistical necessity and certainly not a recognizable step-by-step logic. The surviving sympathy for National Socialism does not need to employ much sophistry to convince itself and others that things could just as well have turned out differently: that what happened was, in fact, due only to mistakes, and that Hitler's downfall was a world-historical accident that the world-spirit might still correct.

On the subjective side, the collective narcissism in the human psyche—national vanity, in a word—was immeasurably exalted by National Socialism. The individual's narcissistic drives, for which a callous world promises less and less satisfaction, which nonetheless persist undiminished as long as civilization refuses them so much, find a substitute gratification in their "identification with the whole."* This collective narcissism was grievously damaged by the collapse of the Hitler regime; a damage which, however, occurred in the realm of simple fact, without each individual becoming conscious of it and thereby getting over it. This is the social-psychological relevance of the talk about an unmastered past. Also lacking is the panic that, according to Freud's theory in *Group Psychology and the Analysis of the Ego*, sets in where collective identifications break down. If the great psychologist's theory isn't to be thrown out, there remains only one conclusion: secretly, unconsciously smoldering and therefore especially powerful, these identifications as well as a group narcissism were not destroyed but continued to exist. Inwardly the defeat has been as little ratified as after 1918. Even in the face of evident catastrophe, the collectivity formed by Hitler held together and clung to chimerical hopes, such as secret weapons, which were in fact possessed by others. From the viewpoint of social psychology, it would also be expected that this damaged group-narcissism is lying in wait to be repaired and grasps at everything in consciousness that might immediately bring the past into harmony with narcissistic wishes—but then it also, if possible, remolds reality as if this injury could be made not to have happened. To a certain degree this was indeed accomplished by economic prosperity and the feeling of "how competent we are."

Yet I doubt whether the so-called economic miracle—which everyone participates in, even as they also speak somewhat disparagingly of it—really extends, in a social-psychological sense, as far as one might think during times of relative stability. Precisely because hunger continues to exist on entire continents (despite the fact that we have the technology to eliminate it), no one can feel all that happy with his own prosperity. Just as individuals may laugh maliciously at a film character licking his chops and tucking his napkin under his chin, so too mankind doesn't grant itself any comfort when it knows too well that it is paid for by lack and misery: ressentiment strikes every happiness, even one's own. Satiety has become a term of rebuke a priori, even though the only thing bad about it would be that there are those who have *nothing* to eat; the supposed idealism that in today's Germany hypocritically attacks a supposed materialism owes much of what it considers to be its profundity only to repressed instincts. A hatred of comfort results in a discomfort with prosperity, at the same time that the past is glorified as tragic. But this malaise in no way issues merely from dark sources, but also again from much more rational ones. Our prosperity is the product of circumstances; no one

---

*Cf. Theodor W. Adorno, "Meinung Wahn Gesellschaft," in *Gesammelte Schriften*, 10/2 (Frankfurt am Main: Suhrkamp Verlag, 1977), pp. 588ff.

trusts in its unlimited duration. If one consoles oneself with the thought that events like the "Black Friday" of 1929 and the subsequent economic crisis could hardly happen again, this already implies trust in a strong state, one that—it is anticipated—will also protect people when their economic and political freedom is no longer there. Even in the midst of prosperity, even during the temporary labor shortage, most people, it seems, see themselves as potentially jobless, as welfare recipients, and therefore ultimately as the objects, and not the subjects, of society: this is the fully legitimate and reasonable basis for their discomfort. And it is clear that at virtually any moment this discontent can be accumulated and turned against the past and misused for the renewal of a disastrous politics.

Today the fascist fantasy undeniably blends with the nationalism of the so-called underdeveloped countries, which already are no longer called that, but rather "developing countries." So also during the war, in slogans about Western plutocracies and proletarian nations, a sympathy was expressed with those who felt that they had come up short in the imperialist competition and wanted to find a seat at the table. It's hard to say if and to what extent this tendency is already embedded in the anti-civilizational, anti-Western undercurrent of the German tradition: whether in Germany too there is a convergence of fascist and communist nationalism. Nationalism today is at once obsolete and current. Obsolete, because individual sovereign nations—at least those in advanced continental Europe—have forfeited their historical selfhood [*Substantialität*] in the face of the obligatory alliance of nations into great-power blocs under the supremacy of the strongest ones, an imperative already dictated by developments in weapons technology. The idea of the nation, in which the joint economic interests of free and independent citizens took a stand against the territorial barriers of feudalism, has itself become a barrier vis-à-vis the obvious potential of a global society [*Gesamtgesellschaft*]. But nationalism is up-to-date only insofar as the traditional and psychically invested idea of the nation (which still expresses a community of interests within the international world of business) has the power to harness hundreds of millions toward goals that they do not immediately perceive as their own.

Nationalism no longer quite believes in itself, and yet is required politically as the most effective means for bringing people around to insisting on objectively outmoded relations. That is why, self-deluded and not comfortable in its own skin, nationalism today puts on such grimacing features. Sure enough, it was never altogether without such features, which were the heritage of barbaric primitive tribal conceptions, but they were kept in check as long as liberalism really confirmed the rights of the individual—also concretely as the condition for collective prosperity. Only in an era when it was already capsizing did nationalism become totally sadistic and destructive. The rage of the Hitlerian world against everything that was different—nationalism as a paranoid delusional system—already manifested this.

The appeal of precisely these features has scarcely diminished today: paranoia, the persecution mania that persecutes those onto whom it projects what it itself desires, is contagious. Collective delusions such as anti-Semitism confirm the pathology of the individual who shows that he is psychologically no longer able to cope with this world, and is thrown back upon a purely illusionary inner kingdom. As the thesis of the psychoanalyst Ernst Simmel puts it, such delusions may well spare half-mad individuals from becoming wholly so. Insofar as the madness of nationalism manifests itself openly today in the reasonable fear of renewed catastrophes, to that extent is its diffusion promoted. Madness is the substitute for the dream that humanity could organize its world humanely, a dream that a man-made world is stubbornly rejecting. Everything that happened from 1933 to 1945 is of a piece with pathological nationalism.

The fact that fascism lives on, and that the much-cited work of reprocessing the past [*Aufarbeitung der Vergangenheit*] has not yet succeeded, and has instead degenerated into its distorted image—empty, cold forgetting—is the result of the continued existence of the same objective conditions that brought about fascism in the first place. Fascism, basically, cannot be deduced from subjective dispositions. Now as then the economic order, and to a large extent the economic organization built upon it, together maintain a majority of people in a state of dependence on conditions over which they have no control, thereby keeping this majority in a condition of political immaturity [*Unmündigkeit*]. If they want to live, they have no choice but to adapt themselves to the given circumstances, to conform; they have to put under erasure their status as autonomous subjects, which the idea of democracy appeals to; they can only maintain that status at the cost of renouncing it. To see through this obfuscatory complex demands of them just that painful intellectual effort which the organization of their everyday life, and not least of all an inflated and comprehensive culture industry, prevents. The necessity of such adaptation, to the point of identifying with the status quo, with the given, with power as such, creates the potential for totalitarianism, and is reinforced by the dissatisfaction and rage which that forced adaptation itself produces and reproduces. Because reality doesn't provide the autonomy or, finally, the possible happiness that the concept of democracy actually promises, people are indifferent to democracy, where they don't secretly hate it. This [democratic] form of political organization is experienced as ill fitted to social and economic realities; if one has to adapt as an individual, then one also wants the forms of collective life to adapt—all the more so since one expects of such adaptation the streamlining on the part of the state apparatus as a giant undertaking among a not-so-friendly competition of all against all. Those whose real powerlessness persists can't bear even the semblance of an improvement in their situation; they'd rather scrap the obligation of an autonomy that they suspect can't be used as a model for living, and they throw themselves into the crucible of the collective ego.

I've exaggerated the dark side, according to the saying that today only exaggeration can be the medium of truth. Please don't misunderstand my fragmentary and often rhaspsodic remarks as so many Spenglerisms (to take after Spengler would be to make common cause with doomsday). My intention was to point out one of the tendencies covered up by the slick façade of everyday life before it overflows the institutional dams that formerly contained it. The danger is an objective one, and does not reside primarily in humanity as such. As I have said, it can be argued that democracy, along with everything that it presupposes, has a more profound hold on people today than it did during the Weimar period. In stressing what is not so obvious, I neglected what sober thinking must nevertheless consider: within German democracy, from 1945 to the present, the material life of society has reproduced itself more richly than at any time in human memory, and this too is not without social-psychological relevance. It would certainly not be over-optimistic to claim that things are not going badly for German democracy, and therefore not so badly for a real coming to terms with the past either—if there were only enough time and things were to remain stable.

Yet there lies in the concept of "having enough time" something naïve, and also contemplative in the worst sense of the word [etwas schlecht Kontemplatives]. We are not mere observers of world history who could romp around more or less untouched in its enormous rooms, nor does world history itself, whose rhythm increasingly simulates that of catastrophe, appear willing to grant its subjects the time in which everything could get better on its own. This leads directly to the question of a democratic pedagogy. Enlightenment about what happened in the past must work, above all, against a forgetfulness that too easily goes along with and justifies what is forgotten. Parents, for example, who must endure embarrassing questions about Hitler from their children, and then, in order to exculpate themselves, speak of the good side and how it really wasn't all that terrible. In Germany it has become a fashion to bad-mouth political education, and, while it surely could be improved, sociology already has data available indicating that political education, seriously conducted and not just as a tiresome duty, produces better results than one had generally thought possible. But if one takes the objective potential for the survival of National Socialism as seriously as I think it has to be taken, then this too will pose limits for a mature political pedagogy. Whether this pedagogy is sociological or psychological in its approach, in practice it will probably reach only those who are already open to it, and for this reason are hardly vulnerable to fascism. On the other hand, it is in no way superfluous to strengthen, through enlightened instruction, even this group against "non-public" opinion. One could well imagine that something like cadres might develop out of this group, whose influence in the most widely varied circles would then reach the whole of society. The chances for this become all the more favorable the more self-conscious these cadres are. Obviously, the process of enlightenment won't content itself with these groups alone.

Here I choose to sidestep a question that is very difficult and burdens us with the greatest kind of responsibility: namely, the extent to which we've succeeded, in attempts at public enlightenment, to explore the past, and whether it's not the case that precisely such insistence on the past doesn't awaken a stubborn resistance and bring about the exact opposite of what is intended. It seems to me that what is conscious can never bring with it as much fatefulness as what remains unconscious, half-conscious, or preconscious. Essentially, it is a matter of the *way* in which the past is called up and made present: whether one stops at sheer reproach, or whether one endures the horror through a certain strength that comprehends even the incomprehensible. For this task it will, however, be necessary to educate the educators.

The problem is aggravated by the fact that what are called the "behavioral sciences" in America are either unrepresented or represented only in the most paltry fashion in Germany. It is imperative to urge the universities to strengthen a sociology that would coincide with historical research on our own epoch. Instead of spouting at second hand pseudo-profundities about "the Being of man," pedagogy ought to take on the task that one so easily accuses "re-education" of having bungled. Criminology in Germany is at the moment nowhere near modern standards. But above all one thinks of psychoanalysis, which remains repressed to this day. Either it's lacking altogether, or it's replaced by tendencies that, while claiming to have overcome the much-abused nineteenth century, actually fall back behind Freudian theory, and so perhaps turn it into its very opposite.

The need for an exact and undiluted knowledge of Freudian theory is as imperative as ever. The hatred for it is directly of a piece with anti-Semitism, not just because Freud was a Jew but because psychoanalysis consists precisely of a critical self-reflection that puts anti-Semites into a seething rage. As unlikely as it is that anything like a mass analysis could be carried out—if only because of the time factor—it would still be therapeutic if rigorous psychoanalysis found its institutional place in, and so influenced, the intellectual climate of Germany—even if this merely consisted of making it self-evident that one shouldn't strike out against others but should reflect on one's self and one's own relation to whatever the hardened consciousness tends to rage at.

In any case, attempts to work subjectively against the objective potential for disaster should not content themselves with "solutions" that scarcely touch upon the real difficulty of what's at stake. References, for example, to the great achievements of Jews in the past, however true they may be, hardly do much good and smack of propaganda. And propaganda—the rational manipulation of the irrational—is the privilege of totalitarians. Those who resist the totalitarians shouldn't imitate them in a way that can only work to their own disadvantage. Speeches in praise of the Jews that segregate them as a group already concede too much ground to anti-Semitism. Anti-Semitism is so difficult to refute because the psychic economy of countless people needed it and, in an attenuated form, still seems to need it today. Whatever happens in the form of propaganda remains ambiguous.

I once heard the story of a woman who, after attending a performance of the dramatization of *The Diary of Anne Frank*, said in a shaken voice: "Yes, but really, at least *that* girl ought to have been allowed to live." Surely, even this was to be welcomed as a first step toward insight. But the individual case, which stands for and illuminates the frightful whole, became at the same time (by virtue of its individualization) an alibi for the whole that the woman forgot. The confounded thing about such observations remains that one wouldn't therefore wish to counsel against performances of the Anne Frank play or the like, since their effect indeed feeds into the potential for improvement—whatever one's objections and however much it seems to be a sacrilege against the dignity of the dead.

I also don't believe that too much is accomplished by social gatherings, encounters between young Germans and young Israelis, and other such organized acts of friendship, however desirable this contact may be. For this sort of activity depends too much upon the assumption that anti-Semitism essentially has something to do with Jews and could be combated through an actual knowledge of Jews. In fact, the genuine anti-Semite is much more defined by his utter incapacity for any kind of experience or his lack of receptivity. Should anti-Semitism be primarily a product of the objective social conditions, and only secondarily of anti-Semites, then—in the sense of the National Socialist joke—they'd have had to invent the Jews if they hadn't already existed.

So long as one wants to struggle against anti-Semitism within individual persons, one shouldn't expect too much from recourse to facts, for they'll often either not be admitted or be neutralized as exceptions. One should rather turn the argument toward the people whom one is addressing. It is they who should be made conscious of the mechanisms that provoke their racial prejudice. Coming to terms with the past in the sense of aiming for enlightenment is essentially that sort of *turn toward the subject*: reinforcement of a person's self-consciousness and, with that, of a sense of self. This should be accompanied by a knowledge of the few durable propaganda-tricks that are exactly attuned to a psychological disposition that we must assume resides in people. Since these tricks are rigid and limited in number, there is no insurmountable difficulty in isolating them, making them known, and using them as a kind of vaccine. The problem of how to achieve, practically speaking, such personal, subjective enlightenment could probably only be solved by the collaborative effort of those teachers and psychologists who do not withdraw, under the guise of "scholarly objectivity," from the most pressing task facing their disciplines today.

Yet considering the social context or the "objective" force behind the still current potential for anti-Semitism, enlightening the individual person as such will not suffice—even should it be planned with greater energy and greater depth than before. If one wants to oppose an objective danger objectively, then a mere idea won't do, not even that of freedom and humanity, which in its abstract form—as we've recently learned—doesn't mean all that much to people. If the potential for fascism is linked to human interests (however limited they may be), then the most effective antidote remains an appeal to whatever truly illuminates those interests, and the most immediate of them. One would really be guilty of a baroque kind of psychologizing if one disregarded the fact that the war and the suffering it brought upon the German population, while insufficient to eliminate the potential for fascism, comes into play as a counterweight. Let us remind people of the simplest things: that open or disguised revivals of fascism will bring about war, suffering, and poverty within a coercive system, and most likely in the end Russian domination over Europe; that, in short, they lead to a politics of catastrophe. This will make a more profound impression upon people than referring to ideals or even to the suffering of others, which, as La Rochefoucauld already knew, is relatively easy to dismiss. From this perspective, the contemporary malaise signifies little more than the luxury of a certain mood. For despite all psychological repression, Stalingrad and the nights of bombing are not so forgotten that one cannot explain to everyone the connection between a revival of the politics that led to them, and the prospect of a third Punic War. Even if one succeeds in making this clear, the danger persists. We will not have come to terms with the past until the causes of what happened then are no longer active. Only because these causes live on does the spell of the past remain, to this very day, unbroken.

Translated by Timothy Bahti and Geoffrey Hartman

EDITOR'S NOTES

This essay is a translation of "Was bedeutet: Aufarbeitung der Vergangenheit," first published in 1959; copyright © Suhrkamp Verlag, Frankfurt am Main, 1963; translation copyright © 1986 by Geoffrey Hartman.

1. Founded in 1923 and associated with the University of Frankfurt (hence the designation "Frankfurt School"), the Institute for Social Research supported Adorno and other intellectuals during the Hitler years. In 1938 it went into exile but maintained a kind of identity, first in Paris, then by its loose affiliation with Columbia University.

2. First published in 1944 in a mimeographed version, and in book form by Querido Press, Amsterdam, 1947. English translation by John Cummings (New York, 1972).

3. Adorno, influenced by Walter Benjamin, uses the word "constellations," suggesting convergence rather than totality or fatality.

4. 1958 film directed by Kurt Hoffmann, popular for his light comedies, about the so-called German economic miracle or wonder.

Primo Levi

The Memory of Offense

Human memory is a marvelous but deceptive tool. This is a threadbare truth, known not only to psychologists but to anyone who has given some attention to the behavior of his neighbors, or his own behavior. Notions lying in our memory are not engraved in stone; not only are they prone to fade away as the years pass by, but they tend to shift, or even to swell, incorporating foreign material. This phenomenon is well known to judges and lawyers; it rarely happens that two eye-witnesses of the same event describe it in the same way and with the same words, even if the event is recent and neither has a personal interest in distorting it to his advantage.

The unreliability of our memories will be fully explained only when we know in what language, in which alphabet, the memories are written: on which material, with what pen they are recorded; and this is a goal that is still very remote. We know some factors that alter memory in particular circumstances: bodily traumas, not only those affecting the brain; interference by other "competing" memories; abnormal states of consciousness; repression. However, even in normal conditions a slow degradation is at work: a dimming out of the records, one might say a physiological oblivion, which few memories can resist. Quite probably we must recognize in this phenomenon, which is so common, one of the great forces of nature, the one that degrades order into disorder and quenches life into death. It is certain that exercising, practicing (in our case, a frequent recalling), keeps a remembrance vivid and bright, in much the same way that a frequently exerted muscle keeps its efficiency. But it is also true that a memory that is recalled too often and that is expressed in a verbal form tends to set as a stereotype—a form tested by experience, crystallized, perfected, and adorned—which settles in the place of the raw record and grows at the expense of the original memory.

It is my intention to review here remembrances of emergencies, of suffered or inflicted offenses. In this case, all or almost all the factors are at work that can cancel or distort the mnemonic record: the memory of a trauma, received or inflicted, is itself traumatic, since its recalling generates pain, or at least a disturbance. He who has been injured tends to remove the memory so as not to renovate the pain; he who has injured his neighbor tends to bury the memory deeply in order to get rid of it, to mitigate his sense of guilt. Here, as in quite a number of instances, we are confronted with a paradoxical analogy between the victim and the perpetrator. I wish to be clear: the two are in the same trap, but the offender, and only he, has set and triggered it, and if he has come to suffer from his deed, it is just that he suffers; whereas it is an iniquity that the victim also suffers, as indeed he or she suffers, even after many years.

Once more we are confronted with a mournful truth: when an offense has been inflicted, there is no healing. It protracts itself endlessly, and the Furies, in whom we cannot help but believe, not only afflict the tormentor (if in fact they do, aided or unaided by human punishment) but perpetuate his work, by denying peace to the tormented. One cannot read without anguish the words written by Jean Améry, the philosopher who was tortured by the Gestapo as a member of the Belgian resistance and then deported to Auschwitz as a Jew:

> Whoever was tortured, stays tortured. . . . Whoever has succumbed to torture can no longer feel at home in the world. The shame of destruction cannot be erased. Trust in the world, which already collapsed in part at the first blow, but in the end, under torture, fully, will not be regained.[1]

For Jean Améry, torture had been an endless dying: he committed suicide in 1978. We, the survivors, do not want confusions, blurs, morbidity, indulgences. The oppressor remains what he is, and so does the victim: they are not interchangeable, they do not overlap. The former must be punished and execrated (but also, as difficult as it may seem, possibly understood); the latter deserves help and pity; but both of them, in the face of the obscenity of the deed that has been irrevocably accomplished, need shelter and defense.

We now have at our disposal a number of witnesses, confessions, and acknowledgments by the culprits. Some were released on the occasion of a trial, others are to be read in books or reports. In my opinion, they are extremely important documents, all of them. Generally speaking, the descriptions of things that have been done or seen are of minor interest. They coincide broadly with the testimony of the victims; they are a closed case, and by now belong to history. Much more important and interesting are the motivations and the justifications: Why did you do it? Were you aware of committing a crime?

The answers to these two questions, or to similar ones, are all alike, irrespective of the background of the person to whom the question is addressed: an ambitious and cultivated professional like Speer, a fanatic, icy officer like Eichmann, obtuse brutes like Boger and Kaduk, the torturers of Auschwitz. These answers can be formulated in different styles and expressed with more or less arrogance, according to the mental and cultural level of the person involved, but they boil down substantially to the same points. "I did it because I was ordered to"; "Others, my superiors, committed worse crimes"; "In view of the education I received and of the environment in which I lived, I could not have acted otherwise"; "If I had refused the orders, another would have fulfilled them with still greater harshness." For the person who reads such justifications, the first feeling is a wave of disgust: these people are lying, they just cannot hope to be believed, they cannot be blind to the imbalance between their pretexts and the huge amount of pain and death they have generated. They lie knowingly; they speak in bad faith.

Now, anyone possessing sufficient worldly experience knows that the distinction between good and bad faith is optimistic and naïve; all the more so when it is applied to men like the ones I have just mentioned. It presupposes a sharpness of ideas that is shared by very few people, and even these few are likely to lose it as soon as, for whatever reason, present or past reality gives rise to anxiety or uneasiness. Under these conditions, some people are prone to lie consciously, so as to falsify the reality in cold blood, but many more are liable to weigh anchor, to take leave (momentarily or forever) from real memories, and to manufacture a truth more suitable to their needs. Here, too, the victim and the oppressor go hand in hand, because both may suffer under the weight of their past. Both tend, for similar yet opposite reasons, to loathe whatever they did or endured; both are inclined to substitute for it a screen-experience.

The substitution can begin in full consciousness, with a scenario that has been overtly faked, or at least deeply touched up, yet is more comfortable than the real one. But, when the description is repeated over and over again, not only to one's neighbors but to oneself, the borderline between truth and falsehood gets progressively blurred. One ends up by fully believing the tale that has been told and retold, polishing and rectifying here and there the details that prove less credible, or internally inconsistent, or inconsistent with established history. This way, initial bad faith has turned into good faith. This silent drift from lie to self-deception is useful: he who lies in good faith lies better, plays his role better, is more easily believed by the judge, by the historian, and by the reader.

The more such events recede into the past, the more the edifice of this self-made truth expands and solidifies. I think it is only in light of this mental process that we can interpret, for instance, the declarations made in 1978 by Louis Darquier de Pellepoix. Around 1942 he was commissary for Jewish questions in the Vichy government and, as such, was personally responsible for the deportation and death of 70,000 Jews. Darquier denies everything: the photos of the heaps of emaciated corpses are artifacts; the statistics of the millions who died have been fabricated by Jews, notoriously avid for publicity and commiseration. The deportations may in fact have taken place. He could not possibly deny them, as his signature appears at the bottom of countless letters giving orders for mass deportation, even of children. But he ignored their end-station, the purpose of such orders and their consequences. Gas chambers in Auschwitz? Yes, they existed, but they served only to kill lice; moreover (and here you can note the consistency of the man), they were built only after the war, as a tool for propaganda.

It is not my intention to extenuate the guilt of this ignoble and dull-witted person, and it hurts me to remember that he has lived for many decades undisturbed in Spain. However, I think we can recognize in him a typical example of one who has been trained in lying publicly, and therefore ends up by lying privately, even to himself, and by constructing a comfortable truth that allows him to live in peace. To keep good and bad faith separate is costly. It requires strenuous sincerity toward oneself, a continuous mental and moral effort. How can we expect such effort from a man like Darquier?

If you read attentively the statements released by Eichmann during the Jerusalem trial, and by Rudolf Höss (the commander of Auschwitz, the inventor of mass poisoning with hydrogen cyanide) in his autobiography, you recognize in both a subtle processing of the past. In essence, their defense was the classical one of rank-and-file Nazis, in fact of all rank-and-files:

> We were educated to absolute obediency, to the Führerprinzip, to hierarchy, to nationalism; we were soaked with slogans, intoxicated with mass parades; we were taught that the only justice is what profits our nation, and the only truth the words of our Leader. What more do you want from us? How can you deem it possible to require from us, *afterwards*, a different behavior from the one we maintained, and everybody maintained who was trained as we were? We were not responsible

for the decisions, since the regime in which we grew up did not allow for individual decision-making. Other people decided for us, and it could not have been otherwise, for our fitness to decide had been *amputated*. Not only were we forbidden to decide, but we became unable to. Therefore, we are not responsible, and we cannot be punished.[2]

Although it is projected against the background of the chimneys of Birkenau, this argument cannot be taken as mere effrontery. The pressure that a modern totalitarian state exerts on a citizen is frightful. Its weapons are fundamentally three: first, propaganda, either direct or masked as education, culture, folklore; second, a heavy barrage against pluralistic information; and third, terror. Nevertheless, it is fully evident that this pressure was not irresistible, particularly given the short term of the twelve years of the Third Reich. In the declarations and justifications of men like Höss and Eichmann, it is easy to perceive an exaggeration, and more precisely an elaboration of their memories. They were born and educated long before the Reich was openly "totalitarian," and their adherence to the regime was a matter of their free choice. Their tampering with the past was done later: it was a gradual procedure, and, very likely, a non-methodical, unplanned one. Wondering if it was accomplished in good or in bad faith is naïve. Faced with their well-deserved death, and faced with their judges, they too constructed a doctored past, and they ended by believing it; especially Höss, who was not very crafty. As he describes himself in his autobiography, he was little inclined to self-control and to introspection. In fact, he fails to perceive that he betrays his coarse anti-Semitism by the very sentences that strive to deny and to renounce it, and he has no inkling of how maudlin his self-portrayal as a model official, father, and husband appears to the reader.

In commenting on these alterations of a traumatic past, indeed of all memories, we must observe that the distortion of facts is inevitably limited by the weight of the facts themselves. For, in most cases, *facts* are supported by witnesses, by documents, by a historically settled context. In contrast, it is easy to alter the *motivations* that have led to an action and the emotions that have accompanied it. These motivations and emotions, being extremely fluid, are subject to deformation even by very weak forces. To the questions "Why did you do it?" and "What did you think while doing it?" there is no reliable reply, because states of mind are intrinsically transient, and still more transient are the memories we keep of them.

The end point of the deformation of the memory of a committed fault is its complete suppression. Here too the borderline between good and bad faith can be hazy; behind the "I don't know," "I don't remember" so often heard in trials, there is often a deliberate intent to lie, but in other cases we are faced with a fossilized lie, an ancient lie frozen into a formula. The acutely conscious person wanted to become forgetful, and has achieved his aim. By steadily denying its existence, he has ejected the obnoxious record as one expels an excretion or a parasite.

Defense lawyers know well that the voids of memory and the faked truths they suggest to their clients tend to become real blanks and firm beliefs. There is no need to look to mental pathology to find cases of this phenomenon. An individual makes statements that are obviously false, but we are at a loss to decide whether he knows or does not know that he is lying. If we absurdly were to suppose that the liar had become truthful for a moment, he himself would be unable to solve the dilemma. While lying, he is an actor totally amalgamated with his character. It is impossible to draw a line between the two.

The best way to resist the invasion of painful memories is to prevent their entry into consciousness, to draw a *cordon sanitaire* all around. It is easier to impede the input of a remembrance than to get rid of it after it is recorded. This was effectively the purpose of several tricks devised by the Nazis to shield the consciences of the men in charge of the dirtiest jobs and to secure actions that were difficult even for the most callous thugs. To the SS men of the Einsatzkommandos, who machine-gunned naked civilians on the edge of mass graves in occupied Russian territory, booze was distributed on request, blunting their sensitivity under a veil of drunkenness. The official language of the Third Reich was studded with euphemisms: the very term "Einsatzkommando" just quoted meant literally "unit for ready employ," but covered a fearful reality; "final solution" meant "extermination"; "special treatment" meant "death by gas"; "transfer" (*Umsiedlung*) meant "mass deportation," and so on. The purpose of this camouflage was twofold: it aimed to lead astray foreign and domestic public opinion, to delude the victims and to prevent their reaction; but at the same time it served to disguise, as far as possible, the crude reality from the very men who were in charge of the bureaucratic machinery. It is a well-established practice: call "murder" by some other name, and it is not murder anymore.

Even among the victims one can observe a manifold alteration of memories; but in this case there is no deliberate intention to deceive. He who is struck by offense or injustice has no need to elaborate a lie to relieve himself of a fault he has not committed, but his innocence does not preclude a distortion of his remembrances. It has been observed, for instance, that many former inmates of German camps, or the victims of other traumatic experiences, unconsciously put their memories through a sieve. When evoking them in conversations, they prefer to dwell on the quiet moments, on grotesque or strange or even comical intermezzos, and to skip over the most painful episodes. These last are reluctantly, rarely, recalled from the reservoir of memory; therefore, as time passes by, they tend to fade away and lose their contours. The behavior of Count Ugolino, in Dante's *Divine Comedy*, is psychologically plausible. Asked to tell the poet about his and his offspring's terrible death by starvation, he hesitates. Eventually he consents to answer the question, not out of self-pity, but only to exact posthumous revenge against his eternal enemy. He explicitly reproaches the poet: "You are asking me to renew my desperate pain by thinking about it."

A fact can be twisted not only by one's memory, but in the very moment it takes place. Throughout the entire year of my imprisonment in Auschwitz, I had as a fraternal friend Alberto, an Italian of my age. He was a robust and courageous youth, much more clearsighted than the average prisoner. Thus, he was very critical toward fellow inmates who were prone to fabricate and feed each other consolatory delusions, such as "within two weeks the war will be over," or "Polish partisans are about to liberate the camp," etc.

Alberto had been deported together with his forty-five-year-old father. Close to the great Auschwitz selection of October 1944, Alberto and I commented on the pending, unavoidable event with fright, anger, and resignation, yet without looking for shelter in doctored truths. The selection came, Alberto's father was chosen for the gas chamber, and within a few hours Alberto underwent a change. Yes, he had heard trustworthy rumors: the Russians were near; surely the Germans wouldn't dare to persist in such slaughter any longer—indeed, *that* selection (which took his father) was quite another thing. It was not for the gas; it was intended to pick out prisoners who were debilitated but still recoverable, like his father, who was weak but not diseased. Somebody had even told him where they would be sent for recovery: not far away, in Jaworzno, was a special camp, a "Schonungslager," for convalescents who would perform only light work.

Alberto's father wasn't seen again, and Alberto himself disappeared in the death march of January 1945, which swallowed almost all the surviving inmates of the camp.

Strangely enough, and without knowing of Alberto's behavior, his relatives, too, who had remained hidden in Italy and escaped deportation, acted more or less as he had. That is, they obstinately dodged a truth too bitter to accept as true. After my (long-delayed) repatriation, I felt it my duty to go immediately to Alberto's town and tell his mother and brother what I knew about him and his father. I was received with affectionate attention, but as soon as I began to speak, Alberto's mother asked me to stop. She already knew everything, at least about Alberto, and it was pointless that I repeat to them the usual horror stories. She *knew* that Alberto alone had miraculously succeeded in fleeing from the march column, without being shot by the SS, and that he had been rescued by the Russians. For the moment, he was cut off from them, but he certainly would write soon. And now, please, would I kindly drop the subject and tell her instead how I myself had managed to survive?

One year later I happened to stop in the same town and paid the family another visit. The truth had slightly changed: Alberto was in a Soviet hospital, he was in good health, but had lost his memory— he had even forgotten his name. But he was recovering and was to return home soon.

Alberto has never returned. Forty years have elapsed, and since then I haven't been able to brace myself to go there again, to set my painful truth against the consolatory truth the relatives of Alberto had constructed.

NOTES

1. Jean Améry, *At the Mind's Limits: Contemplations by a Survivor on Auschwitz and Its Realities*, trans. Sidney Rosenfeld and Stella P. Rosenfeld (Bloomington: Indiana University Press, 1980), pp. 35, 40.

2. *Commandant of Auschwitz: The Autobiography of Rudolf Höss* (London: Weidenfeld & Nicolson, 1959).

SUNDAY, 5 MAY 1985: THE EVENTS AT BITBURG AND BERGEN-BELSEN

John Tagliabue

The Two Ceremonies at Bergen-Belsen

BELSEN, West Germany, May 5—There were two ceremonies at the Bergen-Belsen memorial today.

The first ended when President Reagan's helicopter lifted out of a sea of West German policemen. Rows of invited guests, shaking hands and chatting, then filed out and climbed into the Mercedes-Benz limousines of postwar West German prosperity.

The second ceremony began 20 minutes later, when 50 or so Jews, some former inmates and some the children of victims, entered the concentration camp in a somber procession, each bearing a rose and many in tears. They attended a brief commemorative service that one of their leaders, Menachem Rosensaft, said was to "reconsecrate" the memorial.

Mr. Rosensaft said the memorial had been "desecrated" by the visit of President Reagan and West Germany's Chancellor, Helmut Kohl.

"Never, until today, has anyone dared to prevent survivors and children of survivors from standing beside these mass graves and this monument," Mr. Rosensaft told a gathering at the squat, gray memorial to the more than 50,000 people who died in the camp, "while two politicians violate their sanctity and every principle of decency by coming here on their way to honoring the memory of the SS."

Mr. Rosensaft, the founding chairman of the International Network of Children of Jewish Holocaust Survivors, was born at Bergen-Belsen in 1947, when it served as a camp for displaced persons.

Hundreds of West German policemen, with American Secret Service agents at their side, sealed off the camp for all but the 400 or so invited guests while President Reagan and Mr. Kohl visited the memorial and laid a wreath to its dead.

"Here lie people—Jews—whose death was inflicted for no reason other than their very existence," Mr. Reagan said in his address.

Chancellor Kohl, in his brief remarks, said, "We bow in sorrow before the victims of murder and genocide."

Jewish leaders in the United States, Israel and elsewhere refused to send representatives to the service because of President Reagan's decision to go from the camp to the Bitburg cemetery, where SS soldiers are buried.

On Saturday night, West German policemen removed a group of about a dozen Jews from the camp's document center, where they intended to remain to protest the President's visit. At 5 A.M. today, the West German police carried off about 35 French Jews, some of them former camp inmates, who refused to leave the parking lot where Mr. Reagan's helicopter later landed.

United States Secret Service agents were with the West German police patrols that blocked two forest roads leading to the camp memorial.

The roadblocks infuriated Jewish leaders, like Rabbi Avraham Weiss of the Hebrew Institute of Riverdale, the Bronx, who accused the White House of having ordered the West German police to seal the camp and bar Jews from protesting.

Speaking later by the camp memorial, Mr. Rosensaft said of the President and Chancellor Kohl: "Today, we say to them that they can either honor the memory of the victims of Belsen, or they can honor the SS. They cannot do both."

The absence of Jews at Mr. Reagan's service troubled some official guests, like Friedrich Wöbbeking, Belsen's village pastor, who expressed "distress" and said he had considered staying away. By contrast, Norbert Blüm, Bonn's Minister for Social Affairs, approved the removal of the protesters. "Quiet is important," he said. "Dignity must prevail."

One who remembered less-dignified times was Dimitri Pluchator, 71 years old, a Galician Jew and survivor of Auschwitz, Birkenau and Bergen-Belsen who said he had visited the memorial almost every

Sunday since British soldiers liberated him and other survivors in April 1945.

"For 14 days we wandered through here, stepping over corpses like wood in the forest," he said. "And now, I cannot enter, though I come every Sunday."

Wrapped in a trench coat against a chill wind, he shook his head and repeated, "Sad, sad."

Avraham Weiss

The Peace of the Dead

To the Editor of The Jerusalem Post

Sir,—I was part of a group that observed the first Sabbath at Bergen-Belsen since the end of the Second World War. At Bergen-Belsen, 50,000 Jews murdered by the Nazis lie in mass graves. These graves are punctuated by simple markers: "Here lie 800 dead . . . 1,000 dead . . . 5,000 dead." As you enter the concentration camp, there is a sign, "Visitors are requested to observe the dignity of the memorial grounds and to refrain from disturbing the peace of the dead."

Surrounded, as we were, by the dead, we celebrated the Sabbath in prayer and Tora learning. We sang, danced, and even ate and slept at Bergen-Belsen. We had carried the Tora scroll into the camp and read from it on the Sabbath.

The contrasts were imponderable, at times overwhelming, but we persevered. Our response to death was life; and to those who had sought to extinguish the flame of the Sabbath, we kindled Sabbath lights.

Our Sabbath was specifically designed to coincide with President Reagan's and Chancellor Kohl's visit to Bitburg and Bergen-Belsen, which we viewed as a desecration of the memory of the six million. You cannot honour SS murderers and the murdered at the same time, claiming they are both victims. Our view was shared by almost all Jews. Even the German Jewish community, which is not known for its outspokenness, decided to boycott the president's and chancellor's visit to Bergen-Belsen. It was their way of saying, if you go to Bitburg, you are unwelcome at Bergen-Belsen.

SOURCE: *Jerusalem Post*, May 30, 1985.

The pending visit of the president and chancellor gave our Sabbath special significance. Their visit to Bitburg would defile the dead of Bergen-Belsen. Our Sabbath was meant as a counter-balance, an attempt to maintain the sanctity of the dead. They wish to forget, but we shall always remember.

Why not forget? Because forgetting involves a process of denial. When you deny, you leave open the possibility that other Holocausts will occur. Only by accepting the past can one move boldly towards a better future.

At the end of the Sabbath, German police arrived at Bergen-Belsen. The officer in charge, Friedrich Wilhelm Thieke, told us with great emotion: "We have come peacefully. We have no weapons. You must leave and we have orders to escort you out."

Although this was not the first time that German officers have been heard to say they were "just following orders," the directive to evict us, I was later told, had come from the White House.

Had the West German government not shared in the Bitburg fiasco, we would have left on our own. Were Germany blameless, it would have been unfair to force German police to remove us. But the West German government was guilty, too. Chancellor Kohl's decision to rehabilitate the SS at Bitburg, to give honour to SS murderers should evoke for West Germany remembrances of things past.

In the end, we refused to leave. German police were ordered to expell us. It was overwhelmingly painful for me as a Jew once again to be forced to submit to German authorities. Bergen-Belsen is ours; we had paid dearly for it.

As we left, the young German officer escorting me reached out to shake my hand. "Can you forgive me for doing this to you?" he asked. I shook his hand and responded, "I can forgive you, but I can never forgive those who murdered my people, and those like the chancellor and President Reagan who wish to forget."

I thought of the sign at the gates of Bergen-Belsen, "Please respect the peace of the dead." The president and the chancellor had violated that peace.

Bernard Weinraub

Reagan Joins Kohl in Brief Memorial at Bitburg Graves

BITBURG, West Germany, May 5—President Reagan presided over a wreath-laying today at the base of a brick cemetery tower looming over the graves of nearly 2,000 German soldiers, including 49 SS troops.

Alluding to the controversy aroused by his visit to the cemetery, Mr. Reagan voiced regret in remarks at an American air base afterward that "old wounds have been reopened."

Accompanied by Chancellor Helmut Kohl, Mr. Reagan walked slowly through the narrow, hilltop cemetery, ablaze with tulips and marigolds. Mr. Reagan did not glance at the graves during his eight-minute visit. Mr. Kohl brushed tears from his eyes. Neither made a speech at the cemetery.

Hours earlier, Mr. Reagan stood before an obelisk at the site of the Bergen-Belsen concentration camp, where 50,000 victims of the Nazis are buried in mass graves under mounds of heather.

"Here they lie," Mr. Reagan said in a trembling voice. "Never to hope. Never to pray. Never to love. Never to heal. Never to laugh. Never to cry."

Mr. Reagan's visit to Bergen-Belsen, in addition to the Kolmeshöhe Cemetery at Bitburg, was designed to merge past and present—to pay homage to the millions of victims of Nazi Germany and to honor West Germany's emergence as a powerful democracy and ally of the United States.

"We who were enemies are now friends," Mr. Reagan told about 5,000 American military personnel, their families and local German residents at the Bitburg Air Base, less than one mile from the military cemetery.

"We who were bitter adversaries are now the strongest of allies," Mr. Reagan said. "In the place of fear we have sown trust, and out of the ruins of war has blossomed an enduring peace."

Jewish demonstrators from the United States, France, Britain, West Germany, Belgium, the Netherlands, Israel and other countries protested the President's visit to Bergen-Belsen as well as the stop at Bitburg. They were joined by groups of veterans and politicians, many of them weeping.

Although Roman Catholic and Protestant clergymen took part in the ceremonies at the Bergen-Belsen site, German rabbis refused to attend because of the Bitburg visit.

The Israeli Ambassador to West Germany, Yitzhak Ben-Ari, came to the Bergen-Belsen ceremony—despite anguish, he said, about Mr. Reagan's visit to Bitburg. "I believe the new Germany can be trusted," he said.

White House aides have acknowledged that the Bitburg visit is probably the biggest fiasco of Mr. Reagan's Presidency. The visit, which was made at the insistence of Mr. Kohl, was overwhelmingly opposed by both houses of Congress, Jewish organizations, veterans' groups and others.

Up to the last moment, White House officials sought to minimize the effect of the visit. As Mr. Reagan left Bonn this morning for Bergen-Belsen, officials disclosed that the President and Mr. Kohl would be joined at Bitburg by two prominent retired American and German military officers.

The two were Gen. Matthew B. Ridgway, 90 years old, who led the 82d Airborne Division in Europe and later fought in the Battle of the Bulge, and Lieut. Gen. Johannes Steinhoff, 71, a World War II flying ace who later rose to the highest ranks of the West German Air Force. After the brief ceremony at the military cemetery, the two men shook hands.

Mr. Reagan, starting an official visit to West Germany after the end of the seven-nation economic summit conference in Bonn on Saturday, began his day with an unscheduled drive in the hills overlooking the Rhine to place a wreath at the grave of Konrad Adenauer, West Germany's first Chancellor. White House officials said the idea for the visit had come from Billy Graham, the evangelist.

Mr. Reagan and Mr. Kohl then flew aboard Air Force One to Hanover and traveled 15 minutes by helicopter to the gate of Bergen-

Belsen. Before coming to West Germany, Mr. Reagan initially decided against a visit to a concentration camp site, then reversed the decision amid the furor over his plans to visit the Bitburg cemetery.

Under gray skies and in a light drizzle, Mr. Reagan entered the camp site with his wife, Nancy, as well as leading aides and the United States Ambassador to Bonn, Arthur F. Burns. Mr. Kohl was accompanied by his wife, Hannelore.

The site is an open area with mounds that contain the mass graves of the camp's victims.

Outside, a handful of demonstrators echoed the words voiced by Elie Wiesel, the writer and Holocaust survivor, at the White House two weeks ago. The demonstrators, referring to Bitburg, cried: "You don't belong there. Come back, please, Mr. President. We don't want you to go in there."

Asked about the demonstrators, Mr. Reagan shrugged and said, "It's a free country."

The Premier of Lower Saxony, Ernst Albrecht, escorted the Reagans, the Kohls and their entourage into a document center with photographs and exhibits of the camp, where Jewish, Gypsy, Polish, Russian, French and Dutch inmates died of torture, starvation and disease.

As the Reagans paused in front of a photograph of stacks of bodies found by the British, who liberated the camp in April 1945, Mr. Reagan put his arm around his wife.

Members of Mr. Reagan's staff looked grim during the visit. Robert C. McFarlane, the national security adviser, walked alone, staring at the ground.

Mr. Reagan, standing before the obelisk, his voice low and drained, recounted the story of Anne Frank, the Dutch girl whose moving diary tells of hiding from the Nazis with her family in Amsterdam. She died in Bergen-Belsen at the age of 15.

"Somewhere here lies Anne Frank," Mr. Reagan said. "Everywhere here are memories—pulling us, touching us, making us understand that they can never be erased." Mrs. Reagan, seated with 300 other guests, dabbed her eyes.

"Rising above all this cruelty," Mr. Reagan went on, "out of this tragic and nightmarish time, beyond the anguish, the pain and the suffering for all time, we can and must pledge: Never again."

Mr. Reagan placed a wreath of green ferns near an obelisk at the site. A ribbon on the wreath read, "The People of the United States of America."

Flying to the Bitburg Air Base at midday, Mr. Reagan and his staff found the mood far from somber. Bitburg's German population of 12,500 is almost matched by the 10,600 American military personnel and dependents attached to the 36th Tactical Fighter Wing.

A band played at the runway, and thousands waved American and West German flags.

Mr. Reagan and Mr. Kohl traveled by limousine to the military cemetery, in the town's western suburbs, where they were met by an American and West German honor guard.

As the two leaders walked slowly past the graves, West German Army musicians played a somber drum roll.

Mr. Reagan and Mr. Kohl briefly arranged two large circular wreaths at the foot of the memorial tower before standing to attention.

For several moments silence fell across the cemetery, except for the click of cameras. A trumpeter played a melancholy German soldiers' song, "I Had a Comrade." The song mourns fallen soldiers.

Mr. Reagan stood a few feet from two graves with SS markings.

At the cemetery, Mr. Reagan met families of wartime German resistance leaders. As he left, the President also spoke to General Ridgway.

"Our visit to the soldiers' graves here in Bitburg was not an easy one," Mr. Kohl said later in a speech at the air base before a crowd of Americans and Germans. "I thank you, Mr. President, both on behalf of the whole German people, and I thank you very personally as a friend, for visiting the graves with me."

Mr. Reagan, in his address, said: "I have just come from the cemetery where German war dead lay at rest. No one could visit here without deep and conflicting emotions."

He added: "The evil world of Nazism turned all values upside down. Nevertheless, we can mourn the German war dead today as human beings, crushed by a vicious ideology."

James M. Markham

For Bitburg, Day of Anger Ends Quietly

BITBURG, West Germany, May 5—It was the scene that many had feared. At the main crossroads of this small town, policemen with plastic antiriot shields confronted an advancing crowd of Jews, many of them wearing the badge that accompanied their parents and grandparents to their deaths: a six-pointed yellow star bearing the word Jude.

The Jews came from 21 countries, but many were from France, Belgium and the Netherlands. One big blue banner hoisted in their midst read in French, "Neither hate nor forgetfulness."

Another hand-painted banner, in English, said: "Don't honor SS murderers. My brother's blood cries out to me from the ground."

When the protesters reached the police line they halted, some of them only inches from the policemen. Among them was Irene Quetting, 67 years old, from Traben-Trarbach, West Germany, who said she was half-Jewish.

"If you want to know my impression about the Germans," she said, nodding toward Mötscherstrasse, where Chancellor Helmut Kohl and President Reagan would shortly pass, "they haven't learned from history."

She said she was not speaking of the policemen in green uniforms who were holding back the protesters. "No," she said, "I am talking about my generation and Kohl's, who should have learned but didn't."

The policemen were correct and polite, and clearly uncomfort-

SOURCE: *New York Times*, May 6, 1985. Copyright © 1985 by The New York Times Company. Reprinted by permission.

able. "Personally," said a dark-haired policeman, holding his white helmet to his side, "I would rather be on the other side."

Crosscurrents of emotion swept the streets of Bitburg today, and empathy was not always the predominant one. "If they take off the stars," said Irene Zeller, 32, from Saarlouis, south of Bitburg, "they can come over to this side." She was referring to the Jewish protesters, separated from her by a police cordon.

Two American flags were stuck in the belt of her light blue raincoat.

On the other side of the street, there was this scene: Four young Germans held up a West German flag and an American flag in a gesture of reconciliation. But behind and above them, two protesters held aloft a hand-drawn banner that said, "Never again."

"They did it on purpose," said Wolfgang Röske, a 30-year-old civil servant who had the tip of the German flag in his left hand. "But it is good that they are allowed to hold that up, or anything they want. That is what these two flags guarantee; if the flags were a little redder, it would be very orderly here, and there would be secret police on the streets."

By enlarging the area declared off limits to demonstrations, the jittery White House advance team and Mayor Theo Hallet kept the curious, the sympathetic and the outraged even farther away than had been expected from Kolmeshöhe Cemetery today. As a result, the Presidential caravan approached the cemetery down several blocks of essentially deserted streets.

Held back by a steel fence, David Makovsky, chairman of the World Union of Jewish Students, was furious over what he saw as another step by the Reagan Administration and Mr. Kohl's advisers to neaten up the television imagery out of Bitburg.

"At what price do they have photo opportunities?" asked Mr. Makovsky, whose group summoned young Jews from all over the world to come to Bitburg. Some 1,200 answered the call.

"The whole President's trip is centered around the lens of a camera," he said. "Can we do a trade-off—Bitburg versus Bergen-Belsen?"

Alan G. Hevesi, the deputy majority leader in the New York State Assembly, was positioned with 16 other legislators from New York and New Jersey near to the point where the caravan swept to the cemetery. They all wore small paper badges that read,"We honor the victims of the Holocaust."

The Queens Democrat said 55 members of his family perished in Hitler's death camps; his grandfather was the chief rabbi of Budapest. "Some of my family were saved by Raoul Wallenberg, the greatest hero of the 20th century," said Mr. Hevesi, speaking of the

Swedish diplomat who rescued thousands of Jews in Hungary. "This is personal to me."

For Max Kaplan, a 54-year-old Dutch Jew who survived the war in hiding in Amsterdam, today was his first visit to Germany since the war ended. He wore a sandwich-board sign that read: "God, do not forgive them. They knew what they were doing."

"I haven't spent a mark since I've been here," Mr. Kaplan said.

His 28-year-old daughter, Natasha, wore the same sign and leaned with her father against the steel barrier waiting for Mr. Reagan and Mr. Kohl to emerge from the cemetery. "They are not to blame for what their parents did," Miss Kaplan said, speaking of younger Germans. "But they are responsible that this happened. They should have stopped it."

Many of the people of Bitburg, a town of 12,500 whose population is rivaled in numbers by the population of the adjacent air base, apparently stayed home today. The town, once known for a catchy beer slogan ("Bitte ein Bit"), has found the last few weeks of intense scrutiny traumatic.

Annette Herchen, a 34-year-old Bitburg resident, draped the front of her house on the Presidential route with a gigantic American flag that she said she had borrowed from the base. "I think the Jews have to recognize that we are another generation," she said. "We are happy to have the Americans here. It's an honor, something special, that your President comes to Bitburg."

Another supporter of the visit, Hans-Peter Müller, earnestly grabbed an American reporter and unrolled a banner he wanted to show the American leader. Written in English, like most of the banners on display today, it said: "Thank you. God bless you."

"There is no half-reconciliation," Mr. Müller said emphatically. "We cannot be half-friend, half-enemy. I was never a Nazi."

For those who did not see them on television, Mr. Reagan and his host, Mr. Kohl, were only fleeting presences in Bitburg today. As their caravan emerged from the cemetery and rushed through the center of town, the mostly young Jews gathered there struck up the cry: "Never again! Never again! Never again!"

The cry drowned out a smattering of left-wing demonstrators who had tried to raise the chant of "Out from Nicaragua!" The motorcycles and the Presidential caravan went by in a matter of seconds.

Solemnly, the Jews sang Hatikvah, the Israeli national anthem. Then they went to Bitburg's Jewish cemetery—it has only five graves—to pray.

PHOTOGRAPHS AND CARTOONS

Bitburg Cemetery. (Copyright dpa
Deutsche Presse-Agentur GmbH.)

Mourner in Washington. (*Newsweek*—
John Ficara.)

Opposite. Monument at Bergen-Belsen.
In foreground, marker for mass grave
reading "Here lie 5000 dead." ("Das
Lager Bergen-Belsen." Hannover: Nie-
dersächsischen Minister des Innern.)

The ceremonies at Bitburg Cemetery.
(Photograph by Frank Darchinger; copyright by J. H. Darchinger IFJ.)

Germany's crime of ruin. (Jürgens—
Ost + Europa-Photo.)

Monument and symbolic headstones at
Treblinka, Poland, designed by P.
Duszenko, 1964. Height: ca. 22 feet;
stone. (Photograph by Chuck Fishman.
All rights reserved.)

Monument to the Jewish cemetery, constructed by survivors in Lukow, Poland,
shortly after the war. (Photograph by
Chuck Fishman. All rights reserved.)

Eastern wall of the Warsaw Ghetto Monument, stone bas-relief, by Nathan Rapoport. (Photograph used by permission of Nathan Rapoport, all rights reserved.)

Warsaw Ghetto Monument on Anielewicz Street in Warsaw, Poland. Designed
and constructed by Nathan Rapoport,
1947–48. Height: 36 feet; bronze relief
set in granite blocks. (Photograph by
James E. Young.)

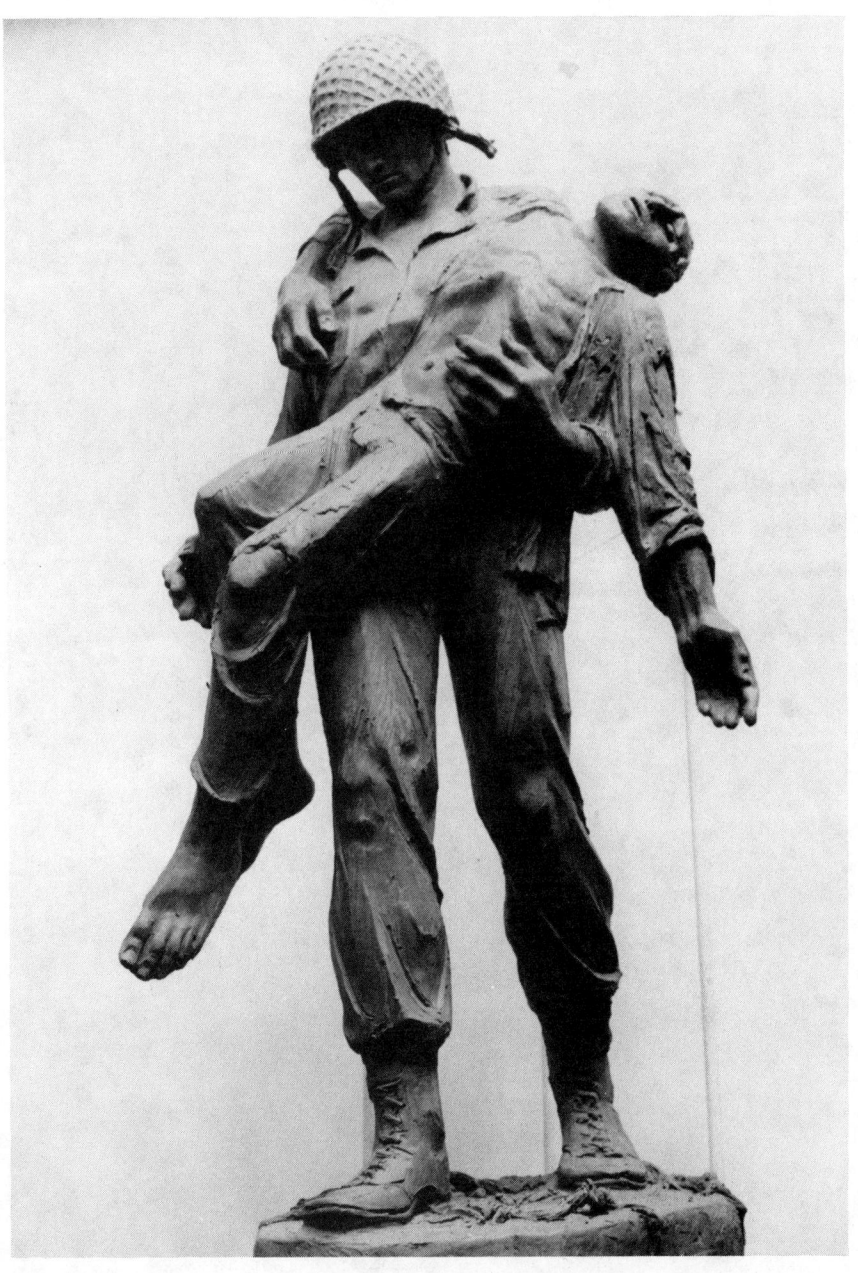

Clay mock-up of Nathan Rapoport's
"Liberation," dedicated in Liberty State
Park, New Jersey, May 1985. (Photo-
graph used by permission of Nathan
Rapoport, all rights reserved.)

Vandalized tombstones at the Jewish
cemetery in Łodz, Poland. (Photograph
by Chuck Fishman. All rights reserved.)

Protest at Mount Zion Cemetery, Cleveland, against President Reagan's visit to Bitburg. (Photograph by Timothy C. Barmann, *Plain Dealer*, Cleveland, Ohio.)

(Paul Conrad, 1985, *Los Angeles Times*.
Reprinted with permission.)

(Paul Conrad, 1985, *Los Angeles Times*.
Reprinted with permission.)

Doonesbury

BY GARRY TRUDEAU

PRESS
COMMENTARIES

EDITORIALS

About Cemeteries

Does Ronald Reagan remember the Holocaust? The answer to that question is undoubtedly yes. But if you think a lapse in memory is the reason the president is in so much political trouble over his proposed visit to a German military cemetery, you haven't delved into the intricacies of this latest Washington *cause celebre*.

Let's start at the beginning. May 8 is the 40th anniversary of V-E Day. Mr. Reagan will be in West Germany that week for the Bonn summit, and the White House wanted some nice gesture toward host Helmut Kohl so he would feel less like a 40th-anniversary wallflower. The cemetery visit would recognize that the Germans also paid a heavy price for Hitler's ambitions and that 40 years on, the Germans are entitled to shed at least some of their guilts.

The Bitburg cemetery, with graves of youths as young as 14 who died in that last futile effort to defend the homeland, bears ample testimony to what World War II cost Germany. But by searching carefully, you also can find among the 2,000 markers some 30 graves of vicious SS storm troopers. Departing White House staffer Michael Deaver is getting the blame for not knowing those graves were there, or if he did, not foreseeing that they carried a different and dangerous kind of symbolism. When the news broke, even the American Legion turned against a president it has usually admired and joined the critics demanding to know how the president could be so insensitive to history as to spend part of his German trip honoring Nazis.

It is not at all plausible that the president, who clearly hates totalitarianism of any stripe, had even the slightest thought of honoring Nazis. But an emotional reaction to even the tiniest suggestion of that is understandable, especially since it came in the context of his decision not to visit a concentration camp. Mr. Reagan has now responded to this sensitivity by planning a stop as well at a German Holocaust site. Modern Germans will not have total absolution from the massive crime of the Austrian-born dictator and his henchmen. But the criticism of the president continues.

For some, the wounds of the Holocaust cannot be healed even by 40 years, and this is understandable enough given the horror of the event. But if Mr. Reagan can be accused of insensitivity, some of his critics might be equally guilty of political cynicism. Mr. Reagan intended a friendly gesture toward the West Germans, who are after all an important link in the resistance to totalitarianism today. Some of his attackers are a great deal less concerned about the Holocaust than about exploiting any weak spot they can find in Mr. Reagan's political armor. The primary audience for this political endeavor is American Jews, torn between their predominantly liberal politics of the past and the modern appeal of hawkish neo-conservatism.

In Europe there is an even nastier game afoot. For 40 years, Russia has been calling the democratic politicians of West Germany neo-Nazis. Even the Holocaust monument at Buchenwald, in East Germany, conveys that message in not-very-subtle fashion. Just last weekend, the East German Communist Party managed to stage a V-E Day commemoration ceremony at that site with much reference to the Western "Nazis" and no mention at all of Jews. Americans attuned to the plight of Jews today in the Soviet Union won't find that particularly surprising.

Mr. Reagan walked into this buzz saw innocently, hoping that with a bit of symbolism 40 years after the fact, he could lay some of the ghosts of the past to rest. But the ghosts are not so easily banished. For some it is because their horrors can never be erased. For others, it is because they remain politically useful.

Conceal Not the Blood

To the 87 million Americans born since 1945, it must seem strange that the President's visit to the monuments of a distant war in remote Bitburg and Bergen-Belsen should awaken so much passion. By the time these Americans reached awareness, (West) German soldiers were their routine allies, Volkswagen and Mercedes were consumer totems and a President had vowed to defend Germany's former capital like "ein Berliner."

What wounds lie raw beneath these bonds? What memories do today's graveyard tributes violate?

Though America's oldest President displays America's shortest memory, most Americans know the answers. Hitler's Germany was no ordinary enemy, and its defeat 40 years ago was no ordinary victory.

Once, but in our time, there was a war transcending greed and miscalculation. Once, in our time, there existed a satanic force that aspired not only to conquer and plunder but to establish a bestial order in half the globe. And in our time, a kindred people fell enthusiastically under the spell of the fascist demon.

In short order, they built him a mighty military machine and fought heroically in his service. They systematically slaughtered, gassed and burned 10 million men, women and children whose genes might pollute the German "race." And they dutifully defended this madman until, at a worldwide cost of 50 million lives, they were vanquished.

Source: *New York Times*, May 5, 1985. Copyright © 1985 by The New York Times Company. Reprinted by permission.

What was to be done with this nation? The Russians, who had to drive back the Germans from the outskirts of Moscow, at a cost of 20 million dead, loosed a terrible vengeance. They seized German men and machines to rebuild their country. They annexed or subjugated vast areas of Eastern Europe, pushed Germany westward and planted their own tyranny on its soil.

Britain, France and the United States, though no less bitter, chose a different response. Believing that vengeance against Germany after Word War I had burdened the Weimar democracy and made Germans more susceptible to Hitler's jingo rantings, the Western allies this time tried generosity.

While punishing thousands of individual Nazi criminals, the allies labored to make their zones of Germany democratic and prosperous. The fear that Soviet Communism might spread across the ravaged continent gave urgency to the effort, but its main inspiration was hope. Peace in Europe, the allies thought, required a democratic union of Europeans, therefore a firm alliance between France and Germany, and a foundation of prosperity financed by the United States.

The policy has been a brilliant success. It left Germany divided but made democrats of the West Germans and made them true partners of the French. It has made Berliners of all Americans, not only John Kennedy, and given Western Europe its longest peace in two centuries.

It is this heroic reconstruction that deserves celebration when Americans and Germans meet, not some gratuitous reconciliation of their warriors in death. The peace to be nourished is planted in the memory of evil, not its forgiveness. It has been fashioned by wisdom, not forgetfulness.

On days of remembrance, the proper prayer is one Mr. Reagan will see today, carved into stone at the Bergen-Belsen concentration camp: EARTH CONCEAL NOT THE BLOOD SHED ON THEE!

The Commemorations

It was not a satisfactory day nor an edifying one and for many it was very hurtful. Both the rhetoric and the fact of reconciliation between this country and the Federal Republic of Germany are well established; the alliance exists and is strong; the postwar West Germans are a different, democratic people; they have long since conceded their nation's crimes. There was nothing new there. What *was* new was costly—to just about everyone involved.

Let us start with the president. We did not think it was a distinguishing day for him. One had been hearing for a while now how Mr. Reagan could not afford to back off the trip to Bitburg because to do so would make him look weak, a man susceptible to pressures, to being pushed around. Yet oddly that is exactly how he looked at Bitburg. The Ronald Reagan who walked stiffly into the cemetery and out again with Chancellor Helmut Kohl seemed almost robot-like, *led.* Our president was in that eight minutes forever being cued, nudged, positioned—stage-managed—by the chancellor. He exuded not wanting to be there. It was not an image of mastery.

Mr. Reagan, in his speeches, said some of the right things. He also resorted to many of those unexceptionable clichés people fall back on when talking about the meaning of the Holocaust, platitudes and pieties that never seem equal to the enormity of the experience nor a fitting idiom in which to discuss it. And his anecdotes struck us as being off-key. But it was, in fact, in the nature of the visit—which is why it was such a bad idea—that no American president could have said what he should have. No such visitor could have spoken raw and relevant truth concerning the systematic starving, maiming, gassing and burning of millions upon millions of defenseless human beings at the hands of the German authorities in World War II. Reconciliation, rehabilitation, ceremony, the political and diplomatic exigencies of 1985—all this would weigh against his citing the true moral.

That moral is not contained in exclamations of bewilderment at the "incomprehensible horror," but rather in facing up to the comprehensible result when a nation permits itself to go the way of the Third Reich. You do not have to believe in collective guilt to believe in social responsibility. Nazi Germany was not, as Mr. Reagan seemed to suggest, the handiwork of "one man" and his regime or even of hundreds or thousands. It remains, in the recollection and understanding of those who dare to recollect and understand, a terrifying—and endlessly instructive—monument to what can happen when a people, for the most part, let it happen. We should add: and also when the world lets it happen. Resistance when it might have made the difference was just too costly, too inconvenient for almost everybody.

It should come as no surprise that those who were prime victims of the Third Reich cannot support, let alone be enthusiastic about commemorations that necessarily so distort and degrade the terrible truths they know concerning the massive indifference and acquiescence that made their fate possible. There was something anguishing and awful in watching Jewish leaders—Elie Wiesel, Hyman Bookbinder—on television yesterday trying not to inflame, not to be spoilsports, not to be disrespectful, not to attract rage or malign attention to the people and the purpose for which they spoke. One of the gratuitous cruelties of this affair has been that it put a burden on Jews yet again to argue their own case for the meaning and magnitude of what happened to them, almost, it sometimes seemed, apologetically, wanting—it was said again and again—not to be misunderstood, not to seem vindictive, not to be at odds with the American president or the country itself. This burden could only deepen a sense of isolation, a sense, as Mr. Wiesel put it, of being "excluded."

The president who went to Bitburg on a well-meant but mistaken mission of reconciliation has much reconciling to do at home.

RECONCILIATION

Lance Morrow

"Forgiveness to the Injured Doth Belong"

The American trajectory generally arcs into the future, not the past. The nation's promise tends to override its memories. The best life lies ahead, like a highway heading west. There are American ghosts, of course, haunted rooms, secrets in the attic. But the virtue of the New World has always been its newness. "Why drag about this monstrous corpse of your memory?" Ralph Waldo Emerson asked. Henry Ford never looked back. "History," he said, "is more or less bunk."

This spring has been the season of the past, however. It is the anniversary of almost everything. Americans have been pitched back into unstable regions of memory, back into Viet Nam and wartime Europe. Sometimes the experience has been disconcerting. The past only looks dead. Ronald Reagan, quintessential American and oldest president, did not seem entirely to grasp that. He displayed a curious insensitivity about the past, as if he did not know how important it is, or how dangerous it can be. As if he did not know that the past has monsters in it. His eyes accustomed to sunshine, Reagan did not peer carefully enough into the shadows.

Once the prospect of his visit to a German military cemetery at Bitburg stirred a violent storm, Reagan, clearly pained, insisted repeatedly that while "we will never forget" the Holocaust, the gesture was a matter not of forgiving and forgetting but of moving forward, of trying to achieve a genuine healing, a reconciliation, of celebrating the 40 years during which the U.S. and West Germany have been strong allies. In a thoroughly American way, Reagan wanted finally to clear the past off the highway, as if it were some sort of old wreck. He wished to proceed, as Lincoln said in his second Inaugural, "with malice toward none, with charity for all."

Yet the symbolism of his visit to the Bitburg cemetery, where 49 SS men are buried, clouded Reagan's goal of bringing about a healing. Before the trip, Reagan made matters worse when he said that young German soldiers were just as much victims of the Third Reich as the Jews were—a grotesque equation even if inadvertent. That statement, coupled with the visit to Bitburg, left an impression that the President of the U.S. was conferring a sort of official forgiveness upon the German army that did Hitler's work.

That is not how forgiveness operates. Once in the middle of the war, Simon Wiesenthal, a prisoner in a forced-labor camp in Lvov, found himself on a work detail in a hospital where a young SS officer lay wounded and dying. The Nazi made Wiesenthal sit and listen while he confessed his atrocities, including burning down a houseful of Jews in the Ukraine and shooting those who tried to escape by leaping from the smoking windows. The SS trooper, tormented by guilt, begged Wiesenthal, as a Jew, to forgive him. Wiesenthal turned and walked away. He survived the camps and has spent the past 40 years hunting Nazi war criminals. But he remained troubled by doubts that he had done the right thing in refusing to forgive the SS trooper. "Forgetting is something that time alone takes care of," he later wrote, "but forgiveness is an act of volition, and only the sufferer is qualified to make the decision."

Christians are taught to turn the other cheek, to forgive. The eye-for-an-eye formula of the Old Testament does not rule out mercy and forgiveness, which are highly valued in Jewish teaching as well. But in Judaism, there are two conditions for repentance: one must go in genuine contrition to the person sinned against, and one must do one's best to compensate for the wrong done. But how can a Nazi, say, compensate a Jew for exterminating his entire family? In that sense, some crimes simply cannot be forgiven.

The summary power of forgiveness resides with God alone. After that, forgiveness gets personal. Pope John Paul II could forgive Mehmet Ali Agca, the man who shot him. The bullet hole in his abdomen gave him the authority to do that. So, in a sacramental way, did his ordination as a priest. Ronald Reagan can forgive John Hinckley (the Pope and the President both being members of the brotherhood of the shot). But Ronald Reagan cannot forgive Agca for shooting the Pope. Nor can he forgive SS men for what they did in Europe while

Reagan was making Army training films in Hollywood. Wrote the poet John Dryden: "Forgiveness to the injured doth belong."

There is a difference between forgiveness and reconciliation, but the distinction between the terms never was very clearly made during the President's trip. Forgiveness implies a kind of moral embrace, a clearing of the books, that is difficult if not impossible in the context of Nazi Germany. Reconciliation is a transaction that can occur between two nations. But forgiveness is between individuals, or between an individual and God. Just as one rejects the notion of collective guilt, so one recoils at the idea of collective absolution. Deeds are done by individuals and must be judged individually. One of the evils of the 20th century has been the practice of totalitarians who create collective categories of people (the "bourgeoisie," for example, or "enemies of the people") in order to legitimize expropriation, imprisonment and mass slaughter.

If Reagan meant to set the past to rest, Bitburg brought it back to angry life. Yet there were many voices muttering, "Must we hear about the Holocaust again?" There have, after all, been other great tragedies in history—the Turkish slaughter of the Armenians, Stalin's liquidation of millions of kulaks and the enforced famine in the Ukraine in 1932–33, the destruction of perhaps 2 million Kampucheans by their own Khmer Rouge countrymen.

One cannot engage in a contest of comparative horrors. Yet there is about the Holocaust a primal and satanic mystery. And no cheap grace can redeem it. The Third Reich was the greatest failure of civilization on the planet. In Freudian terms, it was as if the superego had gone crashing down into the dark, wild id.

Germany represented one of the furthest advances of the culture, yet the Third Reich profoundly perverted the entire heritage of Western achievement. It was as if Goethe had taken to eating human flesh. The scientific method, perfected over centuries, fell into the hands of Dr. Mengele and the engineers of the ovens. Hitler was not alone responsible. More than a few Germans enthusiastically followed him, saluted him and died for him. They seized the accumulated trust of 3,000 years and distilled it into unimaginable evil. They sought to extinguish not only Jews and gypsies and the rest, but all the lights of civilization. That is not easy to forgive.

Arthur Schlesinger, Jr.

The Rush to Reconcile

The Bitburg affair must surely go down as one of the most unnecessary embarrassments in the history of American foreign relations. Mrs. Thatcher is unquestionably right in saying that whatever Mr. Reagan thought he was doing, he was doing with the nicest intentions. But we all know where the road paved with good intentions so often leads.

Why this sudden need in 1985 for "reconciliation" with West Germany? One had supposed that reconciliation was achieved 30 years ago when West Germany was permitted to rearm and to enter the North Atlantic Treaty Organization. Twenty-two years ago John F. Kennedy declared that he too was a Berliner. How much longer will West German leaders keep on demanding further evidence of reconciliation? How many more pilgrimages will American presidents be required to make? Who won the war anyway?

For those of us who supposed that relations between Bonn and Washington have been pretty good, it is hard to understand the sudden need for additional reconciliation in 1985. The 40th anniversary of the end of the Second World War has been mysteriously endowed with sacred significance. One wonders what we will have left to say and do when the 50th anniversary, a far more natural time of commemoration, arrives in 1995. Former Chancellor Helmut Schmidt was quite right in calling the hyping of the 40th anniversary "artificial." We all know the real reason for it. The Christian Democratic Party is facing important elections in North Rhine–Westphalia, and Chan-

Source: Excerpted from *Wall Street Journal*, May 9, 1985.

cellor Helmut Kohl shrewdly manipulated the American president into serving as a Christian Democratic fugleman.

Far from promoting reconciliation, the Bitburg incident has reopened wounds and rekindled animosities, including anti-Semitism in both the U.S. and Germany. Any desire to vindicate Nazism or the SS was obviously the last thing in the president's mind. But, as John Tagliabue reported last week in the New York Times, veterans at the Nesselwang reunion of the Waffen SS Death's Head Division saw the president's visit as a gesture of rehabilitation. Mr. Reagan himself continues to give the impression that he believes Germany to have been an occupied country during World War II, like France or Poland. The German army, he appears to think, was largely made up of men who disliked Nazism and were as much victims of Hitler as the unfortunates in the concentration camps.

This benign view of the German army was not strongly held by Americans who served in the European Theater of Operations at the time. So long as Hitler was doing well, no one could have doubted the devotion of the Wehrmacht to Nazism and the thousand-year Reich. It took defeat to turn German soldiers into anti-Nazis. One surmises that Mr. Reagan's obliviousness to this point derives from his own war, or rather non-war, record. Though he often makes throwaway references to his military career, Mr. Reagan in fact is the only American president who was of military age during the Second World War and saw no service overseas. He fought the war on the film lots of Hollywood, slept in his own bed every night and apparently got many of his ideas of what happened from subsequent study of the Reader's Digest.

William McGurn

V-E Day: East and West

WARSAW, Poland—Almost four decades after a world war that left this once-prosperous capital a smoldering pile of rubble, the rebuilt Cathedral of St. John swells with the triumphant strains of Handel's "Messiah" in an Easter celebration of the Christian Resurrection. Outside, the air is Soviet-bloc gray, but inside . . . inside, the red hat of Jozef Cardinal Glemp, the gleaming gold vestments of his co-celebrant priests and the natural splendor of innumerable fresh flowers combine in a burst of subversive color. The whole celebration gives vent to an East European vibrancy that has yet to be quelled and carries the suggestion that the Polish national struggle might someday enjoy a similar triumph.

As for most Europeans, the significance of this May 8 weighs heavily on Poles: It represents the 40th anniversary of the defeat of Hitler and the reestablishment of democracy on the greater part of this continent. Fittingly, the former allies (including the Soviet Union) are now planning to mark the day by honoring the war dead and recalling the sacrifices made on behalf of the great cause. President Reagan is scheduled to address the Council of Europe in Strasbourg, France, and West Germany's Helmut Kohl says he will celebrate V-E Day as the replacement of tyranny with democracy in his land. Above all, the Western allies plan to emphasize the 40 years of "peace" and "reconciliation" since then.

Talk of peace and reconciliation, however, rings hollow here on the streets of Warsaw, where, as in the rest of Eastern Europe, the only replacement was the hammer and sickle for the swastika. "Like everyone else," says one Pole, "I had two grandfathers. One was shot by the Germans near Gdansk; the other by the Russians at Katyn."

With V-E Day rapidly approaching, signs are that the Western allies are going to let slip yet another opportunity to strengthen their resolve, once again defaulting to the Soviets the advantage. In refusing to draw a clear distinction between the defeat of the German people and the defeat of Nazism (most evidenced in the confusion over President Reagan's decision to visit the Bitburg Cemetery where SS members lie buried), V-E Day is becoming not a touchstone for the future but a burden of the past.

The Western world's reluctance to celebrate a victory it earned through tremendous sacrifice illustrates the same lack of a coherent postwar vision that led to Yalta. Indeed, it was not so much Yalta itself that betrayed Eastern Europe as it was the Allies' failure to enforce it, due largely to an ambivalence toward Soviet imperialistic intentions there. Our refusal to address the fact of a divided Europe today threatens our own future and undermines the efforts of those freedom-loving East Europeans who look westward for inspiration. A forward-looking commemoration of V-E Day would be an expression of solidarity, not merely with one another but with all peoples sharing our principles of freedom, justice and self-determination. We must show that the West is not a place but an idea.

A confident celebration of victory ought not be taken as a call to send our tanks to the Eastern front. Yet it ought to be taken as a reminder that the original task for which the Allies went to war remains unfinished, to be continued by other, less destructive means; in other words, that V-E meant the loss of the East as much as the liberation of the West.

The Reagan administration's repeated public statements that the U.S. does not concede the permanent dominance of Eastern Europe by the Soviets is a healthy first step, but it is not enough. To the peoples here behind the Iron Curtain, the idea of European unity is precious, a cause whose leadership naturally falls to the East Europeans' brothers in the West. One would think that the French in particular, whose own government-in-exile under Col. Charles de Gaulle calls to mind the same struggle, might use V-E Day to show a little more sensitivity toward their fellow Europeans. They could invite representative groups from certain societies—e.g., Solidarity, Charter 77, the various church groups, even Eastern peace groups—to share an honored place at their commemorations, including Mr. Reagan's speech at Strasbourg.

The Soviets and their puppet governments have no such hesitations about exploiting the victory over fascism. Whatever the West's vague pronouncements of "reconciliation," the Soviets know that at the end of World War II someone lost and someone won, and that, despite the 1939 Molotov-Ribbentrop Pact that originally linked the Soviets with Hitler, they came out of the war the real victors. Consequently they are planning large festivities (here in Poland they are calling it the "month of national remembrance") that go heavy on the glorious role of the Red Army in defeating the Hitler menace and light on their 1939 cooperation with that menace.

Not that those here need much reminding. Throughout the Eastern bloc these peoples feel the imprint of the Soviet presence in all of their daily existence, from the foreign troops on their soil to the drabness of the paint that refuses to look bright and cheery even when new. These oppressed peoples need little imagination to see in every official act by their governments an unmistakable continuity in both form and substance with the Third Reich.

Here in the Cathedral of St. John, for example, a black-and-white portrait of the recently canonized Maximillian Kolbe rests atop a side altar; only a few kilometers away lies the fresh grave of another martyred priest, Jerzy Popieluszko. Close by, too, is Warsaw's large Jewish cemetery, testimony to a way of life nearly annihilated by the Nazis. Today the Jews' contributions continue to be slighted, by governments that prefer to warn of the dangers of "world Zionism" and identify Israel with Nazi Germany. Just this past Saturday, in fact, the East Germans held a remembrance at the Nazis' notorious Buchenwald death camp without mentioning the Jews who died there. Throughout the other parts of Eastern Europe it is much the same; only the particulars vary.

No V-E commemoration is going to restore the sovereignty of formerly independent states from Latvia to Hungary; nor is it going to reverse almost a half-century of oppression. But it could call to mind the horrors no sane person ever wants to see again: millions dead, wounded or displaced; millions more brought under the Soviet jackboot; European Jewry nearly extinct.

If the past is to serve the future, V-E Day must rise above ritual to recall not just *that* these things happened but *why*. More than 40 years ago an isolationist America was jolted into recognition that prospects for its own continued peace and security ultimately depended on events across an ocean. This V-E Day, we in the West would do well to realize that in today's world these same freedoms depend no less on events occurring beyond the Elbe.

Mark Krupnick

"Walking in Our Sleep": Bitburg and the Post-1939 Generation

For American Jews like myself, the pain of President Reagan's visit to the German military cemetery at Bitburg is still fresh. Perhaps no event since the Yom Kippur war of 1973, when Israel was nearly overrun by its Arab enemies, has inspired such a sense of Jewish vulnerability. The paradigm of this vulnerability is, of course, the Holocaust.

The writer of a letter that appeared in the *New York Times* on May 2 began by denying that the president had shown "insensitivity" in electing not to cancel his visit to the German military cemetery containing the graves of 49 SS members. The letter went on: "It is forgotten or overlooked that the President is a Christian who follows Christ's teachings, of which *forgiveness* of one's enemies is a cardinal tenet." The letter's emphasis on the specifically Christian element in the president's attitude was followed by a repudiation of the antithetical moral attitude: "According to the Bible, vengeance is reserved for the Lord."

The president's decision to go to Bitburg actually was determined by considerations of politics and power. But once he shifted the terms of public debate to the question of forgiveness, it was inevitable that an implicit contrast be drawn, if only subliminally, between those willing to forget and those who nursed old wounds. It was easy to translate

SOURCE: *The Christian Century*, June 5–12, 1985, pp. 573–74.

that opposition into a contrast between (Christian) forgiveness and (Jewish) vengeance. By marginalizing the Jews, the president contributed to a certain latent American anti-Semitism. Although that factor should not be overstated, it manifested itself in the widespread feeling that "Jewish leaders in the United States protested too much over the [president's] visit." Altogether, 38 per cent of Americans agreed to this statement in a *New York Times* poll.

The appeal to forgiveness was misjudged even when it did not imply an assertion of spiritual superiority. Erna Gans, a concentration camp survivor and president of the Holocaust Memorial Foundation, made the point that needed to be made: "Mr. President, you have no right to forgive in our names. We do not hate. We do not seek vengeance. We did not kill our killers. But we cannot allow you to forgive. We cannot allow the world to forget." It is one thing for the president to forgive his would-be assassin, John Hinckley. It is something else again to arrogate to himself the role, as Harvey Cox described it, of "a kind of high priest of the United States." It would have been more honest had the president said straightforwardly that his visit to Bitburg had less to do with Christian virtue than with the threat represented by the 400,000 Russian soldiers stationed in East Germany.

Those who believe that charity required the American president to honor the dead SS men buried at Bitburg might well have thought that Elie Wiesel was being uncharitable when he said that he was stunned that the president could go from Bergen-Belsen to Bitburg in a single day. Wiesel stated that a concentration camp survivor like himself would have thought that such a journey would have required centuries. What he was saying is not that the Jews will never forgive and forget, but that it will be centuries before they come to terms with their loss. It is impossible to forgive that which one has not fully faced. The trauma of the Holocaust is unparalleled in history; for the future, the most important thing, for the Jews and for all of humanity, is to refuse to forget, to refuse to bury the past. We must not allow ourselves to retreat into the defensive numbness that characterized the immediate postwar period. The important thing is to face the facts, incomprehensible though they are, and to live with them. There is a piety in this attitude, a piety toward the past that has nothing to do with vengefulness.

The Holocaust has been denied—by certain anti-Semitic historians who argue that it never happened; by some Germans who would minimize Jewish suffering so that their own wartime suffering might be more fully acknowledged; by some well-meaning Christians who would substitute a general benignity for direct confrontation of the historical record; and, not least of all, by Jews themselves, whose behavior as a people is incomprehensible except against the background of the Holocaust, but who continue to find it painful to face. Jews are more reconciled with the new generation of Germans than they are with their own recent past. We Jews can't really believe that something so terrible as the Holocaust can have happened to us. To feel and to assimilate the reality of the loss, its irreversibility, is too much to accomplish in 40 years. Self-preservation, the law of life itself, seems to require denial.

A true forgiveness can come only when the irreparability of this disaster is more fully acknowledged. The president of West Germany, himself the son of a man tried for war crimes, made the point most poignantly by quoting a Hasidic master: "The secret of redemption lies in remembrance."

But it is delusive to think that there was a principled debate over Bitburg, an opposition between those who argue for forgiveness and those who find their piety in memory. In fact, most Americans were simply indifferent. Many were willing to forgive and forget because they cared so little. Indeed, the *New York Times* poll was most interesting for what it revealed of American ignorance and confusion about the reasons for the outcry.

According to the poll, though 41 per cent of Americans opposed the president's visit to Bitburg, only 9 per cent of this group gave as their reason the role of the SS in the killing of the Jews. The *Times* should have tried to measure the intensity of American feelings for and against the Bitburg visit, for 12 per cent of those who opposed the president's trip marked "don't know" when asked to give reasons for their opposition. The president, attentive as always to the national mood, concluded with some justification that his cemetery visit was not "of that much concern" to many Americans. The press had blown it up, he said, but the people themselves weren't very involved. For the administration, the implication was that it was politically safe to ride out the mainly Jewish protests. After all, the number of Jewish voters is small, and two out of three had voted for Mondale in the last election.

In the Bitburg affair, the greatest pain for Jews was just this incommensurability between their anguish and the relative indifference of everyone else. But, ironically, the effect of the decision of President Reagan and West Germany's Chancellor Helmut Kohl to sacrifice the Jews to political expediency has been mainly positive. I say that despite knowing that many Jewish concentration camp survivors and relatives of those who did not survive cannot possibly agree. My judgment is founded on the premise that the Jewish piety toward the past cannot depend solely on those who experienced the Nazi terror at firsthand.

The Bitburg fiasco has awakened a whole new generation of American-born Jews to the isolation and vulnerability of the Jewish condition. Jews of my generation and younger (I was born in 1939) have been walking in their sleep. They have been nearly as indifferent to the Jewish past as have non-Jewish Americans. Now, after Bitburg, it is not only concentration camp survivors like Elie Wiesel who can say that they have felt "excluded," "rejected" and "unnecessary." American Jews, the privileged fraction of Diaspora Jewry who have previously flattered themselves on their exemption, have had their first taste of real humiliation. Altogether, Ronald Reagan's blundering over Bitburg has done more than the Holocaust Council itself to awaken American Jews like us to the terror of the Jewish past and the vulnerability of the Jewish present.

With a by-election (that his party has now lost) coming up, Chancellor Kohl was seeking short-term political advantage; the American president wanted to shore up the crumbling NATO alliance; and the Jews, as always, were caught in the middle. It was "the abandonment of the Jews" all over again. Rabbi David Polish does not seem to have exaggerated in comparing the Reagan-Kohl decision on Bitburg to "the complicity of governments and national leaders" during the World War II years "in the rejection of desperate Jewish cries for rescue." Once again we heard the Jewish cries. This time, as Rabbi Polish writes, they were answered with "a call to forget." Younger American Jews found themselves suddenly and alarmingly awakened out of their own indifference by the official indifference of Reagan and Kohl. The effect of that official unresponsiveness has been to shock a new generation into an awareness of what it has meant and continues to mean to be Jews. We have been shocked into a long-repressed sense of identity with those Jews of Bergen-Belsen and Auschwitz who came before us.

Max Kohnstamm

The Old Songs Filled with Anger

For many people who lived through the 1930s and 1940s well aware of what was going on, it was—and still is—so difficult to come to terms with the past that they prefer to avoid looking back altogether. "The old songs filled with anger, the bad dreams filled with woe"[1] once again threaten to overwhelm us. And yet now I cannot help but go up that path again to review images from a past now more than forty years old.

Why? Because it suddenly seemed as if I were being forced to choose between Dachau and Bitburg, as if the one had to exclude the other. On the one hand, Dachau or Bergen-Belsen, where the victims of Hitler and National Socialism, from all the peoples of Europe, suffered and were murdered; on the other, Bitburg, where the German soldiers who had fallen in Hitler's war lie buried.

In the beginning, forty years ago and more, there was hate. I remember as clearly as if it were yesterday with what joy I greeted the sight of the Allied planes arriving in the air above my concentration camp and later flying back into the evening sun. When in May 1945 the terror came to an end, I mourned not for others, but for my own dead. Two years later I came to Germany for the first time. My hatred and my belief in the collective guilt of the German people were confronted with the rubble heaps of German cities, with children who lived and played among these ruins, who went to school there. It slowly dawned on me that there could be no future for my country, for Europe, without the reconstruction of Germany.

Translation of "Die alten, bösen Lieder: Das Hin und Her um die Vorbereitungen der Reagan-Reise öffnet schon verheilte Wunden," *Die Zeit* 18, April 26, 1985.

The reconstruction of Germany—-was this really necessary? A shared future—was this really possible? Or would this only mean building up the industry on the Rhine to the point where it could once again produce bombs destined for Rotterdam? Was there even a way out of the vicious circle of hate and violence? For me, the answer lay in the Schuman Plan[2] and in cooperating with our former enemy in the "Montan-union."[3] In the Old Testament there is a curious story. God decides to lay waste to Sodom and Gomorrah; he allows only Abraham, Lot, and their families to flee these cities. But they are forbidden to look back. When Lot's wife does this nevertheless, God transforms her into a pillar of salt. In the Europa School in Luxembourg, our children sang Hindemith's "Wir bauen eine neue Stadt" (We're building a new city). The future overwhelms the past but it is forbidden to look back—looking back is lethal, because it is a threat to the future.

Maybe we were right after all: the past was too close, too horrible. None of us had ourselves come to terms with it. It would probably have been impossible to approach this past together in a way that was more than just work toward a collective future. In any case, I know that I kept the door that led to the most horrible memories locked for many years.

During these forty years of collaborative work on Europe's future, many borders have been successfully crossed. But in the last few days it has become strikingly clear that the borders that separate our pasts have not yet been penetrated or, if so, then only to a very limited extent. Is it even necessary for us to do this? Would it not be enough simply to let my generation die out? Wouldn't the problem then simply work itself out? I do not believe so. We in Europe cannot and may not live without our history. There is much talk about the necessity of defining Europe's identity more precisely. Identity, according to the psychologist Erik H. Erikson, means knowing what one wants to do with oneself. This also involves knowing where one comes from, which is one's own past and what this past means to one.

Dachau, Bergen-Belsen, Amersfoort, Vught, Westerbork—adding to the German names only the names of the places of terror built on Dutch soil—these names cannot and may not ever be forgotten. But also Bitburg and the names of innumerable other military cemeteries that are everywhere between the Urals and the Atlantic—we cannot and may not forget them either. Does this mean a parallel, an equation: victim of National Socialism here, victim of National Socialism there? Such simplification does violence to reality and does not help us to master the past together. To die in war is not the same as being destroyed because of one's supposed "race" or because one was a Gypsy or a Jehovah's Witness.

In Bitburg there are also graves of members of the SS. Victims or agents of Hitler's deeds? There is no answer to this question—the dead took it with them to their graves. I only know that at these graves too there were mothers and fathers who mourned for their sons, women who mourned for their husbands, children who mourned for their fathers.

In the Amersfoort camp we would sometimes hear at dawn the summons "Let the dead be buried, let the living line up!" Is it not possible for us, the living, the survivors, to come together on May 8 and honor our dead, to mourn them and bury them? "The old songs filled with anger, the bad dreams filled with woe, let's bury them now— get hold of a mighty coffin, ho!" Indeed the coffin must be very, very big to have enough room for the pain.

Images from the past that I want to forget but may not: for instance, the approximately fifty prisoners of war—God knows from where or why they were delivered to our camp—who were all shot one day. A visit more than twenty years ago to Auschwitz, one of these places of terror where the most terrible things occurred. For the pain from all this, for the millions upon millions, there must be room in the coffin.

Translated by Thomas Levin

TRANSLATOR'S NOTES

1. The first line of poem LXV in Heine's *Buch der Lieder* (Book of songs), here in the translation by Hal Draper in Heinrich Heine, *The Complete Poems: A Modern English Version* (Boston: Suhrkamp/Insel, 1982).

2. A plan announced on May 9, 1950, to coordinate cooperation between Western European nations with regard to coal and steel. Named after the Foreign Minister Robert Schuman (1886–1963), who conceived it, the Schuman Plan was one of the first stages in the economic integration of Western Europe.

3. An agreement reached in 1951 between France, Italy, Belgium, West Germany, the Netherlands, and Luxembourg to reduce trade barriers in order to facilitate industrial production.

Meir Merhav

Honouring Evil

President Reagan, it's said, has been trapped by the stage managers on whom, as a veteran actor, he relies blindly, and by the insistence of the German chancellor, Helmut Kohl, into a grand act of reconciliation with Germany by visiting the military cemetery of Bitburg.

Reconciliation with whom, and by what symbolic act? Reconciliation with the new Germany which, as Nobel laureate Heinrich Boell said, became converted to democracy within five minutes on May 8, 1945? The Germany that has ever since been sworn to freedom, human dignity and peace on earth? Surely there is no need for a reconciliation with *those* values, and surely the men who lied buried at Bitburg did not die for them. They gave their lives for history's most diabolic negation of those values.

Much has been made of the fact that among the dead of Bitburg there are 49 members of the Waffen-SS, possibly the very murderers of Malmedy, of Oradour, of Le Paradis, and of the countless other places where these "elite" murderers of Hitler committed their crimes against humanity. The rest are "merely" soldiers of the Wehrmacht. This tenuous distinction has now been overtaken by the obscenity, thoughtlessly repeated by Reagan at the prompting of the German chancellor, of calling them all "victims" of Hitler's tyranny and war, no different from the 50 million other victims of all nationalities, including, of course, six million Jews.

Hitler's war? Yes, but it was also Germany's war, at least as long as Hitler won victory after victory, and it remained so for most Ger-

SOURCE: *Jerusalem Post*, May 3, 1895.

mans even when the Thousand-Year Reich was already being buried in ruins and ashes. Those who lie at Bitburg, if victims, were willing victims—the executors of Hitler's will and his executioners.

Ronald Reagan's visit to Bitburg, an unspeakable insult not only to us Jews, but to all humanity, has been depicted as a regrettable flap by the amiable Great Communicator, an error by a great friend of Israel and of the Jews, many of whom were among his best friends. The insult has been compounded by the last-minute decision to include a "compensatory" visit to Bergen-Belsen in the itinerary of the American president.

Error it is, and a leader less dependent on stage managers and with more of a sense of history might have avoided it. Yet it is not quite the product of a phenomenal insensitivity, nor merely a thoughtless pandering to Helmut Kohl's desire to be forgiven for what, as he keeps reminding us unceasingly, he personally and two-thirds of the other Germans living today bear no guilt, because they were not there when it all happened.

There is system in the error, both on Reagan's and on Kohl's part. If there were any doubts about what President Reagan is about to honour at Bitburg, it was the letter of Alfred Dregger, the faction leader of Kohl's Christian-Democratic party, to U.S. senators who had protested against the visit, that clarified what the act of "reconciliation" was all about. The soldiers buried at Bitburg, Dregger intimated, had fought against the Communists. His brother had died on the Eastern front, and he himself (a Wehrmacht officer wounded four times) had fought to the last minute in Silesia to defend the fatherland against the Russian hordes.

So now we know. True, the "victims of Bitburg" did not die for freedom, for democracy, for human dignity, for peace, against tyranny and inhumanity. But they died in the fight against Bolshevism, against the "empire of evil." That is their redeeming sacrifice, that is what earns them the respect of an American president, and that is the nexus between the new, the other Germany of today, and the old Germany, that which elected and adored Hitler, rejoiced in his victories and followed him enthusiastically when not blindly. Ronald Reagan is not the first American president to have made anti-Communism the touchstone of American friendship and support.

We may perhaps overlook the fact that the millions of Alfred Dreggers did not fight "Bolshevism" in a crusade for freedom, but in the service of a tyranny compared with which even Stalin's dictatorship looks good. They fought for *Lebensraum* in the east, where the "subhuman" Slavs, and of course the Jews, the gypsies and all those not counted as part of the *Herrenvolk* were to be exterminated or reduced to slavery.

An American president who would like to see the "empire of evil" relegated to the dustheap of history may be indifferent to the fact that the war in which the Dreggers served so loyally cost the Soviet Union 20 million lives. But what an American president should not have forgotten is that it was this war, with its devastation and these millions of victims, that left the Soviet Union obsessed with the will to be militarily invincible. It was this war, and the ultimate victory over Nazi Germany, that catapulted the Soviet Union into the status of a superpower 50 years ahead of time, and it was this war which made it possible to launch a Manhattan Project and to bequeath to the entire world the fear of a terminal nuclear holocaust.

There is no point in demanding a global historical perspective from Chancellor Helmut Kohl. He is the most parochial of all German chancellors since the Federal Republic emerged from the ashes of the Reich's defeat. He wants, above all, to be accepted. Miffed at having been left out of the assembly of the leaders of the Allies in Normandy last July (what did a German have to celebrate there, on the anniversary of the Allied invasion of Europe?), he gloried in his "reconciliation" with President François Mitterrand at Verdun, where France and Germany had bled each other white in the First World War. It seems to have escaped him that any French president will be glad to hold hands with a German chancellor, for the ruins of Germany will, after all, be the last barrier between France and any possible onslaught of the Soviets. Nevertheless, Mitterand wisely chose Verdun, which does not figure in the annals of the last war.

Helmut Kohl did not see the subtlety of the choice of location for the hand-holding ceremony with Mitterand. What mattered to him, the self-styled political grandson of Konrad Adenauer, was that it looked like a repeat of the first German post-war chancellor's embrace with de Gaulle at Chartres in 1953. What he wanted as a follow-up was an equivalent symbolic act of full acceptance from the U.S. at any cost.

Full acceptance, for Helmut Kohl, means to bracket the Nazi era out of history, to make it appear as some act of nature, in which there are only victims, no victimizers. He does not tire of reminding all listeners that he was only a boy of 15 when the Thousand-Year Reich collapsed. He, like nearly all Germans, of course rejects collective guilt, but he often speaks of historical responsibility, even of collective shame, as Theodor Heuss called it, as he did recently in a speech at Bergen-Belsen.

Of course there is no collective guilt or responsibility for the past, in the sense that all Germans who lived then are individually culpable for what was done in their name. Even less can the sins of the fathers be visited upon their sons. If there is collective guilt and responsibility—and there is—it belongs to the omissions and commissions of the *present*, not the crimes of the past. And there is an undischarged collective responsibility of the Germans of today, of those 60 per cent who were not yet born or too young to have taken part in the crimes of Nazi Germany, for what they have *not* done to settle accounts with the perpetrators, accomplices, ideologists and supporters of those crimes.

Instead of judging them and casting them out, they have forgiven them and often reinstated them in honours, wealth and power from the first days of the new German republic under Adenauer. That is where the guilt of the new Germany lies—and it is collective because it is only through the collective political process that it might have been discharged.

The new Germany has not done that. Not collectively, not politically, and not by mere omission and indifference, but by design: so as to "reintegrate" all except a few of the murderers (mostly the small fry) and some of the most embarrassingly vociferous shouters of "*Heil Hitler*."

There are many Germans of the younger generation, as decent, humane, and peace-loving people as one can find anywhere, who are anguished not only by the sins of their parents and grandparents, but by the impotence, the refusal, of the political system in their own generation to look into the face of the ignominious past. Helmut Kohl does not belong with them. He belongs to the generation of the in-betweens, those who believe that individual culpability is enough, and who have, for a whole generation shut their eyes and ears to the past.

That is why one of the first acts of Helmut Kohl as chancellor was to defend the decision of his interior minister to take HIAG, the association of former Waffen-SS members, off the list of subversive organizations under the surveillance of the *Verfassungsschutz*, Germany's FBI. For Helmut Kohl they were merely an innocuous mutual aid society of old soldiers.

That is why Helmut Kohl, then chairman of his party, remained almost to the last moment a stout defender of the premier of Baden-Wuerttemberg, Hans-Karl Filbinger, whom playwright Rolf Hochhuth had in 1978 exposed as a murderous judge in Hitler's navy. And that is why, if we believe the unrefuted chapter in Kohl's political biography written by Bernt Engelmann, Helmut Kohl did not, early in his political career, spurn the patronage of one Fritz Ries, an industrialist who had amassed his wealth from taking over "aryanized" Jewish enterprises and from slave labour in factories near Auschwitz, and whose legal adviser and *chef de bureau* was the Goebbels assistant Eberhard Taubert, the man who made the film in which the Jews were depicted as flies and rats.

I am sure that when Helmut Kohl, as premier of the Rhineland-Palatinate, conferred the star of Germany's highest civil decoration, the *Bundesverdienstkreuz*, the federal cross of merit, on this Fritz Ries, he did not know anything about the man's past. I am also sure that Kohl was careful not to ask.

If the German chancellor wanted a reaffirmation of the alliance with the U.S. and its allies in the free world, he might have suggested to President Reagan that he visit the graves of those who died resisting Hitler, not those who fought for him.

Reagan will go to Bitburg. But if a last-minute request may be made of an American president who is a friend of Israel and the Jewish people, it is this: Please spare us your visit to Bergen-Belsen. Do not drag our dead into your reconciliation with Kohl's Germany. Do not mention our victims in the same breath with those who lie at Bitburg.

Timothy Garton Ash

Germany After Bitburg

HANNOVER, West Germany—Chancellor Helmut Kohl, though a historian, is not famous for his historical tact. When in Israel, Kohl declared that young Germans do not feel responsible for Nazi crimes. The Bitburg debacle was essentially of his making; and it was certainly Kohl who kept the president to his foolish promise. If Kohl sometimes gives the impression of disowning the Nazi past—"nothing to do with me"—then in this, as in so many respects, he is quite typical of contemporary West Germany. All the polls suggest that the majority of West Germans thought he was right to push ahead with Bitburg. Now here he is in Hannover, addressing a mass rally of Germans expelled from Silesia in 1945 (people who say of that now Polish territory, "Silesia remains ours") and walking across a mine field of East European sensibilities that his best advisers urged him to avoid. His speech is a sermon on the future of Europe, but it illustrates the terrible muddle into which he and his government have gotten themselves of late; whether they are talking about the past, the present, or the future of Europe.

In a way one must sympathize. It is so difficult to be a German after Hitler. "Wherever we set foot," writes Günter Grass, "we run into harsh reminders of the past. Hardly a patch of ground without its pitfalls, hardly a word without a double meaning." And so the old German Silesians here prefer to talk of Polish guilt for their expulsion, or Stalin's guilt, or the culpability of those who appeased Hitler, or the injustice of the Versailles Treaty. A provincial Christian Demo-

SOURCE: *The New Republic*, July 15 & 22, 1985, pp. 15–17. Reprinted by permission of THE NEW REPUBLIC, © 1985, The New Republic, Inc.

cratic leader is hissed and booed when he suggests that the division of Germany was the result of a war *Hitler* began. A brave Young Liberal who suggests in a public discussion that the Versailles Treaty was also the result of a war Germany began is met with hoots of derisive laughter. What, *Germany* began the First World War? Preposterous suggestion! As James Fenton puts it in his poem "A German Requiem": "How comforting it is, once or twice a year, / To get together and forget the old times."

But it is not just old rightists and Silesians who feel the compulsion, if not to evade the blame or guilt altogether, then at least to spread it around. In my experience it is above all young leftists who have hastened to equate American conduct in Vietnam with Nazi war crimes, and more recently, to equate the first Sabra and Shatila massacres with Auschwitz and Treblinka—this latter, grotesque equation being made with an almost audible sigh of relief, as if they are really saying: at last, even the Jews have done it too! You see, we are all guilty—therefore we are all innocent.

The problem of guilt was recently addressed in an exemplary fashion by Federal President Richard von Weizsaecker in his magnificent speech to the Bundestag on May 8. Talking about the persecution of the Jews in the Third Reich he said: "Anyone who kept his eyes and ears open could not fail to see the deportation trains. The nature and scale of the destruction may have exceeded human imagination, but too many people . . . tried not to notice what was happening. There were many ways of not burdening one's conscience, of shunning responsibility, looking the other way, keeping silent. When the unspeakable truth of the Holocaust then became known at the end of the war, all too many of us claimed that we had not known anything. . . . " However, von Weizsaecker continued, echoing Burke, "There is no such thing as the guilt or innocence of a whole people. Guilt, like innocence, is not collective but personal." What there is collectively is historical responsibility.

This is a theme that, to be fair, was first addressed by Chancellor Kohl, on his original visit to Bergen-Belsen in April. "Germany bears historical responsibility for the crimes of the Nazi tyranny," he said there, and "forty years later, we continue to acknowledge that historical liability." In what does this collective responsibility consist? In the duty to remember: both chancellor and president quote the Jewish saying, "Seeking to forget makes exile all the longer; the secret of redemption lies in remembrance." In ensuring that a war will never again begin "from German soil." In working everywhere for those human rights on which Nazi Germany trampled. But there is also a particular European vision that arises from this sense of historical responsibility. In this vision, Germany, the nation that took old European nationalism to its lunatic extreme, will now be the first to overcome that nationalism, to point the way forward beyond the outmoded nation-state. It will be the first to give up its sovereignty into a (West) European Union; and then, by overcoming the division of Europe in a European way, we will finally overcome the division of Germany.

How did this unfold in the version Kohl presented to the Silesians? "Just recently we have made significant steps forward in the European community," he said. "With every further renunciation of nation-state sovereignty we come closer to the goal of European Union." Coming just a few days after his government had for the first time used its right of veto in the EEC, over the issue of cereal prices, this sounded like a bad joke. Turning from Western to Eastern Europe, he talked at length about his desire for reconciliation. As Konrad Adenauer achieved the historic reconciliation with Germany's *Erbfeind* France, so Kohl, "Adenauer's grandson," would dearly love to go down in history as the man who achieved Germany's historic reconciliation with Poland, the old enemy in the East. The people of West Germany and Poland, he said, have recently come closer together, because the West Germans sent so many food parcels. He would like to see more German-Polish youth exchanges. The Poles must rest assured that West Germany will never try to change the post-1945 German-Polish frontier by force; and he repeated (to boos and hisses) his pledge that the Federal Republic neither has now, nor will have in the future, any territorial claims on the Polish People's Republic.

Yet he also insisted (to applause) that West Germany "can not and may not" give up its "legal position," which is that legally the German nation still recognizes the frontiers of 1937 (i.e., including about one-third of present-day Poland). In short, they do acknowledge the Polish frontiers, but then again they don't. One is bound to ask: "Why not?" Why "can not" West Germany change its "legal position"? No higher power prevents it. The constraint is imposed by a German court using German and international law. What is at stake, however, is a political and historical change for which there is no adequate German or international law (just as there was—and still is—no adequate German or international law to cover Nazi crimes against humanity). So this "can not" does not refer to some external objective truth, it refers to the subjective truth of German *national feelings*.

Then again he declared that what is vital for overcoming the division of Germany and Europe is the question of freedom for the people living east of the iron curtain, not the question of sovereignty rights. But what is the sacred "legal position" if not a question of sovereignty rights? And freedom for whom? Historically, West Germany has engaged itself first and foremost for the freedom of the *Germans* in Eastern Europe—above all, for their freedom to emigrate to West Germany. Today the Kohl government insists that there are still 1.2 million Germans living in Poland (mostly in Silesia)—a contention that not only the Polish Communist government but also the Polish Catholic Church flatly denies. Curiously enough, Bonn's definition of a "German" in Poland is based directly on Hitler's definition of a "German" in Poland; they have used Nazi card indexes to determine eligibility. "This national minority exists," Kohl trumpeted, to loud applause. "We are its trustee." And this is to be the basis for a historic German-Polish reconciliation?

To say "scratch the European rhetoric and you find a national interest" would be to suggest a clearheaded cynicism that the Kohl government does not have. Indeed, the chancellor himself is a wondrous muddleheaded sort of man. But I think it is fair to say that, contrary to first appearances, national interests and national feelings play quite as large a part in West German politics as they do in British or French politics, although they are expressed here in a much more complex way. This is equally true of the Social Democrats, who also gave a top priority to the specific interests of the *Germans* in Eastern Europe when they ran the Ostpolitik, and who, let it not be forgotten, fought the last general election on the slogan "In the German Interest." But whereas the leading members of the Brandt and Schmidt governments at least agreed upon a common way to present the equation between German and European interests, the leading members of the Kohl government speak with several tongues. If the Free Democratic Party leader and foreign minister, Hans-Dietrich Genscher, says one thing, the Christian Socialist Union leader Franz Josef Strauss is sure to say another; and then Chancellor Kohl is sure to say that they are both right. This disarray certainly contributed to the Christian Democratic Union's serious defeat in the recent North Rhine-Westphalia election. Just three days before coming to Hannover, Kohl met with his two equally weighty coalition partners, Genscher and Strauss—Bonn wits dubbed it the "meeting of the elephants"—to try to restore a semblance of coalition unity.

His Hannover performance was thus important for his domestic as well as his foreign political position. On both scores it must be accounted an embarrassment. It will be recalled that he had threatened not to come unless the organizers changed their original, truly revanchist motto, *"Schlesien bleibt unser"*—"Silesia remains ours." And to be sure, the large backcloth behind him bore the official compromise motto: "Silesia remains our future in a Europe of free peoples." But as soon as he began to speak, placards were raised saying, yes, "*Schlesien bleibt unser*" and "*Schlesien bleibt Deutsch.*" The ushers did nothing. Then, just in front of the press seats, two girls hoisted a red flag that said "*Schlesien bleibt Polnisch.*" Immediately, several ushers hurried to tear it down, with some violence, while the chancellor intoned, "We are peaceful democrats. . . . " Later, as he stumbled nervously through his muddled text—an elephant in a mine field—a group of neo-Nazis interrupted him with chants of "*Wi-der-stand!*" ("Resistance!") and raised their arms in a close approximation to the Hitler salute. The ushers did nothing. It was not a numerous group—at most, a few hundred—but it was large enough to fill a million television screens. Kohl must have wished he had never come.

Flora Lewis

The Anxious Germans

BONN—The economic summit conference here has been overwhelmed by the emotions of the German problem. It is a deep irony that the attempt to close a chapter of history 40 years after World War II has only revealed how much the wounds still fester.

Chancellor Helmut Kohl and President Reagan planned an unnecessary, ill-advised gesture to demonstrate that Germans and Americans have no grudges two generations after the fighting stopped. It boomeranged, not only because some SS troops are buried in the German military cemetery that Mr. Reagan is determined to visit, but also because the symbolism forced attention to hidden feelings and unspoken facts.

The central fact is the reversal of alliances. That is why it was impossible to hold a ceremony honoring 40 years of peace among all the victors and the vanquished. Both the Soviet Union and the United States decided to use the anniversary to bolster their rival alliances.

For the Russians, this 40th anniversary has been an occasion to insist on the permanence of the partition of Germany and of Europe. There has been a long propaganda campaign, vilifying modern West Germany and extolling the Pax Sovietica.

That was in the background of the Reagan-Kohl decision, intended to counter this Moscow line as well as to make a show of reconciliation in the West and of German-American friendship. Trying to go too far in setting aside the past inevitably opened wounds.

Even though old enemies are friends and old allies are adversaries now, World War II is more than history. It is the foundation of modern Europe, of the frontiers, the grievances, the tensions of the everyday present and of the foreseeable future.

SOURCE: *New York Times*, May 3, 1985.

There is no way to understand why Germany is divided, why there is a line of East-West confrontation, without acknowledging that Germany started the war with aggression to the East and to the West, and that it was defeated after causing vast suffering.

True, there was a brave but small German resistance. True, in the end the German people also suffered. But it is not true, as Alfred Dregger, floor leader of Mr. Kohl's Christian Democratic Union in the Bundestag, said last week, that none of the evil would have happened if it weren't for Hitler. All the blame cannot be heaped on one dead man, nor can those who fought and died in his name be equated as victims with those whom they tortured and murdered in cold blood.

A particularly ugly bit of rhetoric that has surfaced in the German debate stirred by Mr. Reagan's visit is the charge that American complaints about SS graves at Bitburg amount to "selection of the dead." The ordinary German word for selection is "auswahl," but in this phrase the word "selektion" is used, the word used at Auschwitz to separate those who were to be gassed immediately from those who were to be forced to work.

The past is permeating the present again; it won't go away. The issue isn't only the guilt of a vanishing generation. That should not be laid upon the children. But the children cannot escape the results of what was done, nor pursue their restless search for identity by asking for absolution of the past.

West Germans are uneasy, unsure of the standing of their nationality. For all their economic and political power, they feel vulnerable because of this burden. That is why Mr. Reagan's cemetery visit evokes so much satisfaction here. It seems to say that what happened doesn't matter any more because now there is freedom and democracy and good will. It seems to encourage pride in German nationalism.

There lies a dilemma. For a long time, the rest of the world denounced German nationalism as the root of great evil. Now West Germans are told it is good, for fear that the peace movement and the neutralists will renounce the defense of this country and thus undermine the security of all the West.

West German television and the press have been recalling for the last several months the unimaginable atrocities of Nazi Germany. It isn't that people ignore the truths of 40 years ago. But having to deal with it for their individual sense of themselves and their country provokes profound anxiety. This was seldom admitted. Now it is bared. The pain is understandable. But it is an insult to the past and a dangerous confusion for the future to gloss over the real cause.

Claire Tréan

The Liberator Is Still There . . .

EAST BERLIN—The workers in the petrochemical plants are going to increase their output, the watchmakers are going to produce more watches, the schoolchildren are going to redouble their efforts, especially in Russian. . . .

If one were to believe the headlines that have been making the front page of *Neues Deutschland* (New Germany), the party's daily paper, for the last month, all of East Germany (officially known as the German Democratic Republic or GDR) is accelerating its pace and frenetically celebrating the fortieth anniversary of the fall of Nazism. People are certainly understanding each other better in the East and in the West at this time of commemoration. While President Reagan and Chancellor Kohl become pitifully entangled in the elaboration of a common program of ceremonies, the East is hauling out the big propaganda artillery, strutting its finery. Everybody is hanging out their banners and flags; everyone is expected to make a show of public spiritedness. It is true, however, that the task is easier because what is being celebrated here on the anniversary of the fall of the Hitler regime is the liberation by the Soviet Army.

In East Germany, as in the other sister nations, the celebrations are all the more ostentatious since, forty years later, the liberator is still there, and really there.

While Chancellor Kohl seems to want to do away with Germany's past, officially at least the East Germans have long since dismissed the question and have replaced mourning or shame with celebration. As if Nazism had never had any followers in Prussia, in Saxony, or in

Translation of "Le libérateur est toujours là . . . ," *Le Monde*, April 27, 1985, no. 12517.

Thuringia. . . On such grand occasions the GDR exults in its patriotism without the slightest reservation, without the slightest allusion to the fathers and grandfathers of those participating in the festivities, unless they were members of the Resistance. The Democratic Republic defines itself as "the concretization of antifascist forces." So where could any possible problems of conscience come from since the only political past with which it is concerned begins precisely in May 1945?

The entire country is covered with slogans in white lettering on a red background, proclamations of friendship and of gratitude toward the USSR, incantatory declarations in favor of peace. There is not one building or business whose windows are not hung with alternating flags of red, black, yellow, and red—the colors of East Germany.

The few spots that the celebration of May Day usually leaves vacant are this year occupied by the fortieth anniversary. The country is crammed, saturated with propaganda. Every marathon and every bike race has a place within the frame of the May 8 celebrations. Even the discotheques received a circular from the party encouraging them to do their part for the celebrations. On an almost daily basis, television viewers are treated to the victorious advance of the Russian front toward Berlin.

A film about the year 1945, produced using materials obtained exclusively from Soviet archives, was premiered with great fanfare in East Berlin. Since the beginning of April ceremonies have been organized at the former concentration camps—Buchenwald, Sachsenhausen, and Brandenburg—timed to coincide with the anniversaries of their liberation.

Out of all this, what the East Germans have to hold onto are the images of Red Army soldiers sharing their rations with starving Berlin children, the fact that the war essentially took place between the Oder and the Spree, and that it took twenty million Soviet lives.

There is no mention, obviously, of the atrocities inflicted on civilian populations by the Red Army as it passed through. No mention of the Jews, an almost unknown word in the abundant literature produced for the commemorative occasion. Like others, they are merely part of "the nationals of twenty countries" who were massacred in the camps. The Jews have no individual fate and are subsumed under the general term of "antifascists." If Nazism is thus merely one barbarism among others, it becomes possible, on this occasion, to establish its relations to American imperialism. This was one of the points made on April 11 by Herman Axen, a member of the Politburo, in a veritable prewar speech announcing the imminence of nuclear catastrophe.

That does it for the big artillery. There remain nevertheless a few nuances with which the GDR discreetly distinguishes its particular message from the chorus of the East Bloc countries. One of the high points of the program of ceremonies was the get-together on Thursday between American and Soviet veterans in Torgau, a small market town on the banks of the Elbe, where the two armies met on April 25, 1945.

While the brass band from Leipzig played the *Internationale* and the *Marche Funèbre*, photographs from 1945 were brought out and the "Elbe Oath" was recalled, the oath of peace pronounced by Joseph Polowsky, former member of the Sixty-ninth Infantry Division and a cab driver in Chicago who was buried a few years ago, according to his wishes, in Torgau. All this would have almost been pulled off if the death of the American colonel Nicholson—slain by Russians a few weeks earlier in the GDR—had not provided the American, French, and British officials with a pretext to boycott a demonstration that, in any case, they had hardly been eager to attend.

What is essential is the much greater publicity given to this ceremony than to others by the East German authorities. The point was to show that the German Democratic Republic had succeeded where the Federal Republic of Germany had failed: that is, in bringing together the former victors on German soil. The telegrams sent to Torgau by Gorbachev and the East German head of state Erich Honecker calling for a "coalition of reason and realism," stressed this point instead of the usual anti-Hitler coalition. More than any other country in the East Bloc, the GDR has become the mouthpiece for calls for peace and disarmament. It also tries to give the impression that it is particularly committed to détente. As a result, Honecker's speeches are much more moderate toward the West than are those of Axen. The anniversary in February of the bombing of Dresden by the American and British air forces provided an opportunity for a harangue against the West, which, however, the GDR let go by unnoticed. Similarly, there was hardly any reaction in East Berlin to the rather confusing signals now coming from the Federal Republic.

The meeting of the leaders of the two German states in Moscow on the occasion of Chernenko's funeral officially marked for the GDR the resumption of dialogue after a period of cool relations. This should not be forgotten even if the Federal Republic of Germany is open to criticism: after the statements made by one of the leaders of the Christlich-Demokratische Union (CDU), according to which May 8, 1945, had been "a catastrophe for Germany," and after the statements about the former territories of Silesia made by other representatives of the Right in West Germany, the proposed visit by Chancellor Kohl and President Reagan to the Bitburg cemetery, where SS soldiers are buried, could have been a veritable godsend for the propaganda against "the politics of revenge."

While in the West those on the Right recall that Germany suffered and still suffers under the Soviets, in the East a state, born virginal and without memory a little less than forty years ago, today celebrates its "eternal" friendship with the USSR.

Translated by Thomas Levin

Yevg Bovkun

History, Washington Style

Bergen-Belsen and Bitburg. From the perspective of the American president, the virtually simultaneous visit to Hitler's concentration camp and a cemetery for Hitler's soldiers, which caused indignation in the entire world, must have looked like "a gesture of reconciliation." Whose and with whom? That of a victorious power with a former adversary, explained Reagan in his address to a select audience on the territory of an American military base in Bitburg, where one of America's air force units is stationed.

He did not utter a word about the joint struggle of the states in the anti-Hitler coalition, or about the decisive role of the Soviet Union in bringing about the victory over fascism, which cost the lives of 20 million Soviet citizens.

On the other hand, conservative circles in West Germany heard from Reagan about the necessity "of protecting democracy and freedom" against encroachments from "totalitarian regimes in the East"—music to their ears.

The head of the American administration also intolerably distorted historic truth in Bergen-Belsen, where he confined the crimes of the Nazi regime solely to the extermination of the Jewish population. Speaking about the horrors of the war, the president did not mention the immeasurable human sacrifices and destruction that the Second World War, unleashed by the Nazis, inflicted on nations.

And there was yet another "amendment to history": listening to Reagan one would have thought that the United States, which set foot

SOURCE: *Izvestia*, May 7, 1985.

on European soil only after the turning point in the war, had almost singlehandedly liberated our continent from the brown tyranny.

The "reconciliation" performance in Bergen-Belsen and Bitburg also has another side. It is hard to resist an impression that for the American president and some people in Bonn this was an attempt to reconcile the executioners with their victims on the foundation of anticommunism.

If the rightist camp welcomed "amendments to history," however, the democratic public of West Germany met them with angry condemnation. Despite the measures adopted by the security services and the police, which erected a multilayered cordon around Bitburg, thousands of people came to express their protests against attempts retroactively to justify criminals from the SS. Demonstrations of protest were held in many cities of West Germany including Neustadt (close to Bitburg), where a peace festival was organized by the GSDP during Reagan's visit. A mass gathering in Dachau came as a stern reminder of the monstrous crimes of the Nazis.

This is how hundreds and hundreds of thousands of citizens of West Germany reject Reagan's concept of "overcoming the past," which is thrust upon them with absurd amendments to the history of World War II made for the sake of today's Reaction.

Translated by Roman Pipko

William Safire

'I Am a Jew . . .'

LOS ANGELES—To President Kennedy's "Ich bin ein Berliner," a powerful and personal statement of identification with people struggling for freedom, President Reagan added: ". . . I am a Jew in a world still threatened by anti-Semitism, I am an Afghan, and I am a prisoner of the Gulag, I am a refugee in a crowded boat foundering off the coast of Vietnam, I am a Laotian, a Cambodian, a Cuban and a Miskito Indian in Nicaragua. I, too, am a potential victim of totalitarianism."

The poet-theologian John Donne made that point in his "no man is an island" passage, and Ernest Hemingway used a phrase from Donne in his title of a book about resistance to fascism, "For Whom the Bell Tolls." Many Jews will remember the lesson from the seder service that requires commemoration of the need for personal identification, during which it is recounted that an arrogant son asks, "What did the Almighty do for you?" and is castigated for not asking as a Jew, "What did the Almighty do for me?" To understand humanity, you have to be an active part of it.

Ronald Reagan, a month ago, had no real grasp of the moral priorities of the Holocaust or the fear of forgetting that prevents forgiveness. His journey to understanding—his own "painful walk into the past"—opened the minds of millions to the costs of reconciliation in a way that no other process could have accomplished. In driving home the lessons of history, his incredible series of blunders turned out to be a blessing.

At first, he did not want to go to a concentration camp. Too

SOURCE: *New York Times*, May 6, 1985. Copyright © 1985 by The New York Times Company. Reprinted by permission.

gloomy to be part of an upbeat trip. Like so many, he praised "remembrance" so long as it involved no personal pain.

The discovery of the SS graves in the scheduled cemetery visit saved him from the sin of avoidance. At that point, Mr. Reagan—and the world—had to go to a death camp and bear witness.

Then some invisible pedagogic hand led him to equate the victims of the death camps with the dead soldiers of the Third Reich. He soon learned, along with millions who had never given the matter any thought, that no reconciliation could ever come about by glossing over the enormity of the crimes committed by the Nazis and all the Germans who enthusiastically abetted them. Feeling sadness at the grave of soldiers is on a different order of magnitude from feeling agony at the slaughter of innocents.

The President absorbed the point. In an inspiring instructional penance in the Oval Office, he led a huge audience in listening to the testimony of Elie Wiesel, the quintessential survivor.

The invisible teaching hand would not let go. An ignoble motive (fear of appearing weak and subject to pressure) merged with a noble motive (the concern about insulting a new generation of Germans) to send him to a place tainted with the graves of storm troopers. This posed a test: Would he understand, and be able to articulate both the need for remembrance and the requirement for reconciliation?

In part one of this amazing exam, he stood at Bergen-Belsen alongside the German Chancellor, a man of relentless repentance, "to confront and condemn the acts of a hated regime of the past." The Jewish prayer for the dead speaks not of the dead, but determinedly of faith in God; fittingly, the President stressed the message of the doomed Anne Frank, "I still believe that people are really good at heart." No horror photograph can be as affecting as that example of intelligent innocence and pure hope snuffed out: The ritual "never again" had context.

In the final part of the test, at the Bitburg cemetery, he acknowledged the presence of the Nazi graves first by turning his back on them, then by contrasting them with the remains of young draftees, and left the judgment to Heaven. He did not equate them with their victims or with the soldiers who fell in a moral cause. One false note was an extended anecdote about the suspension of hostilities on a holiday—as if the Wehrmacht had been made up mainly of sentimental boys—but he drew the central lesson clearly: "that freedom must always be stronger than totalitarianism, that good must always be stronger than evil."

That followed his uplifting "I am a Berliner, I am a Jew in a world still threatened by anti-Semitism" passage, and for me redeemed the thoughtless early planning of this trip.

In seeking at first to sidestep the smouldering resentments, the President brought on a firestorm 40 years after a Holocaust, which in turn forced a forgetful world through a most necessary grief.

Anthony Lewis

The One-Track Mind

BOSTON—The essence of Ronald Reagan was exposed at Bitburg. Confronted by the most profound questions of man's nature and responsibility, he responded with narrow ideology and distorted history.

"I am a Jew in a world still threatened by anti-Semitism," Mr. Reagan said after visiting the German military cemetery. "I am an Afghan, and I am a prisoner of the Gulag, I am a refugee in a crowded boat foundering off the coast of Vietnam, I am a Laotian, a Cambodian, a Cuban and a Miskito Indian in Nicaragua. I, too, am a potential victim of totalitarianism." So freedom-loving people around the world must say today.

The rhetoric of that passage was much noted, and it was brilliantly effective rhetoric. But think about the message.

Every victim Mr. Reagan mentioned, after the reference to anti-Semitism, was a victim of Communism. He was saying that the serious violations of human rights—the only ones worth mentioning in the shadow of the Holocaust—are all the work of Communist governments.

Not a thought there for those who have suffered and died at General Pinochet's hands in Chile, for the Bahai and other victims of religious terror in Iran, for the South Africans who live under institutionalized racist tyranny. Not a word of memory for the Armenians who died at the hands of Turks in this century's first genocide.

The point is not to play down the existence of cruelty in Communist regimes. It is to recognize that inhumanity of appalling kinds

SOURCE: *New York Times*, May 9, 1985. Copyright © 1985 by The New York Times Company. Reprinted by permission.

may appear in all kinds of societies and systems—and must be opposed regardless of ideology.

That is one of the most obvious lessons of the history of the Nazi period. There were people who argued, then, that we should not object too strongly to Hitler's racial ideas, because after all he was anti-Communist. Some political excuse can always be presented for closing one's eyes to the horror of an Idi Amin, of the Khmer Rouge, of the torturers in the Argentine generals' regime, of Stalin.

The concept of human rights must be universal to have meaning: If we have not learned that, we have learned nothing from what Hannah Arendt called this terrible century. But Ronald Reagan, speaking in the shadow of its most terrible crime against humanity, saw an occasion to make an anti-Communist point.

Along with the zealot's one-eyed view of human rights, Mr. Reagan offered an extraordinary version of the great crime that left its imprint all around him: Nazism. In his edited history, Nazi Germany was not a system, not a terrifying mass phenomenon, but the work of one man.

"One man's totalitarian dictatorship" was the President's phrase for it. But Hitler was not alone. Millions voted for him, mouthed his ideas, hated and killed with him. The horror of Nazism was that ordinary men, or ones who would have been thought ordinary, pushed Jews into gas chambers. And there are still advocates of fascism today.

In the Reagan memory, as displayed at Bitburg, there were mostly good Germans: teen-agers drafted into the army, "soldiers to whom Nazism meant no more than a brutal end to a short life," the mother and son in the Reader's Digest story told by Mr. Reagan—who welcomed both American and German soldiers to their cottage in the woods on Christmas Day 1944.

"We do not believe in collective guilt," the President said, and he was right. But neither can we rightly close our minds to the terrible knowledge that millions followed Hitler. It is by facing that fact that successive generations of West German political leaders have done so much to create a healthy Federal Republic. A perfect symbol of Mr. Reagan's attitude was his refusal to meet one of the bravest of those leaders, an early anti-Nazi, former Chancellor Willy Brandt.

In his speech at the U.S. air base in Bitburg, the President said he had received many letters about his planned visit to the cemetery: some supportive, some concerned, some opposed. He described only one, from a young Jewish woman who recently had had her bat mitzvah. "She urged me," Mr. Reagan said, "to lay the wreath at Bitburg cemetery in honor of the future of Germany, and that is what we have done."

The young woman was later identified by the White House press office as Beth Flom, of Marlboro Township, N.J. Miss Flom told The Associated Press that in her message to the President she told him she disapproved of his plan to visit Bitburg.

Charles William Maynes

Facing the Dark Side of Nationalism

WASHINGTON—The White House has now corrected its original mistake not to include in the President's West German schedule next month a visit to a site associated with the Holocaust. But this whole episode, and particularly the general reaction to it, raises troubling questions about the degree to which the United States—from the President on down—understands the significance of the Holocaust.

The country has largely viewed the issue of the President's West German schedule as a public-relations problem. Has a President who is the most skillful open-field political runner of his generation now committed a bonehead fumble and alienated most of American Jewry? Has he compounded that political error by visiting a German military cemetery that contains the bodies of some Waffen SS troops? (Presumably, all German military cemeteries have graves of some SS soldiers.) As the arguments unfolded, American Jewish leaders expressed their outrage in growing numbers; finally, joined by the American Legion, they proved to have enough political muscle to bring the President, if not to his knees, then to his senses.

Regrettably, that is probably how the President's new schedule will be viewed: He will be seen as visiting a site associated with the Holocaust only because of Jewish pressure. This is unfortunate because non-Jews as well need to understand that the purpose of a presidential visit to a concentration camp is not to mollify Jews or condemn Germans but to face up to a dark side of modern nationalism that is not found only in Germany.

SOURCE: *Los Angeles Times*, April 21, 1985.

The historical relationship between Jews and Germans has been troubled. Germany's greatest religious figure, Martin Luther, denounced Jews in terms that now seem taken from manifestoes of the Nazi period. Luther, attacking this "damned, rejected race" who had wealth because "they have robbed and stolen from us by their usury," called for a "merciful severity" that would include "setting fire to their synagogues and schools and covering over what will not burn with earth so that no man will ever see a stone or cinder of them again."

But Luther was not the only religious leader—nor Germany the only culture—to define another people as lying outside the circle of the community. It is a characteristic of modern nationalism for each people to ascribe to itself qualities it denies can exist in others. The first European settlers in North America who believed themselves a chosen people regarded blacks as inferior and exterminated the Indian tribes that stood in the way of white Christian settlement. The Western colonial powers, convinced of their superiority, felt no qualms in their ruthless use of force to bring "civilization" to "lesser breeds without the law."

Today Iraqi generals speak of Iranian soldiers as "insects." Most Arab leaders, through their extreme rhetoric, attempt to dehumanize Israel and its citizens. A former Israeli army chief of staff recently called for a policy of control over the Palestinians on the West Bank that would treat them like "drugged roaches in a bottle."

During the siege of Beirut, Palestine Liberation Organization leader Yasser Arafat was interviewed over American television and, to the annoyance of the American correspondent, ignored the questions posed to say repeatedly: "We are not rats. We are human beings." Most American viewers were probably puzzled by the exchange, but this was an important distinction. Toward rats, human beings will show no mercy. The goal is extermination. Toward fellow human beings, even in war, the goal should be victory, not elimination.

Franklin D. Roosevelt once observed that the presidency is not merely an administrative job; it is "pre-eminently a place of moral leadership." The purpose of a presidential visit to a concentration camp site is not to remind the world of German crimes, but to honor the dead and instruct the living. The presidential role should be that of educator, not accuser.

In performing that role, Reagan can help all to remember a period in world history that should be unforgettable but unfortunately, is not. In the mid-1970s, teachers at 110 schools in West Germany asked students in different grades to explain what they had heard about Hitler. The results were astonishing.

Many had never heard of him. Some believed he was born in the early 19th century or thought he was an Italian. Some suggested that he put his opponents, called Nazis, in gas chambers; that he made the first moon landing, or that he had fought in the Thirty Years' War.

Gordon A. Craig, an eminent scholar of Germany, has correctly pointed out that young American students might produce similar inanities if asked to write about Franklin D. Roosevelt. The point, while true, is not reassuring. In the 1930s and the 1940s, Western civilization broke down. It almost disappeared. Ignorance of that period—in particular, an abandonment of efforts to determine the reasons for the breakdown—can pose a much greater threat to this country's survival than similar ignorance about any other period in modern history.

Many non-Germans find solace in a belief that Hitler's success could have taken place only in Germany. Since German officials carried out the Holocaust, the German nation does shoulder a special responsibility. But we all know that extreme movements of the National Socialist variety exist in many countries.

In truth, Hitler represents an evil deformation of modern nationalism, to exalt one's own community at the expense of those outside it. The distorted form has already plunged us into two world wars and could bring on a third. Identifying in Hitler and in his society what may remain in our own is, therefore, essential to our survival.

The President did commit a fumble but so did the rest of us; and this last fumble was not political but moral.

Tyler Marshall

Germans Decry Bitburg Furor

BONN—Bitterness grew in West Germany on Monday over attacks on President Reagan's plan to visit a German military cemetery, and a Foreign Ministry official called on American clergymen to defend the trip.

In addition, newspapers warned of the effect of the controversy on U.S.–West German relations, and government officials decried what they called false information about the visit.

Alois Mertes, the member of Parliament for Bitburg and a state secretary in the West German Foreign Ministry, said Roman Catholic bishops in the United States should support Reagan's visit to the cemetery.

"I ask where the Catholic Church and other churches are in this debate," he said in a radio interview Monday, "especially the U.S. Catholic bishops, who have plenty to say about strategic and economic issues but have not brought the joyful news that God's blessing also extends to the buried SS soldiers."

He added: "A grave is a grave. Allowing the dead to rest in peace is a basic principle of our Christian-Judeo civilization."

Chancellor Helmut Kohl's hope that Reagan's stop at the Bitburg cemetery would help seal the reconciliation between the former enemies has instead erupted into a major controversy, tearing open old wounds. West German leaders have been clearly stunned by the intensity of the reaction, but Kohl has staunchly stood by the visit.

At a news conference Monday, government spokesman Peter

Boenish labeled as "scandalous" references in the international press to Bitburg as a "Nazi city."

Boenisch read a plea to Kohl, signed jointly by Bitburg Mayor Theo Hallet and Rhineland Palatinate Premier Bernhard Vogel, to counter what they see as the defamation of the town.

"Make it clear to the world public (that) in Bitburg live people who resisted Nazism as hardly any other city, (and that) in Bitburg people live who have had friendly ties as hardly any other city for decades with thousands of American soldiers living here," the appeal said.

The U.S. Air Force 36th Tactical Fighter Wing is based nearby.

State Secretary Mertes has released figures showing that the staunchly Roman Catholic Bitburg constituency gave a lower percentage of its vote—14.7%—to the Nazi Party than any other city in prewar Germany's last free election in 1932.

The controversy has centered on the presence of 49 graves of Waffen SS troops among the 1,887 World War II dead, mostly teenage draftees, buried at Bitburg. The Waffen SS was a combat branch of Hitler's elite force, a separate branch of which ran Nazi concentration camps.

Boenisch, calling irrelevant the presence of one SS grave for every 39 of those of regular soldiers, said: "Even if someone who is lying there was guilty of anything, there is no worse punishment than death."

Jewish communities in the United States and other countries have expressed outrage, charging that Reagan's plans to lay a wreath at the cemetery is tantamount to honoring those who carried out the Holocaust.

Assurances that the wreath will be laid far from the few SS graves and changes in Reagan's itinerary to include a stop at the Bergen-Belsen concentration camp memorial have failed to dampen the controversy.

West Germans, who make sharp distinctions between the SS concentration camp units and the SS combat divisions to which those buried at Bitburg belonged, have taken the controversy as a national insult.

In a public opinion poll to be released today, West Germans were asked if they viewed those buried at Bitburg as Germans or Nazis, and 94% answered Germans.

"This goes to the heart of every family," said Elisabeth Noelle-Neumanan, who heads the Allensbach Opinion Research Institute that conducted the poll. "In almost every (German) living room there is a picture of someone who died in the war."

The reaction is also a severe setback for a country that has strived so hard for international acceptance since the war.

The respected Frankfurter Allgemeine Zeitung said in a front-page commentary that the Bitburg controversy is "a trauma that won't be soon forgotten."

The commentary exuded disillusionment and talked of Washington giving Japan respect while "treating its most loyal European ally as a vassal."

"There has been clumsiness on both sides, but the reaction has been immoderate and hysterical," the newspaper said. "The U.S.A. should be aware of growing anti-Americanism" that could be fueled by the controversy over Bitburg.

The Bonner Rundschau newspaper said the planned cemetery visit has "created hysteria without end."

Kohl also warned about possible lasting damage to U.S.–West German relations, saying he hoped this would not happen either on a governmental or personal basis. But if it did, he added in a magazine interview, "then we would have to ask ourselves whether or not we have been building (relations) on sand these past decades."

At his news conference, government spokesman Boenisch hinted at a possible expansion of Reagan's state visit program but insisted the cemetery trip will not be canceled.

"I assume individual parts of the program will remain unchanged," he said. "We are going to complete what we said we would do in the first place."

Martin E. Marty

'Storycide' and the Meaning of History

CHICAGO—Society, lacking group memory, keeps stories alive through ceremonies and rituals. One never "merely" lays a wreath at a cemetery. Some script must provide for the human need to walk through the past without walking over it. Such rites, on human scales, help us remember what often gets overlooked when the mannequins of state follow conventional scripts.

As "Bitburg Sunday" recedes in memory, many are saying good riddance to media coverage and debate over the event. On May 5, President Reagan laid a wreath at a German military cemetery as a gesture of reconciliation with Germany. That event left unreconciled the Jews, American veterans, the Congress and the majority of citizens, who had expressed outrage over that gesture. They were angered over his ability to overlook the graves of fallen SS men, agents of the Nazi horror.

The President's original plan not to visit a concentration camp of Nazi victims did change. He went to Bergen-Belsen to cool the outrage and to balance the symbolism: one stop for the victims, one for the agents whose deeds, after 40 years, were now to be obscured. His reference to the fact that the killers had already been judged by a higher judge was an effort to lift the issue to a plane where no one could criticize. Not all accepted his theology or regarded it as a way to keep moral issues alive in the affairs of humans.

As the visits fade from prime time and front-page coverage, they leave two issues. The first and familiar one is anti-Semitism. The sec-

SOURCE: *Los Angeles Times*, May 12, 1985.

ond, less familiar but just as important, is the issue of neglecting and forgetting the Jewish story, this time of the Holocaust. Anti-Semitism did not become the major issue. Not even his most severe critics accused the President or his advisers of wanting to contribute to the hatred of Jews.

There were chills, of course, when the popular German magazine, *Quick*, headlined its suggestion that the influence of Jews on the President was the problem behind the Bitburg debate. The fact that SS veterans holding their annual meeting at a German resort toasted Reagan was an abhorrent notion, but not something that found counterparts elsewhere. Letters to the editor in U.S. newspapers here and there underscored the *Quick* theme, but such expressions were rare. Some Jews complained of overhearing remarks about Jewish influence, but they had heard worse. There was no outbreak of swastika-painting on synagogues, and the woebegone American Nazi Party, Ku Klux Klan and other hate groups did not find a way to exploit the day.

Instead, the second issue is what lives after the Bitburg and Bergen-Belsen visits. As lethal as anti-Semitism to Jews is the idea that their story could be forgotten. Jews live by story. So, of course, do other peoples. Americans recall Abraham Lincoln telling the story of what happened "four score and seven years ago," whenever they seek new resolve. Yet Jews have not much *but* their story to give them coherence and hope. They lack numbers. Only 17 million live on after Hitler, most in the United States and Israel. They lack weaponry. The guns of Israel point more to precariousness than to the security of the people. They do have story.

Early chapters of the story live on in annual observances of recall wherever there are Jews. Passover and Exodus are the most familiar of these. It took a few years to integrate the two newest chapters into the story: the Holocaust before 1945 and the rebirth of Israel after 1948. Thus, in 1966, *Commentary*, a magazine of Jewish intellectuals, asked many younger Jewish writers and religious leaders about their belief. The Holocaust, writes Nathan Glazer, "did not figure" much among the questions or answers. Then, Glazer added, "suddenly, 1967 raised sharply the possibility of real genocide again."

Why 1967? That was the time of the Six-Day War, when Israel's existence was threatened. That war brought Jewish consciousness of a possible end to a new stage; now, Bitburg is likely to reinforce Jewish fears and resolves. Bitburg was a nonviolent, calculatedly gentle and solemn event, yet one might say that 1985 raised sharply the possibility of Jewish "storycide." The dictionary does not include or need that term, but the world needs such a concept. If a story sustains Judaism, then to distort, neglect, mute or forget that story would be to help end the people and all it holds dear.

Urgent questions arose this spring across the spectrum of otherwise often divided American Judaism. Have we made the point of the Holocaust story so weakly, so forgettably? After only 40 years, can a President and his advisors, people adept at manipulating symbols, have so misunderstood ours? Can they not have learned other ways to "reconcile" than to walk past the SS graves and "balance" the death of drafted German youth with the weight of 6 million innocents led to death? If our story is thus downgraded and devalued, and if that story matters for our existence, are we secure? Will we survive when greater tests come?

Such questions sound, to some, too defensive and urgent. Had the President understood what was at stake, many said, he would have stepped back. Other balancing statements did help quiet Jewish fears. This time, for one thing, Christian leadership from fundamentalists through liberals supported Jews in a spirit of common cause seldom evident. U.S. military veterans, who long ago showed creative ways to let years help healing between nations, showed that they could "forget" some wounds of war without confusing that war's symbols.

The story of the 1967 war brings tears to the eyes of Jews who mourned new deaths as a result. Yet it also brings resolve. Philosopher—and death camp survivor—Emil L. Fackenheim has ever since argued that "Jews are forbidden to hand Hitler posthumous victories. They are commanded to remember the victims of Auschwitz lest their memory perish." He adds, for us all, "They are forbidden to despair of man and his world, and to escape into either cynicism or other worldliness, lest they cooperate in delivering the world over to the forces of Auschwitz."

Voices like his have gained a fresh hearing. Unwittingly and ironically, Reagan, German Chancellor Helmut Kohl and their planners and public relations people, through ineptness, served to keep the story fresh in its 40th year. The form their contribution took embarrassed them and grieved millions but recall of the day will challenge conscience more profoundly in years to come. In the kind of trick that history can play, the debate over Bitburg, 1985, will likely achieve more good than a proper observance would ever have done.

William McGurn

Samuel Pisar: Of Bitburg and Liberation

President Reagan is expected to lay a wreath Sunday at a German war cemetery in Bitburg, West Germany, that includes the remains of 49 Waffen SS soldiers.

Earlier this week, William McGurn of The Wall Street Journal/Europe discussed the Reagan visit with one of the youngest survivors of Dachau and Auschwitz, Polish-born Samuel Pisar, author of a memoir titled "Of Blood and Hope." Today a graduate of Harvard Law School and an international lawyer with offices in Paris and New York, Mr. Pisar was liberated by American troops shortly after his 16th birthday in 1945 and was made a U.S. citizen by a special act of Congress in June 1961.

Mr. Pisar: My childhood seems to me eons removed from the universe in which I live and work today, where my daily preoccupations are with international law, the world economy, trade, finance, technology and things of that kind.

But at moments like this I can't forget that I was saved from extermination by the U.S. Army under most dramatic circumstances. Forty years ago I ran toward an approaching tank bearing that glorious white star, shouting "God Bless America," words my mother taught me when dreaming of deliverance—which for her and the rest of my family never came. Then a tall, black, helmeted American soldier crawled out of the hatch of his vehicle and pulled me down into the womb of freedom.

At that moment, after knowing two years of Soviet occupation and four years of Nazi slavery, I became an American. The congressional vote granting me U.S. citizenship years later merely formalized what was already a reality.

What are your concerns about the president's coming visit to Germany?

There are two basic issues here. The first is the moral authority of the president, which mustn't be allowed to be sapped. The other is that this entire situation must not diminish the fantastic moment 40 years ago when liberty triumphed over evil.

Do you think the president was right to go to Bitburg?

About the visit to the cemetery where Nazi SS are buried, I have not one good word. There is no way I can characterize it but as a mistake. I still wish he wouldn't go, though he says he will.

What about the president's statement that some of the German soldiers were victims, too?

This was, to say the least, maladroit. But I think I know what he was trying express, the idea of the "peace of the brave"—that the dead of the victors and the dead of the vanquished provide an occasion for reconciliation.

But he did not measure the crucial difference here. I do not want to be emotional, but this was not a peace of the brave, with two sides fighting under equal conditions on the field of honor. In this case there were millions of unarmed defenseless men, women and children targeted for systematic extermination. They, and the few who survived, are essential parties to any reconciliation.

So while the president's intention was noble, the execution was horrible.

Why was that?

He is a politician who gets advice, and in this case he had atrocious advice. Now, I know Reagan to be a great friend of the Jewish people, a great friend of Israel. This is a president who helped rescue the Falashas from Ethiopia, who speaks up for the Russian Jews. The compassion is obviously there; he has proved that over and over. So it is most unfortunate that he got caught in this situation.

What happened under the Nazis and SS had no precedent. Let me put it this way: In their hands, the ship of European civilization went under. That great country, Germany, that flower of European culture that gave us Gutenberg, Beethoven, Goethe, went momentarily mad.

So Reagan is a victim in a sense, not only because of his failure to grasp the awesome implications of what this visit means but also a victim of a protocol Chancellor Kohl negligently forced on him. Because the chancellor is not taking Reagan to a cemetery—he is taking him to a mine field.

What would have been an ideal commemoration?

Oh, there were so many possibilities. He could have gone to Adenauer's grave, even von Stauffenberg's. Or the grave of the brother and sister Scholl, who started a student resistance movement at the University of Munich and were executed.

You don't then believe in collective guilt?

No, I don't believe in the collective guilt of the German people. Nor do I believe in guilt by attribution to a generation of Germans who are struggling with the tremendous burden of the evil perpetrated by their fathers and grandfathers.

What could the president say at Bitburg to get himself out of this predicament?

I don't think he should say much at the cemetery. I think he would be making a terrible mistake to speak there.

What about at the Bergen-Belsen death camp now on the itinerary?

I think the president has to find a way to transcend all political calculus on this occasion. He must speak to the whole world at the loftiest humanistic level. All the more reason why he must not make a speech about how we Americans, we Germans, have made NATO stronger, etc.

The president must rise above all this. If he can, we will come out of this divisive, heart-rending national experience more humble, better instructed, and at peace. The catharsis may yet turn out to be a positive thing.

So you think the president can still make the day into something constructive?

If at Bergen-Belsen he can transcend the momentary needs of diplomacy or strategy or politics, then the event could become a moment of beauty and greatness. And the place to do it, to say "never again," is the place of agony and martyrdom, the death camps of World War II.

Back in 1975, you accompanied then-President of France Giscard d'Estaing to Auschwitz. How does that compare with today?

It happens that I was privy to the difficult decision Giscard had to make about going to Auschwitz because he shared it with me. Now, I would not say that he is less sensitive or more sensitive than Ronald Reagan, more humble or less humble, but what impressed me was the tremendous care he took personally to try to understand what a thing of this kind is made of. I think he understood that Auschwitz was something beyond his experience, his reach, something immense, unfathomable. As I said in my book, there Eichmann's grim reality eclipsed Dante's vision of hell.

Giscard was like marble. Some people thought it was because he is by nature aristocratic and cold, but I knew the other side. As I walked with him through the camp, I showed him the barracks where I lived, the chimneys; he said nothing. What could he have done: ask questions? make comments?

What was the reaction?

Everyone perceived that pilgrimage as a moment of great healing, both in France and abroad. The proof was that, shortly thereafter, François Mitterrand—at the time Giscard's greatest political enemy— said to me: For once Giscard spoke in the name of all Frenchmen, all mankind, and he spoke well.

Are you aware that two weeks ago, at an East German commemoration at Buchenwald, the officials did not mention the Jews who perished there?

Yes, and it is outrageous. It is the same at Babi Yar, on the outskirts of Kiev, where almost 100,000 Jews were slaughtered by the Nazis. As a heartbreaking poem goes, "There is no monument at Babi Yar. . . ." So you can imagine how such a commemoration as the one at Buchenwald hits us. Outrageous, and yet unreported.

Do you see a difference between something like that and what has happened to Mr. Reagan?

Yes, because in this case, it is systematic official policy. Whereas with the president, it was spontaneous, human. The president's decision hurt, but it was not calculated to hurt. There is a great difference in that.

What is your hope for the outcome of this visit?

I still fervently hope that at the last minute Reagan will decide not to go to Bitburg; there is a consensus that he not go. In the long run, it would not be perceived as giving into pressure but as a human act of courage.

It is to the barbed wire fence that he must go—with the world's eyes upon him— to bow his head and meditate on justice, tolerance and respect for human rights. For he will be standing in the presence of six million innocent souls.

If Reagan can transcend the painful controversy by speaking to all men at Bergen-Belsen—and this is something he does well— then not only will he recapture his moral authority, he will have made it a moment of inspiration and greatness. It is essential that the president return home with his moral authority intact, a leader who has commemorated the triumph of that five-pointed white star that 40 years ago gave people like me life and freedom.

Marvin Kalb

'New' SS Wreaths, Old Anti-Semitism

WASHINGTON—The controversy over the Reagan visit to Bitburg is receding, no longer a front-page embarrassment. But do you hear an echo from the past?

I visited the cemetery the morning after President Reagan and Chancellor Helmut Kohl placed wreaths of reconciliation in front of its chapel. For years, the cemetery had been largely ignored; now, it was an instant shrine, a focus of political debate. Small flower pots marked many flat graves, 49 of them honoring Waffen SS troops. By the end of my visit, many hundreds of Germans and occasional Americans from the nearby Air Force base paused before the wreaths. Some took pictures. Mothers hushed children. A religious air seemed to saturate the scene.

But look and listen: all around there were the sights and sounds of the new Germany—and old. Six feet to the left of the President's wreath stood an equally impressive one. Across its banner: "To the Waffen SS who fell at Leningrad." No more than a foot to the right of the Chancellor's was another wreath: "For the fallen comrades of the Waffen SS."

These two wreaths had been placed in the chapel, out of sight, hours before the President arrived. They were restored to their original places of honor only hours after he left. In the ensuing tranquillity, the Waffen SS could again be honored in the springtime sun.

A middle-aged visitor from Nuremberg said the Waffen SS were simply soldiers—young conscripts doing their duty. "Let them rest in peace. For us, a dead soldier is a dead soldier, not a hero."

A native of Bitburg, who looked to be in his 20's, expressed a view I was to hear with disturbing regularity. "We Germans and Americans had been cooperating very well"—he lowered his voice—"until the Jews began to make trouble."

Another Bitburger zeroed in on Elie Wiesel. "Imagine the nerve of a Jew lecturing President Reagan. I saw him on television, making trouble the way they all do."

An old woman complained that Mr. Reagan had spent only eight minutes at the cemetery. "You know why the visit had to be cut back? Because of the Jews." She stalked away to join a group of friends nodding in agreement.

A man with a cane stopped and said: "If they don't like it here, the Jews, let them go away. We were better off without them in Germany." There are only 28,000 left, he was reminded. "Too many," he replied.

The people of Bitburg are pleased that Mr. Reagan came to visit, that he didn't yield to pressure. But it's clear they resent their new notoriety—and equally clear whom they consider responsible for the unwelcome change: the Jews and the media. The Jews are seen as a group separate from Germans and Americans—an indigestible lump, a foreign body. The media are seen as intrusive and irresponsible and, somehow, controlled by the Jews.

So it went. A few days later, a Munich newspaper editor explained that anti-Semitism is an "anthropological phenomenon" in Germany. The controversy seems only to have uncorked the venom once again. There is a sad irony. Bitburgers consider themselves remarkably enlightened. In 1933, when Hitler won a critical election, this conservative Catholic town voted overwhelmingly against him.

Is Bitburg an aberration? It is impossible to judge and dangerous to generalize. But a number of leading West German politicians and professors—several close to Mr. Kohl—think anti-Semitism was on the rise even before Bitburg. "The Jews were getting too impertinent," one politician said, citing, among other things, their opposition to West German tank sales to Saudi Arabia. "We've listened to them much too long. It's enough."

The pursuit of reconciliation by way of Bitburg has been a failure. What should have been obvious from the beginning is that reconciliation is a long process—not a single photo opportunity, an event, a moment frozen in time. Bitburg, exposing clumsiness and poor political judgment in Bonn and Washington, in the process lifted the scab on dark corners of recent German history. There is a time to know when to leave well enough alone.

As I entered the cemetery, I noticed a sign: "Please do not disturb the peace and rest of the dead." Too late.

Miles Kington

Alas, poor Ronald, I knew him well

Scene, a graveyard. Enter Prince Ronald Reagan, with Horatio, a scriptwriter. They stand and watch the grave-diggers.

First Grave-digger: *(holding a skull)*
Here's a fellow gone to dust,
American, Slav or Dane,
He ran for office twice, I trust;
He'll not be running again.

Ronald: This fellow has a gloomy tone. I like not his speech, Horatio.

Horatio: Had I written his speech, it would have been far cheerier.

Ronald: Well said! These European graveyards get me down.

Grave-digger: Having been got down, thou'll never get up again in this place. When a fellow goes to ground here, 'tis underground he stays, for having been ground down. . .

Ronald: OK, I get the point. This fellow's talk is full of gags, Horatio, as if he had a team who wrote them for him.

Grave-digger: *(tossing skull)*
Two hundred-million Russians said,
This man is lord and boss,
But now that he is surely dead,
We account him little loss.

Ronald: To go from world leader to skull in one fell movement, Horatio, this is bitter indeed! I knew a fellow once, from Africa, who was a prince at home, with some strange name like Mary. . .

Horatio: President Nimeiry.

Source: *London Times*, May 3, 1985.

Ronald: Aye, that was him. One moment he was in my house, talking and laughing, a king of the world, the next moment in Cairo airport, sans title, sans land, sans anything . . . I would not like to be deposed in my absence, Horatio.
Horatio: We have people working on that, my lord.
Ronald: Good, good. What do I say next?
Horatio: Whose skull was this?
Ronald: Whose skull was this?
Grave-digger: Why, sir, a hero of the war.
Ronald: A hero of the war? I knew him well! We stormed the heights of Iwo Jima, he and I, brave like two hawks! Up Normandy beaches swam we together, in Africa's sandy deserts fought we well, and went on furlough once in London. . .
Horatio: You were in Hollywood, sir. You knew him not.
Ronald: Why, then, I saw the film!
Grave-digger: I think not so. He was a *German* hero of the war.
Ronald: Oh, was he now? That's different. Horatio, give me a speech. Get me out of this hole.
Grave-digger: Being once in this hole, thou'll never get out, for he who is wholly in this hole. . .
Ronald: Stop thy prating. Here comes old King Kohl.
Enter old King Kohl, with mourners. Kohl speaks.
Soon comes Prince Ronald, with his black suit on.
I wish to God he'd stayed in Washington.
Exit old King Kohl, with mourners, plus TV crews, media folk etc.
Ronald: Alas, I have committed one too many gaffes.
Horatio, where's thy supply of laughs?
Horatio: None good enough to get you off the hook.
It could be said that we are both in schtuck.
Ronald: Oh, cruellest stroke of fate for the US. . .
Grave-digger: To be defeated now by the SS!
Ronald: Yes, well, something like that.
Enter a messenger, bleeding badly. Well, not very well, at least.
Messenger: I come from Nicaragua, my lord,
Where we take arms against the Commie horde.
Ronald: How goes the battle with the Soviet trash?
Messenger: Not well, my lord. We need a lot more cash.
Ronald: OK, you've got it. Here's a billion dollars.
Now go and hit the enemy till he hollers!
Exit Horatio, wondering how he can explain to the world that Prince Ronald is commemorating the last war, not planning the next.

ESSENTIAL
DOCUMENTS

Remarks of President Reagan to Regional Editors, White House, April 18, 1985

. . . Q Regarding the upcoming trip to West Germany, 53 Senators have signed a letter requesting that you drop the trip to the cemetery, and in light of this and waves of other opposition, would it damage German-American relations to seek some other gesture of reconciliation and drop that visit and, secondly, would you say that is was a failure of political analysis to realize the fallout that resulted from the itinerary as it was scheduled?

THE PRESIDENT: . . . Helmut Kohl, sometime ago, back, I guess, when we were celebrating or observing the Normandy landings last June, he and president Mitterand went to a military cemetery together in Verdun. Now, here were the representatives of the two countries that have been at odds for the War of 1870, the First World War, the Second World War. The impact on all of Europe was so great to see them standing together at this ceremony that Helmut Kohl told me about this and told me how deeply he felt about it.

Now, the Summit places us in Bonn in Germany close to the time of the anniversary. And he invited me to accept an invitation to be a state visitor following the Summit meeting. And he suggested to me this visit, as he had done with Mitterand, to a cemetery there. The cemetery that was picked, Bitburg, was picked because at the same time, also, there has been a church service with our military at Bitburg—we have a base there and our Americans—and I'm going there and go to church with them and have lunch with them. And the Kohls will be with us also.

When the invitation to visit a concentration camp was offered, whether it was my confusion or the way in which it was done, I thought that the suggestion had come from an individual and was not a part of the state visit. And I thought there was no way that I, as the guest of the government at that point, could on my own take off and go someplace and, then, run the risk of appearing as if I was trying to say to the Germans, "Look what you did," and all of this when most of the people in Germany today weren't alive or were very small children when this was happening.

And I know the feeling they have. And I know this government that for 40 years—what he'd asked me to do in the cemetery was that we should start this day now, observing this day as the day that 40 years ago the world took a sharp turn, an end to the hatred, an end to the obscenities of the persecution and all that took place. And today, after 40 years of peace, here we are, our staunchest allies in that

Summit are the countries that were our enemies in World War II. Now, their leaders have come here and visited Arlington. They have— leaders from Germany, from Italy, from Japan. And this cemetery— we only found out later, someone dug up the fact that there are about 30 graves of SS troops. These were the villians, as we know, that conducted the persecutions and all. But there are 2,000 graves there. And most of those—the average age is about 18. These were those young teenagers that were conscripted, forced into military service in the closing days of the Third Reich, when they were short of manpower, and we're the victor and they're there. And it seemed to me that this could be symbolic, also, of saying—what I said about the— what this day should be. And let's resolve, in their presence, as well as in the presence of our own troops that this must never happen again.

Well, when the furor erupted and got as far as Germany, Helmut Kohl sent me a cable. And the cable informed me that there was a mistake, that the Dachau was a part of the state itinerary, the planned trip. Well, I immediately communicated and said, "Fine, that's fine with me. If it is you, the government, that is inviting me to do this, I am more than happy to do it because I have said repeatedly, and I would like on that occasion to say again, the Holocaust must never be forgotten by any of us. And in not forgetting it, we should make it clear that we're determined the Holocaust must never take place again. And—

Q Does that mean you're still going to Bitburg?

THE PRESIDENT: I think that it would be very hurtful and all it would do is leave me looking as if I caved in in the face of some unfavorable attention. I think that there's nothing wrong with visiting that cemetery where those young men are victims of Nazism also, even though they were fighting in the German uniform, drafted into service to carry out the hateful wishes of the Nazis. They were victims, just as surely as the victims in the concentration camps. And I feel that there is much to be gained from this, and—in strengthening our relationship with the German people, who, believe me, live in constant penance, all these who have come along in these later years for what their predecessors did, and for which they're very ashamed.

Remarks of Elie Wiesel at Ceremony for Jewish Heritage Week and Presentation of Congressional Gold Medal, White House, April 19, 1985

Mr. President, Mr. Vice President, Secretary Bennett, Mr. Agresto, Mr. Regan, very distinguished members of the Senate, my friends—and of the House—

Mr. President, speaking of reconciliation, I was very pleased that we met before, so a stage of reconciliation has been set in motion between us. But then, we were never on two sides. We were on the same side. We were always on the side of justice, always on the side of memory, against the SS and against what they represent.

It was good talking to you and I'm grateful to you for the medal. But this medal is not mine alone. It belongs to all those who remember what SS killers have done to their victims. It was given to me by the American people for my writings, teaching, and for my testimony.

When I write, I feel my invisible teachers standing over my shoulders, reading my words, and judging their veracity. And while I feel responsible for the living, I feel equally responsible to the dead. Their memory dwells in my memory.

Forty years ago, a young man awoke and he found himself an orphan in an orphaned world. What have I learned in the last 40 years? Small things. I learned the perils of language and those of silence. I learned that in extreme situations when human lives and dignity are at stake, neutrality is a sin. It helps the killers, not the victims.

I learned the meaning of solitude, Mr. President. We were alone, desperately alone. Today is April 19th, and April 19, 1943, the Warsaw Ghetto rose in arms against the onslaught of the Nazis. They were so few and so young and so helpless. And nobody came to their help. And they had to fight what was then the mightiest legion in Europe.

Every Underground received help, except the Jewish Underground. And yet, they managed to fight and resist and push back those Nazis and their accomplices for six weeks.

And yet, the leaders of the free world, Mr. President, knew everything and did so little, or nothing, or at least nothing specifically to save Jewish children from death.

You spoke of Jewish children, Mr. President. One million Jewish children perished. If I spent my entire life reciting their names, I would die before finishing the task.

Mr. President, I have seen children—I have seen them being thrown in the flames alive. Words—they die on my lips.

So I have learned. I have learned, I have learned the fragility of the human condition. And I'm reminded of a great moral essayist—the gentle and forceful Abe Rosenthal, having visited Auschwitz once wrote an extraordinary reportage about the persecution of Jews, and he called it, "Forgive them not Father, for they knew what they did."

I have learned that the Holocaust was a unique, a uniquely Jewish event, albeit with universal implications. Not all victims were Jews, but all Jews were victims. I have learned the danger of indifference, the crime of indifference. For the opposite of love, I have learned, is not hate, but indifference. Jews were killed by the enemy, but betrayed by their so-called allies who found political reasons to justify their indifference or passivity.

But I've also learned that suffering confers no privileges. It all depends what one does with it. And this is why survivors of whom you spoke, Mr. President, have tried to teach their contemporaries how to build on ruins, how to invent hope in a world that offers none, how to proclaim faith to a generation that has seen it shamed and mutilated. And I believe, we believe, that memory is the answer—perhaps the only answer.

A few days ago on the anniversary of the liberation of Buchenwald, all of us Americans watched with dismay and anger as the Soviet Union and East Germany distorted both past and present history. Mr. President, I was there. I was there when American liberators arrived. And they gave us back our lives.

And what I felt for them then nourishes me to the end of my days and will do so. If you only knew what we tried to do with them then, we who were so weak that we couldn't carry our own lives—we tried to carry them in triumph!

Mr. President, we are grateful to the American Army for liberating us. We are grateful to this country—the greatest democracy in the world, the freest nation in the world, the moral nation, the authority in the world. And we are grateful especially to this country for having offered haven and refuge and grateful to its leadership for being so friendly to Israel.

Mr. President, do you know that the Ambassador of Israel, who sits next to you, who is my friend and has been for so many years, is himself a survivor? And if you knew all the causes we fought together for the last 30 years, you could be prouder of him. And we are proud of him.

And we are grateful, of course, to Israel. We are eternally grateful to Israel for existing. We needed Israel in 1948 as we need it now.

And we are grateful to Congress for its continuous philosophy of humanism and compassion for the underprivileged.

And as for yourself, Mr. President, we are so grateful to you for being a friend of the Jewish people, for trying to help the oppressed Jews in the Soviet Union, and to do whatever we can to save Scharansky and Abe Stolyar, and Josef Begun, and Sakharov, and all the dissidents who need freedom. And, of course, we thank you for your support of the Jewish state of Israel.

But, Mr. President, I wouldn't be the person I am, and you wouldn't respect me for what I am, if I were not to tell you also of the sadness that is in my heart for what happened during the last week. And I am sure that you, too, are sad for the same reasons. What can I do? I belong to a traumatized generation. And to us, as to you, symbols are important. And furthermore, following our ancient tradition—and we are speaking about Jewish heritage—our tradition commands us "to speak truth to power."

So may I speak to you, Mr. President, with respect and admiration of the events that happened. We have met four or five times. And each time I came away enriched, for I know of your commitment to humanity. And, therefore, I am convinced, as you have told us earlier when we spoke that you were not aware of the presence of SS graves in the Bitburg cemetery. Of course, you didn't know. But now we all are aware. May I, Mr. President, if it's possible at all, implore you to do something else, to find a way—to find another way, another site. That place, Mr. President, is not your place. Your place is with the victims of the SS.

Oh, we know there are political and strategic reasons. But this issue, as all issues related to that awesome event, transcends politics and diplomacy. The issue here is not politics, but good and evil. And we must never confuse them, for I have seen the SS at work, and I have seen their victims. They were my friends. They were my parents. Mr. President, there was a degree of suffering and loneliness in the concentration camps that defies imagination. Cut off from the world with no refuge anywhere, sons watched helplessly their fathers being beaten to death. Mothers watched their children die of hunger. And then there was Mengele and his selections, terror, fear, isolation, torture, gas chambers, flames, flames rising to the heavens.

But, Mr. President, I know and I understand, we all do, that you seek reconciliation. So do I. So do we. And I, too, wish to attain true reconciliation with the German people. I do not believe in collective guilt, nor in collective responsibility, only the killers were guilty. Their sons and daughters are not. And I believe, Mr. President, that we can and we must work together with them and with all people. And we must work to bring peace and understanding to a tormented world that, as you know, is still awaiting redemption.

I thank you, Mr. President.

Address by Helmut Kohl, Chancellor of the Federal Republic of Germany, during the Ceremony Marking the 40th Anniversary of the Liberation of the Concentration Camps at the Site of the Former Bergen-Belsen Concentration Camp, April 21, 1985

"O earth, cover not thou their blood"—these words, taken from the Book of Job and inscribed on the Jewish memorial over there, have today summoned us here to mourn, to remember, to seek reconciliation. We are gathered here in memory of the many innocent people who were tortured, humiliated and driven to their deaths at Bergen-Belsen, as in other camps. This site's admonition to us must not go unheard or be forgotten. It must be heeded by us as we define our basic political principles and requires each of us to examine his own life and way of thinking in the light of the suffering sustained here. Reconciliation with the survivors and descendants of the victims is only possible if we accept our history as it really was, if we Germans acknowledge our shame and our historical responsibility, and if we perceive the need to act against any efforts aimed at undermining human freedom and dignity.

For twelve years, the light of humanity in Germany and Europe was concealed by ubiquitous violence. Germany under the National Socialist regime filled the world with fear and horror. That era of slaughter, indeed of genocide, is the darkest, most painful chapter in German history. One of our country's paramount tasks is to inform people of those occurrences and keep alive an awareness of the full extent of this historical burden. We must not nor shall we ever forget the atrocities committed under the Hitler regime, the mockery and destruction of all moral precepts, the systematic inhumanity of the Nazi dictatorship. A nation that abandons its history forsakes itself. The presence of history is illustrated in a particularly cogent manner by the survivors of Bergen-Belsen who are here today at the invitation of the Central Jewish Council.

We recall above all the persecution and murder of the Jews, the pitiless war which man, in the final analysis, waged against himself. Bergen-Belsen, a town in the middle of Germany, remains a mark of Cain branded in the minds of our nation, just like Auschwitz and Treblinka, Belzec and Sobibor, Chelmno and Majdanek and the many other sites testifying to that mania for destruction. They epitomize what man can do against his fellow beings out of hatred and blindness. We do not know exactly how many people perished here at Bergen-Belsen. They numbered more than 50,000. But what does this figure tell us about how death befell every individual, his next of kin, his family? Vicariously for them all I name Anne Frank. She was 15 years old when she died here a few days before the liberation of the camp. We do not know exactly how her life was extinguished. But we know what awaited people here, how they were maltreated, what pain they suffered. Their lives, their human dignity were wholly at the mercy of their tormentors.

Despite their own great suffering, many inmates found the strength to stand by others, to turn to their fellow beings and offer them solace and consolation. An old Jewish saying goes: "Whoever saves a human life saves the whole world." A few known and many unknown detainees afforded their fellow beings strength at that time of great agony. We also recall those courageous people who, in their everyday lives under the Nazi dictatorship, gave the persecuted a refuge at the risk of their own lives. They all helped to save our conception of man as God's image on earth.

Forty years ago, Bergen-Belsen was liberated. But for thousands of people in this camp, salvation came too late: too drained were their bodies, too deeply scarred their souls. The National-Socialist despisal of mankind was demonstrated not only in the concentration camps. It was ubiquitous, just as the dictatorship was totalitarian. Violence prevailed everywhere, and everywhere people were shadowed, persecuted and abducted, they were incarcerated, tortured and murdered. They were people from all walks of life, people of many nationalities, faiths and creeds, and with highly different political convictions. From the very outset, the terror of the totalitarian regime was directed against the Jews in particular. Envy and crude prejudice, nurtured over the centuries, culminated in an ideology of manic racism. The mass graves here show us where that led to.

Today, forty years later, it is still our duty to ask ourselves how a culture could disintegrate, to whose development and maturity German Jews in particular made an outstanding contribution. Many of them clearly professed themselves German patriots. Throughout the world they were representatives and ambassadors of German and Western culture. When the forces of evil seized power in Germany, the Jews were deprived of their rights and driven out of the country. The regime officially declared them "subhumans" and condemned them to the "final solution." Those have become Nazi terms in the German language—in the language of Goethe and Lessing, of Immanuel Kant and Edmund Husserl, of Dietrich Bonhoeffer and Leo Baeck. That misanthropic regime also violated our language.

But even before that it poisoned the spirit of the nation. The rulers were the henchmen of anarchy. With their arrogant use of power and their unbridled demands, they blinded the nation and then plunged an entire continent into misery. The deepest cause of this destruction was the accelerating disintegration of values and morals. In the final analysis, the totalitarian State was the product of the re-negation of God. The Nazi regime's hypocritical invocation of "godly providence" merely served to gloss over their own arbitrariness. That was and remains indeed the gravest perversion of religious faith: contempt for the living God professed by the great religions.

This darkest chapter of our history must always serve as a reminder to us, not because of the question of why those who risked their lives in opposing the terror ultimately failed in their efforts. The decisive question is, instead, why so many people remained apathetic, did not listen properly, closed their eyes to the realities when the despots-to-be solicited support for their inhumane programme, first in back rooms and then openly out in the streets. The intentions of the National-Socialists were apparent well before 9 November 1938, when 35,000 Jews were abducted to concentration camps. We ask ourselves today why it was not possible to take action when the signs of National-Socialist tyranny could no longer be overlooked—when books regarded as great cultural works of this century were burned, when synagogues were set on fire, when Jewish shops were demolished, when Jewish citizens were denied a seat on park benches. Those were warnings. Even though Auschwitz was beyond anything that man could imagine, the pitiless brutality of the Nazis had been clearly discernible. At the Barmen Synod in 1934, Hans Asmussen clear-sightedly warned of the designs of the new rulers: "They claim to be redeemers, but prove to be the tormentors of an unredeemed world."

The truth of this utterance is clear to us today. Millions of Jews fell victim to the National-Socialist terror. The horror of this occurrence is still with us today. In view of such depravity, one could use the words of St. Augustine who once said: "To myself I have become a land of misery."

Like the Jews, many other innocent people fell victim to persecution. We cannot separate the ashes of the murdered. Let us here remember those victims, too. The racial hatred of the National-Socialists was also directed against gypsies. In the mass graves before our eyes lie countless Sinti and Romany gypsies. The inscription here at Bergen-Belsen reads: "Their violent death exhorts the living to oppose injustice." We mourn all those who lost their lives under the totalitarian regime because of their unswerving faith—among them many who refused to render military service on religious grounds.

A totalitarian State claims to possess the absolute truth, to be alone in knowing what is good and what is bad. It does not respect the individual's conscience. It seeks to provide its own answers not only to the penultimate questions, those of politics, but also to the final questions, those concerning the meaning and value of our lives. Only in this way could there arise the demonic official dogma that certain lives are not worth living. Only in this way could Mengele and others perform horrifying experiments on living people.

We recall the persecution of the mentally handicapped, of those people who were branded as social outcasts, and of the many others who, for highly different reasons, were slaughtered—some of them simply because they expressed doubts about the so-called final victory.

When this camp was set up, Russian prisoners-of-war were first brought here. Their accommodation and treatment amounted to no less than torture. Over 50,000 died alone in this region around Bergen. This we must also remember today and in the future: Of the almost 6 million Soviet soldiers who were captured by the Germans as prisoners-of-war, far less than half survived. Hence at this hour we also reflect on the suffering inflicted in the name of Germany on the peoples of Central and Eastern Europe. We commemorate the 20 million people from the Soviet Union who died during the war. We remember the crimes perpetrated against the Polish nation. And we also mourn those people who suffered from Nazi injustice being repaid with new injustice, those Germans who fled their home regions and perished during the flight. But we would not have learned anything from history if we were to set off atrocities against each other.

Germany bears historical responsibility for the crimes of the Nazi tyranny. This responsibility is reflected not least in never-ending shame.

We shall not let anything in this context be falsified or made light of. It is precisely the knowledge of guilty involvement, irresponsibility, cowardice and failure that enables us to perceive depravity and nip it in the bud. The totalitarianism that prevailed in Germany from 30 January 1933 onwards is not an unrepeatable deviation from the

straight and narrow, not an "accident of history." An alert and sensitive stance is needed above all towards any views and attitudes that can pave the way for totalitarian rule:
—belief in ideologies which claim to know the goals of history and promise paradise on earth,
—the failure to exercise freedom responsibly, and
—apathy about violations of human dignity, basic rights and the precept of peace.

Peace begins with respect for the unconditional, absolute dignity of the individual in all spheres of life. The suffering and death of people, the victims of inhumanity, urge us to preserve peace and freedom, to promote law and justice, to perceive man's limits and to follow our path in humility before God.

What Konrad Adenauer said here at Bergen-Belsen in February 1960 remains valid: "I believe we could not choose a better place than this one to give a solemn pledge to do our utmost so that every human being—irrespective of the nation or race to which he belongs—enjoys justice, security and freedom on earth in the future."

The collapse of the Nazi dictatorship on 8 May 1945 was a day of liberation for the Germans. It soon became apparent, however, that it did not mean freedom for everyone. We in the free part of our fatherland have, following the experience of Hitler's dictatorship, made it a rule that especially in central political questions man must decide on and for himself. We have established a free republic, a democracy based on the rule of law. The founders of our democratic country perceived and took advantage of the moment which Werner Nachmann spoke of. By possessing the strength to face up to the responsibility imposed by history, they restored for us the value and dignity of freedom that is exercised responsibly. For this reason, we have also linked ourselves irrevocably to the community of free Western democracies based on shared values and entered into a permanent alliance with them. This was only possible because those nations—and not least former concentration camp inmates and the relatives of victims of the Nazi dictatorship—reached out their hands to us in reconciliation. Many of those nations directly experienced Nazi terror in their own country. There was bitter hatred for those who had come to subjugate and maltreat them—hatred which ultimately was directed against the entire German nation. We in the free part of Germany realize what it means, following Auschwitz and Treblinka, to have been taken back into the free Western community. Those nations did so not least with the justified expectation that we will not disown the crimes perpetrated in the name of Germany against the nations of Europe.

Today, forty years later, we continue to acknowledge that historical liability. Precisely because we Germans must never dismiss from our minds that dark era of our history, I am today addressing you and our fellow countrymen as Chancellor of the Federal Republic of Germany. We have learned the lessons of history, especially the history of this century. Human dignity is inviolable. Peace must emanate from German soil.

Our reconciliation and friendship with France is a boon to the Germans and the French, to Europe and the world as a whole. We also wish to attain such a peaceful achievement in our relations with our Polish neighbours.

We are grateful that reconciliation was possible with the Jewish people and the State of Israel, that friendship is again growing particularly among young people. And we respectfully pay tribute to those men and women who, looking to the future, were prepared to surmount the strength of hatred with the force of humanity. We are especially thankful to eminent representatives of the nation of Israel like Nahum Goldmann and David Ben Gurion. We are also grateful to Konrad Adenauer. They all sought reconciliation.

Reparations were paid to secure a homeland for the Jews and to assist the survivors of the Holocaust. However, today we know just as we did then: suffering and death, pain and tears are not susceptible to reparations. The only answer can be collective commemoration, collective mourning, and a collective resolve to live together in a peaceful world.

In his memorial address at the Cologne Synagogue on 9 November 1978, Nahum Goldmann recalled the creative mutual influence of Jews and Germans and spoke of a "unique, historical occurrence." This co-existence of Jews and Germans in particular has a long, eventful history. It has been examined only little until now and is scarcely known to many people. For this reason we intend to promote the establishment of an "Archive for the study of Jewish history in Germany." We want to trace German-Jewish interaction through history. Over many centuries, Jews made decisive contributions to German culture and history. And it is an accomplishment of historical import that, even after 1945, Jewish compatriots were prepared to assist us in building the Federal Republic of Germany. We wish to preserve this memory, too, in order to strengthen our resolve to live together in a better future. It is therefore essential to make it clear to the upcoming generation that tolerance and an open-minded attitude towards one's fellow beings are irreplaceable virtues without which a polity cannot survive. Emulating each other in the quest for humanity is the most pertinent answer to the failure of an era marked by intolerance and the abuse of power. At Yad va-Shem, the words of a Jewish mystic of the early 18th century became firmly impressed upon my mind: "Seeking to forget makes exile all the longer; the secret of redemption lies in remembrance."

For this reason, the exhortation expressed here at Bergen-Belsen rightly is "O earth, cover not thou their blood."

Interview of President Reagan by Representatives of Foreign Radio and Television, White House, April 29, 1985

Q   Mr. President, . . . The controversy over your intended Bitburg cemetery visit is sharpening and it overshadows the economic summit and it spoils your idea of reconciliation. The Congress urge you not to go. The veterans urge you not to go. And the Holocaust victims urge you not to go. And the majority of the American people are against this visit. Mr. President, how does this turmoil of emotions affect you personally and politically, and has the final word been spoken on Bitburg?

THE PRESIDENT: The final word has been spoken, as far as I'm concerned. I think it is morally right to do what I'm doing and I'm not going to change my mind about that.

I don't believe it actually has affected a majority of the people here. As a matter of fact, some of our own people have done polls and surveys and reveal that this is not of that great of concern.

I can understand how some of the people feel because, very frankly, I don't believe that many of your American colleagues—in that sense, I mean in the press—have been quite fair about this. I think they've gotten a hold of something, and like a dog worrying a bone, they're going to keep on chewing on it. But this all came about out of a very sincere desire of Chancellor Kohl and myself to recognize this 40th anniversary of the war's end—and incidentally, it's the 30th anniversary of our relationship as allies in NATO—that shouldn't we look at this and recognize that the unusual thing that has happened, that in these 40 years since the end of that war, the end of that tragedy of the Holocaust, we have become the friends that we are, and use this occasion to make it plain that never again must we find ourselves enemy, and never again must there be anything like the Holocaust.

And if that is what we can bring out of these observances and the trip that has been planned, then I think everything we're doing is very worthwhile.

Q But there have been made mistakes in Bonn and in Washington, and isn't it yours and Chanceller Kohl's obligation to correct these mistakes and solve this crisis?

THE PRESIDENT: I'm not sure that I agree about mistakes. There have been mistakes with regard to information that was given on the various locales. Let me just point out one place in which I think the whole distortion started. And it started with me, perhaps, in answering incompletely a question.

When the invitation came to a state visit—and for the purpose that I've mentioned, because the Chancellor and I had talked about this—that there's no longer, after 40 years, a time when we should be out shooting off fireworks and celebrating a victory or commiserating a victory or a defeat.

This is a time to recognize that after years and years, centuries, indeed, of wars being settled in such a way that they planted the seeds of the next war and left hatreds that grew and grew until there would be another war, that the miracle that has happened, that has brought 40 years of peace and 40 years of alliance, that those countries that were of the axis and the countries of the allies, we're sitting down together in the summit, and do this every year, and we're friends and allies, that this was the thing that we were seeking to do.

But the distortion came when I received what seemed to be a private invitation to go to one of the concentration camps, and I didn't see any way that I, as a guest of the state, and of the government of Germany, could take off on my own and go, and that might then look as if I was trying to do something different than the purpose that we had in mind. And I received a cable from Chancellor Kohl, that no, such a visit to—and it will be Bergen-Belsen—was included in the trip, and I immediately accepted. I thought it was appropriate in that way.

The thing I thought was inappropriate, when it seemed that someone else was asking me to simply step away from the plans that were being made for me as a guest, and go off on my own, and— than that mistake, I think that what has been planned is all in the spirit of recognizing what has been achieved. Your country now has the most democratic government it has ever had in its existence. You are and have been for 30 years one of the principal Allies in the NATO defense for Western Europe and of the United States. And this is what we're seeking to recognize.

But at the same time, I think I'm free to say, just as your own people have said, and that is that we all must never forget what did take place and be pledged to the fact it must never take place again.

Q Mr. President, I'm sorry to insist on that, but the new report published in The New York Times says that some SS buried in Bitburg maybe participated in a massacre in Oradour. Oradour is a village in the South of France. And there were altogether 642 victims. Did you know that? How would you comment on that?

THE PRESIDENT: Yes, I know all the bad things that happened in that war. I was in uniform for four years myself. And, again, all of those—you're asking with reference to people who are in the cemetery—were buried there. Well, I've said to some of my friends about that, all of those in that cemetery have long since met the Supreme Judge of right and wrong. And whatever punishment or justice was needed has been rendered by One who is above us all.

And it isn't going there to honor anyone. It's going there simply to, in that surrounding, more visibly bring to the people an awareness of the great reconciliation that has taken place and, as I've said before—too many times, I guess—the need to remember in the sense of being pledged to never letting it happen again.

Address by Chancellor Helmut Kohl to President Reagan during the Visit to the Former Concentration Camp at Bergen-Belsen, May 5, 1985

Mr. President:

You have come here to pay homage to the victims of National Socialist tyranny. Bergen-Belsen was a place of unimaginable atrocities. It was only one of the many sites testifying to a demonic will to destroy.

At a ceremony here two weeks ago, I, in my capacity as Chancellor of the Federal Republic of Germany, professed our historical responsibility.

You, Mr. President, represent a country which played a decisive part in liberating Europe and ultimately the Germans, too, from Hitler's tyranny. We Germans reverently commemorate the soldiers of your nation who lost their lives in that act of liberation.

We bow in sorrow before the victims of murder and genocide.

The supreme goal of our political efforts is to render impossible any repetition of that systematic destruction of human life and dignity. With their partners and friends, the Americans and Germans therefore stand together as allies in the community of shared values and in the defense alliance in order to safeguard man's absolute and inviolable dignity in conditions of freedom and peace.

Remarks of President Reagan at Bergen-Belsen Concentration Camp, May 5, 1985

Chancellor Kohl and honored guests. This painful walk into the past has done much more than remind us of the war that consumed the European continent. What we have seen makes unforgettably clear that no one of the rest of us can fully understand the enormity of the feelings carried by the victims of these camps.

The survivors carry a memory beyond anything that we can comprehend. The awful evil started by one man, an evil that victimized all the world with its destruction, was uniquely destructive of the millions forced into the grim abyss of these camps.

Here lie people—Jews—whose death was inflicted for no reason other than their very existence. Their pain was borne only because of who they were and because of the God in their prayers. Alongside them lay many Christians—Catholics and Protestants.

For year after year, until that man and his evil were destroyed, hell yawned forth its awful contents. People were brought here for no other purpose but to suffer and die. To go unfed when hungry—uncared for when sick—tortured when the whim struck—and left to have misery consume them when all there was around them was misery.

I'm sure we all share similar first thoughts. And that is: What of the youngsters who died at this dark stalag? All was gone for them forever. Not to feel again the warmth of life's sunshine and promise; not the laughter and the splendid ache of growing up; nor the consoling embrace of a family. Try to think of being young and never having a day without searing emotional and physical pain—desolate, unrelieved pain.

Today, we've been grimly reminded why the commandant of this camp was named, "The Beast of Belsen." Above all, we're struck by the horror of it all—the monstrous, incomprehensible horror. And that's what we've seen, but is what we can never understand as the victims did. Nor with all our compassion can we feel what the survivors feel to this day and what they will feel as long as they live.

What we've felt and are expressing with words cannot convey the suffering that they endured. That is why history will forever brand what happened as the Holocaust.

Here, death ruled. But we've learned something, as well. Because of what happened, we found that death cannot rule forever. And that's why we're here today. We're here because humanity refuses to accept that freedom of the spirit of man can ever be extinguished. We're here to commemorate that life triumphed over the tragedy and the death of the Holocaust—overcame the suffering, the sickness, the testing, and, yes, the gassings.

We're here today to confirm that the horror cannot outlast hope—and that even from the worst of all things, the best may come forth. Therefore, even out of this overwhelming sadness, there must be some purpose. And there is. It comes to us through the transforming love of God.

We learn from the Talmud that, "It was only through suffering that the children of Israel obtained three priceless and coveted gifts: The Torah, the Land of Israel, and the World to Come." Yes, out of this sickness—as crushing and cruel as it was—there was hope for the world as well as for the World to Come. Out of the ashes—hope. And from all the pain—promise.

So much of this is symbolized today by the fact that most of the leadership of free Germany is represented here today. Chancellor Kohl, you and your countrymen have made real the renewal that had to happen. Your nation and the German people have been strong and resolute in your willingness to confront and condemn the acts of a hated regime of the past. This reflects the courage of your people and their devotion to freedom and justice since the war. Think how far we've come from that time when despair made these tragic victims wonder if anything could survive.

As we flew here from Hanover, low over the greening farms and the emerging springtime of the lovely German countryside, I reflected—and there must have been a time when the prisoners at Bergen-Belsen, and those of every other camp, must have felt the springtime was gone forever from their lives. Surely we can understand that when we see what is around us—all these children of God, under bleak and lifeless mounds, the plainness of which does not even hint at the unspeakable acts that created them. Here they lie. Never to hope. Never to pray. Never to love. Never to heal. Never to laugh. Never to cry.

And too many of them knew that this was their fate. But that was not the end. Through it all was their faith and a spirit that moved their faith.

Nothing illustrates this better than the story of a young girl who died here at Bergen-Belsen. For more than two years Anne Frank and her family had hidden from the Nazis in a confined annex in Holland where she kept a remarkably profound diary. Betrayed by an informant, Anne and her family were sent by freight car first to Auschwitz and finally here to Bergen-Belsen.

Just three weeks before her capture, young Anne wrote these words: "It's really a wonder that I haven't dropped all my ideals because they seem so absurd and impossible to carry out. Yet I keep them because in spite of everything I still believe that people are good at heart. I simply can't build up my hopes on a foundation consisting of confusion, misery and death. I see the world gradually being turned into a wilderness. I hear the ever approaching thunder which will destroy us too; I can feel the suffering of millions and yet, if I looked up into the heavens I think that it will all come right, that this cruelty too will end and that peace and tranquility will return again." Eight months later, this sparkling young life ended here at Bergen-Belsen.

Somewhere here lies Anne Frank. Everywhere here are memories—pulling us, touching us, making us understand that they can never be erased. Such memories take us where God intended his children to go—toward learning, toward healing, and, above all, toward redemption. They beckon us through the endless stretches of our heart to the knowing commitment that the life of each individual can change the world and make it better.

We're all witnesses. We share the glistening hope that rests in every human soul. Hope leads us, if we're prepared to trust it, toward what our President Lincoln called, "the better angels of our nature." And then rising above all this cruelty, out of this tragic and nightmarish time, beyond the anguish, the pain and the suffering for all time, we can and must pledge . . .

Never again.

Address by Chancellor Helmut Kohl to German and American Soldiers and Their Families at Bitburg, May 5, 1985

Mr. President,
Members of the U.S. Armed Forces,
Members of the Bundeswehr,
Excellencies,
Ladies and Gentlemen,
Dear American friends,
Fellow Countrymen:

It is not often that the link between the past, present and future of our country reaches us as vividly as during these hours at Bitburg.

A few minutes ago, the President of the United States of America and I paid homage at the military cemetery to the dead buried there and thus to all victims of war and tyranny, to the dead and persecuted of all nations.

Our visit to the soldiers' graves here in Bitburg was not an easy one. It could not but arouse deep feelings. For me it meant first and foremost deep sorrow and grief at the infinite suffering that the war and totalitarianism inflicted on nations, sorrow and grief that will never cease.

Stemming from them is our commitment to peace and freedom as the supreme goal of our political actions. And the visit to the graves in Bitburg is also a reaffirmation and a widely visible and widely felt gesture of reconciliation between our peoples, the people of the United States of America and us Germans, reconciliation which does not dismiss the past but enables us to overcome it by acting together.

Finally, our presence here testifies to our friendship, which has proved to be steadfast and reliable and is based on our belief in shared values.

I thank you, Mr. President, both on behalf of the whole German people, and I thank you very personally as a friend, for visiting the graves with me. I believe that many of our German people understand this expression of deep friendship, and that it presages a good future for our nations.

The town of Bitburg witnessed at first hand the collapse of the Third Reich. It suffered the year 1945. It was part of the reconstruction in the years of reconciliation. For 25 years now, Bitburg has been the site of joint ceremonies in which American, French and German soldiers and citizens of this town and region commemorate the victims of the war and time and again affirm their friendship and their determination to preserve peace jointly. Here close and friendly relations have evolved in a special way in these years between the U.S. Forces and the German population.

Bitburg can be regarded as a symbol of reconciliation and of German American friendship.

Members of the Bundeswehr, most of you have been born since May 8, 1945, you have not yourselves experienced the war and tyranny in this country, you grew up in the years in which we built our republic, at a time when friendship re-emerged and developed between us and the American nation. You got to know our American friends as helpers, as partners and allies.

Days like this are a suitable way of reminding our people's young generation in particular that this development—so favorable for us—was not a matter of course and that the preservation of peace and freedom requires our very personal dedication.

You, the members of the U.S. forces in the Federal Republic of Germany, serve your country, the United States of America, and our republic alike.

The security of the Federal Republic of Germany is closely linked to the partnership and friendship of the United States of America. We know what we owe you and your families. We also know that serving overseas means sacrifice for many of you. Let me assure you that you are welcome guests in our country, in the Federal Republic of Germany. Do not let a small and insignificant minority give you a different impression. We sincerely welcome you here as friends, as allies, as guarantors of our security.

Relations have developed over many years between the U.S. armed forces and the Bundeswehr and are closer than ever before. I should like to thank you, the American and German soldiers, for this partnership we now almost take for granted. It strengthens our joint determination to defend the peace and freedom of our nations, and this partnership—as I wish expressly to state here at Bitburg—thus is a source of mutual understanding of our peoples, generating many personal friendships.

I wish the members of the U.S. forces, I wish our soldiers of the Federal Armed Forces, I wish for us all that together we make our contribution to the peace and freedom of our country and of the world—and may God's blessing be with us.

Remarks of President Reagan at
Bitburg Air Base, May 5, 1985

Thank you very much. I have just come from the cemetery where German war dead lay at rest. No one could visit there without deep and conflicting emotions. I felt great sadness that history could be filled with such waste, destruction and evil. But my heart was also lifted by the knowledge that from the ashes has come hope and that from the terrors of the past we have built 40 years of peace, freedom, and reconciliation among our nations.

This visit has stirred many emotions in the American and German people, too. I've received many letters since first deciding to come to Bitburg cemetery; some supportive, others deeply concerned and questioning, and others opposed. Some old wounds have been re-opened, and this I regret very much because this should be a time of healing.

To the veterans and families of American servicemen who still carry the scars and feel the painful losses of that war, our gesture of reconciliation with the German people today in no way minimizes our love and honor for those who fought and died for our country. They gave their lives to rescue freedom in its darkest hour. The alliance of democratic nations that guards the freedom of millions in Europe and America today stands as living testimony that their noble sacrifice was not in vain.

No, their sacrifice was not in vain. I have to tell you that nothing will ever fill me with greater hope than the sight of two former war heroes who met today at the Bitburg ceremony; each among the brav-est of the brave; each an enemy of the other 40 years ago; each a witness to the horrors of war. But today, they came together, Amer-ican and German, General Matthew B. Ridgway and General Johan-nes Steinhoff reconciled and united for freedom. They reached over the graves to one another like brothers and grasped their hands in peace.

To the survivors of the Holocaust: your terrible suffering has made you ever vigilant against evil. Many of you are worried that reconciliation means forgetting. Well, I promise you, we will never forget. I have just come this morning from Bergen-Belsen where the horror of that terrible crime, the Holocaust, was forever burned upon my memory. No, we will never forget, and we say with the victims of that Holocaust: "Never again."

The war against one man's totalitarian dictatorship was not like other wars. The evil war of Nazism turned all values upside down. Nevertheless, we can mourn the German war dead today as human beings, crushed by a vicious ideology.

There are over 2,000 buried in Bitburg cemetery. Among them are 48 members of the SS. The crimes of the SS must rank among the most heinous in human history. But others buried there were simply soldiers in the German army. How many were fanatical followers of a dictator and willfully carried out his cruel orders? And how many were conscripts, forced into service during the death throes of the Nazi war machine? We do not know. Many, however, we know from the dates on their tombstones, were only teenagers at the time. There is one boy buried there who died a week before his 16th birthday.

There were thousands of such soldiers to whom Nazism meant no more than a brutal end to a short life. We do not believe in collective guilt. Only God can look into the human heart and all these men have now met their Supreme Judge and they have been judged by Him as we shall all be judged.

Our duty today is to mourn the human wreckage of totalitarianism and today in Bitburg cemetery we commemorated the potential good in humanity that was consumed back then, 40 years ago. Perhaps if that 15 year old soldier had lived, he would have joined his fellow countrymen in building this new Democratic Federal Republic of Germany devoted to human dignity and the defense of freedom that we celebrate today. Or perhaps his children, or his grandchildren might be among you here today at the Bitburg Air Base where new generations of Germans and Americans join together in friendship and common cause, dedicating their lives to preserving peace and guarding the security of the free world.

Too often in the past each war only planted the seeds of the next. We celebrate today the reconciliation between our two nations that has liberated us from that cycle of destruction. Look at what together we've accomplished. We who were enemies are now friends; we who were bitter adversaries are now the strongest of allies. In the place of fear we've sown trust, and out of the ruins of war has blossomed an enduring peace. Tens of thousands of Americans have served in this town over the years. As the Mayor of Bitburg has said, in that time, there have been some 6,000 marriages between Germans and Americans, and many thousands of children have come from these unions. This is the real symbol of our future together, a future to be filled with hope, friendship, and freedom.

The hope that we see now could sometimes even be glimpsed in the darkest days of the War. I'm thinking of one special story—that of a mother and her young son living alone in a modest cottage in the middle of the woods. And one night as the Battle of the Bulge exploded not far away, and around them, three young American soldiers arrived at their door—they were standing there in the snow, lost behind enemy lines. All were frostbitten, one was badly wounded. Even though sheltering the enemy was punishable by death, she took them in and made them a supper with some of her last food.

And then, they heard another knock at the door. And this time four German soldiers stood there. The woman was afraid, but she quickly said with a firm voice, ". . . there will be no shooting here." She made all the soldiers lay down their weapons, and they all joined in the makeshift meal. Heinz and Willi, it turned out, were only 16; the corporal was the oldest at 23. Their natural suspicion dissolved in the warmth and the comfort of the cottage. One of the Germans, a former medical student, tended the wounded American.

But now, listen to the rest of the story through the eyes of one who was there, now a grown man, but that young lad that had been her son. He said, "The Mother said grace. I noticed that there were tears in her eyes as she said the old, familiar words, 'Komm, Herr Jesus. Be our guest.' And as I looked around the table, I saw tears, too, in the eyes of the battle-weary soldiers, boys again, some from America, some from Germany, all far from home."

That night—as the storm of war tossed the world—they had their own private armistice. The next morning the German corporal showed the Americans how to get back behind their own lines. And they all shook hands and went their separate ways. That happened to be Christmas Day, 40 years ago.

Those boys reconciled briefly in the midst of war. Surely, we allies in peacetime should honor the reconciliation of the last 40 years.

To the people of Bitburg, our hosts and the hosts of our servicemen, like that generous woman forty years ago, you make us feel very welcome. Vielen Dank.

And to the men and women of Bitburg Air Base, I just want to say that we know that even with such wonderful hosts, your job is not an easy one. You serve around the clock far from home, always ready to defend freedom. We are grateful and we are very proud of you.

Four decades ago we waged a great war to lift the darkness of evil from the world, to let men and women in this country and in every country live in the sunshine of liberty. Our victory was great and the Federal Republic, Italy and Japan are now in the community of free nations. But the struggle for freedom is not complete, for today much of the world is still cast in totalitarian darkness.

Twenty-two years ago President John F. Kennedy went to the

Berlin Wall and proclaimed that he, too, was a Berliner. Well, today freedom-loving people around the world must say, I am a Berliner, I am a Jew in a world still threatened by anti-Semitism, I am an Afghan, and I am a prisoner of the Gulag, I am a refugee in a crowded boat foundering off of the coast of Vietnam, I am a Laotian, a Cambodian, a Cuban, and a Miskito Indian in Nicaragua. I, too, am a potential victim of totalitarianism.

The one lesson of World War II, the one lesson of Nazism, is that freedom must always be stronger than totalitarianism and that good must always be stronger than evil. The moral measure of our two nations will be found in the resolve we show to preserve liberty, to protect life, and to honor and cherish all God's children.

That is why the free, democratic Federal Republic of Germany is such a profound and hopeful testament to the human spirit. We cannot undo the crimes and wars of yesterday, nor call the millions back to life, but we can give meaning to the past by learning its lessons and making a better future. We can let our pain drive us to greater efforts to heal humanity's suffering.

Today I have traveled 220 miles from Bergen-Belsen, and, I feel, forty years in time. With the lessons of the past firmly in our minds, we have turned a new, brighter page in history.

One of the many who wrote me about this visit was a young woman who had recently been Bat Mitzvahed. She urged me to lay the wreath at Bitburg Cemetery in honor of the future of Germany. And that is what we've done.

On this 40th anniversary of World War II, we mark the day when the hate, the evil and the obscenity is ended and we commemorate the rekindling of the democratic spirit in Germany.

There's much to make us hopeful on this historic anniversary. One of the symbols of that hate—that could have been that hope, a little while ago, when we heard a German band playing the American national anthem and an American band playing the German national anthem. While much of the world still huddles in the darkness of oppression, we can see a new dawn of freedom sweeping the globe. And we can see in the new democracies of Latin America, in the new economic freedoms and prosperity in Asia, in the slow movement toward peace in the Middle East and in the strengthening alliance of democratic nations in Europe and America that the light from that dawn is growing stronger.

Together, let us gather in that light and walk out of the shadow. Let us live in peace.

Thank you, and God bless you all.

Speech by Richard von Weizsäcker, President of the Federal Republic of Germany, in the Bundestag during the Ceremony Commemorating the 40th Anniversary of the End of the War in Europe and of National Socialist Tyranny, May 8, 1985

I

Many nations are today commemorating the date on which World War II ended in Europe. Every nation is doing so with different feelings, depending on its fate. Be it victory or defeat, liberation from injustice and alien rule or transition to new dependence, division, new alliances, vast shifts of power—May 8, 1945, is a date of decisive historical importance for Europe.

We Germans are commemorating that date amongst ourselves, as is indeed necessary. We must find our own standards. We are not assisted in this task if we or others spare our feelings. We need and we have the strength to look truth straight in the eye—without embellishment and without distortion.

For us, the 8th of May is above all a date to remember what people had to suffer. It is also a date to reflect on the course taken by our history. The greater honesty we show in commemorating this day, the freer we are to face the consequences with due responsibility. For us Germans, May 8 is not a day of celebration. Those who actually witnessed that day in 1945 think back on highly personal and hence highly different experiences. Some returned home, others lost their homes. Some were liberated, while for others it was the start of captivity. Many were simply grateful that the bombing at night and fear had passed and that they had survived. Others felt first and foremost grief at the complete defeat suffered by their country. Some Germans felt bitterness about their shattered illusions, while others were grateful for the gift of a new start.

It was difficult to find one's bearings straightaway. Uncertainty prevailed throughout the country. The military capitulation was unconditional, placing our destiny in the hands of our enemies. The past had been terrible, especially for many of those enemies, too. Would they not make us pay many times over for what we had done to them? Most Germans had believed that they were fighting and suffering for the good of their country. And now it turned out that their efforts were not only in vain and futile, but had served the inhuman goals of a criminal regime. The feelings of most people were those of exhaustion, despair and new anxiety. Had one's next of kin survived? Did a new start from those ruins make sense at all? Looking back, they saw the dark abyss of the past and, looking forward, they saw an uncertain, dark future.

Yet with every day something became clearer, and this must be stated on behalf of all of us today: The 8th of May was a day of liberation. It liberated all of us from the inhumanity and tyranny of the National Socialist regime.

Nobody will, because of that liberation, forget the grave suffering that only started for many people on May 8. But we must not regard the end of the war as the cause of flight, expulsion and deprivation of freedom. The cause goes back to the start of the tyranny that brought about war. We must not separate May 8, 1945, from January 30, 1933.

There is truly no reason for us today to participate in victory celebrations. But there is every reason for us to perceive May 8, 1945, as the end of an aberration in German history, an end bearing seeds of hope for a better future.

II

May 8 is a day of remembrance. Remembering means recalling an occurrence honestly and undistortedly so that it becomes a part of our very beings. This places high demands on our truthfulness.

Today we mourn all the dead of the war and the tyranny. In particular we commemorate the six million Jews who were murdered in German concentration camps. We commemorate all nations who suffered in the war, especially the countless citizens of the Soviet Union and Poland who lost their lives. As Germans, we mourn our own compatriots who perished as soldiers, during air raids at home, in captivity or during expulsion. We commemorate the Sinti and Romany Gypsies, the homosexuals and the mentally ill who were killed, as well as the people who had to die for their religious or political beliefs. We commemorate the hostages who were executed. We recall the victims of the resistance movements in all the countries occupied by us. As Germans, we pay homage to the victims of the German resistance—among the public, the military, the churches, the workers and trade unions, and the Communists. We commemorate those who did not actively resist, but preferred to die instead of violating their consciences.

Alongside the endless army of the dead, mountains of human suffering arise—grief over the dead, suffering from injury or crippling or barbarous compulsory sterilization, suffering during the air raids, during flight and expulsion, suffering because of rape and pillage, forced labor, injustice and torture, hunger and hardship, suffering because of fear of arrest and death, grief at the loss of everything which one had wrongly believed in and worked for. Today we sorrowfully recall all this human suffering.

Perhaps the greatest burden was borne by the women of all nations. Their suffering, renunciation and silent strength are all too easily forgotten by history. Filled with fear, they worked, bore human life and protected it.They mourned their fallen fathers and sons, husbands, brothers and friends. In the years of darkness, they ensured that the light of humanity was not extinguished. After the war, with no prospect of a secure future, women everywhere were the first to set about building homes again, the "rubble women" in Berlin and elsewhere. When the men who had survived returned, women had to take a back seat again. Because of the war, many women were left alone and spent their lives in solitude. Yet it is first and foremost thanks to the women that nations did not disintegrate spiritually on account of the destruction, devastation, atrocities and inhumanity and that they gradually regained their foothold after the war.

III

At the root of the tyranny was Hitler's immeasurable hatred against our Jewish compatriots. Hitler had never concealed this hatred from the public, but made the entire nation a tool of it. Only a day before his death, on April 30, 1945, he concluded his so-called will with the words: "Above all, I call upon the leaders of the nation and their followers to observe painstakingly the race laws and to oppose ruthlessly the poisoners of all nations: international Jewry." Hardly any country has in its history always remained free from blame for war or violence. The genocide of the Jews is, however, unparalleled in history.

The perpetration of this crime was in the hands of a few people. It was concealed from the eyes of the public, but every German was able to experience what his Jewish compatriots had to suffer, ranging from plain apathy and hidden intolerance to outright hatred. Who could remain unsuspecting after the burning of the synagogues, the plundering, the stigmatization with the Star of David, the deprivation of rights, the ceaseless violation of human dignity? Whoever opened his eyes and ears and sought information could not fail to notice that Jews were being deported. The nature and scope of the destruction may have exceeded human imagination, but in reality there was, apart from the crime itself, the attempt by too many people, including those of my generation, who were young and were not involved in planning the events and carrying them out, not to take note of what was happening. There were many ways of not burdening one's conscience, of shunning responsibility, looking away, keeping mum. When the unspeakable truth of the holocaust then became known at the end of the war, all too many of us claimed that they had not known anything about it or even suspected anything.

There is no such thing as the guilt or innocence of an entire nation. Guilt is, like innocence, not collective, but personal. There is discovered or concealed individual guilt. There is guilt which people acknowledge or deny. Everyone who directly experienced that era should today quietly ask himself about his involvement then.

The vast majority of today's population were either children then or had not been born. They cannot profess a guilt of their own for crimes that they did not commit. No discerning person can expect them to wear a penitential robe simply because they are Germans. But their forefathers have left them a grave legacy. All of us, whether guilty or not, whether old or young, must accept the past. We are all affected by its consequences and liable for it. The young and old generations must and can help each other to understand why it is vital to keep alive the memories. It is not a case of coming to terms with the past. That is not possible. It cannot be subsequently modified or made not to have happened. However, anyone who closes his eyes to the past is blind to the present. Whoever refuses to remember the inhumanity is prone to new risks of infection.

The Jewish nation remembers and will always remember. We seek reconciliation. Precisely for this reason we must understand that there can be no reconciliation without remembrance. The experience of millionfold death is part of the very being of every Jew in the world, not only because people cannot forget such atrocities, but also because remembrance is part of the Jewish faith.

"Seeking to forget makes exile all the longer. The secret of redemption lies in remembrance." This oft-quoted Jewish adage surely expresses the idea that faith in God is faith in the work of God in history. Remembrance is experience of the work of God in history.

It is the source of faith in redemption. This experience creates hope, creates faith in redemption, in reunification of the divided, in reconciliation. Whoever forgets this experience loses his faith.

If we for our part sought to forget what has occurred, instead of remembering it, this would not only be inhuman. We would also impinge upon the faith of the Jews who survived and destroy the basis of reconciliation. We must erect a memorial to thoughts and feelings in our own hearts.

IV

The 8th of May marks a deep cut not only in German history but in the history of Europe as a whole. The European civil war had come to an end, the old world of Europe lay in ruins. "Europe had fought itself to a standstill" (M. Stürmer). The meeting of American and Soviet Russian soldiers on the Elbe became a symbol for the temporary end of a European era.

True, all this was deeply rooted in history. For a century Europe had suffered under the clash of extreme nationalistic aspirations. At the end of the First World War peace treaties were signed but they lacked the power to foster peace. Once more nationalistic passions flared up and were fanned by the distress of the people at that time.

Along the road to disaster Hitler became the driving force. He whipped up and exploited mass hysteria. A weak democracy was incapable of stopping him. And even the powers of Western Europe—in Churchill's judgment unsuspecting but not without guilt—contributed through their weakness to this fateful trend. After the First World War America had withdrawn and in the thirties had no influence on Europe.

Hitler wanted to dominate Europe and to do so through war. He looked for and found an excuse in Poland. On May 23, 1939, he told the German generals: "No further successes can be gained without bloodshed. . . . Danzig is not the objective. Our aim is to extend our Lebensraum in the East and safeguard food supplies . . . so there is no question of sparing Poland. And there remains the decision to attack Poland at the first suitable opportunity . . . the object is to deliver the enemy a blow, or the annihilating blow, at the start. In this, law, injustice or treaties do not matter."

On August 23, 1939, Germany and the Soviet Union signed a non-aggression pact. The secret supplementary protocol made provision for the impending partition of Poland. That pact was made to give Hitler an opportunity to invade Poland. The Soviet leaders at the time were fully aware of this. And all who understood politics realized that the implications of the German-Soviet pact were Hitler's invasion of Poland and hence the Second World War.

That does not mitigate Germany's responsibility for the outbreak of the Second World War. The Soviet Union was prepared to allow other nations to fight one another so that it could have a share of the spoils. The initiative for the war, however, came from Germany, not from the Soviet Union. It was Hitler who resorted to the use of force. The outbreak of the Second World War remains linked with the name of Germany.

In the course of that war the Nazi regime tormented and defiled many nations. At the end of it all only one nation remained to be tormented, enslaved and defiled: the German nation. Time and again Hitler had declared that if the German nation was not capable of winning the war it should be left to perish. The other nations first became victims of a war started by Germany before we became the victims of our own war.

The division of Germany into zones began on May 8. In the meantime the Soviet Union had taken control in all countries of Eastern and South Eastern Europe that had been occupied by Germany during the war. All of them, with the exception of Greece, became socialist states. The division of Europe into two different political systems took its course. True, it was the postwar developments which cemented that division, but without the war started by Hitler it would not have happened at all. That is what first comes to the minds of the nations concerned when they recall the war unleashed by the German leaders. And we think of that too when we ponder the division of our own country and the loss of huge sections of German territory. In a sermon in East Berlin commemorating the 8th of May, Cardinal Meissner said: "the pathetic result of sin is always division."

V

The arbitrariness of destruction continued to be felt in the arbitrary distribution of burdens. There were innocent people who were persecuted and guilty ones who got away. Some were lucky to be able to begin life all over again at home in familiar surroundings. Others were expelled from the lands of their fathers. We in what was to become the Federal Republic of Germany were given the priceless opportunity to live in freedom. Many millions of our countrymen have been denied that opportunity to this day.

Learning to accept mentally this arbitrary allocation of fate was the first task, alongside the material task of rebuilding the country. That had to be the test of the human strength to recognize the burdens of others, to help bear them over time, not to forget them. It had to be the test of our ability to work for peace, of our willingness to foster the spirit of reconciliation both at home and in our external relations, an ability and a readiness which not only others expected of us but which we most of all demanded of ourselves.

We cannot commemorate the 8th of May without being conscious of the great effort required on the part of our former enemies to set out on the road of reconciliation with us. Can we really place ourselves in the position of relatives of the victims of the Warsaw Ghetto or of the Lidice massacre? And how hard must it have been for the citizens of Rotterdam or London to support the rebuilding of our country from where the bombs came which not long before had been dropped on their cities? To be able to do so they had gradually to gain the assurance that the Germans would not again try to make good their defeat by use of force.

In our country the biggest sacrifice was demanded of those who had been driven out of their homeland. They were to experience suffering and injustice long after the 8th of May. Those of us who were born here often do not have the imagination or the open heart with which to grasp the real meaning of their harsh fate.

But soon there were great signs of readiness to help. Many millions of refugees and expellees were taken in who over the years were able to strike new roots. Their children and grandchildren have in many different ways formed a loving attachment to the culture and the homeland of their ancestors. That is a great treasure in their lives. But they themselves have found a new home where they are growing up and integrating with the local people of the same age, sharing their dialect and their customs. Their young life is proof of their ability to be at peace with themselves. Their grandparents or parents were once driven out. They themselves, however, are now at home.

Very soon and in exemplary fashion the expellees identified themselves with the renunciation of force. That was no passing declaration in the early stages of helplessness but a commitment which has retained its validity. Renouncing the use of force means allowing trust to grow on all sides. It means that a Germany that has regained its strength remains bound by it. The expellees' own homeland has meanwhile become a homeland for others. In many of the old cemeteries in Eastern Europe you will today find more Polish than German graves. The compulsory migration of millions of Germans to the West was followed by the migration of millions of Poles and, in their wake, millions of Russians. These are all people who were not asked, people who suffered injustice, people who became defenseless objects of political events and to whom no compensation for those injustices and no offsetting of claims can make up for what has been done to them.

Renouncing force today means giving them lasting security, unchallenged on political grounds, for their future in the place where fate drove them after the 8th of May and where they have been living in the decades since. It means placing the dictate of understanding above conflicting legal claims. That is the true, the human contribution to a peaceful order in Europe which we can provide.

The new beginning in Europe after 1945 has brought both victory and defeat for the notion of freedom and self-determination. Our aim is to seize the opportunity to draw a line under a long period of European history in which to every country peace seemed conceivable and safe only as a result of its own supremacy, and in which peace meant a period of preparation for the next war.

The peoples of Europe love their homelands. The Germans are no different. Who could trust in a people's love of peace if it were capable of forgetting its homeland? No, love of peace manifests itself precisely in the fact that one does not forget one's homeland and is for that very reason resolved to do everything in one's power to live together with others in lasting peace. An expellee's love for his homeland is in no way revanchism.

VI

The last war has aroused a stronger desire for peace in the hearts of men than in times past. The work of the churches in promoting reconciliation met with a tremendous response. The "Aktion Sühnezeichen," a campaign in which young people carry out atonement activity in Poland and Israel, is one example of such practical efforts to promote understanding. Recently, the town of Kleve on the Lower Rhine received loaves of bread from Polish towns as a token of reconciliation and fellowship. The town council sent one of those loaves to a teacher in England because he had discarded his anonymity and written to say that as a member of a bomber crew during the war he had destroyed the church and houses in Kleve and wanted to take part in some gesture of reconciliation. In seeking peace it is a tremendous help if, instead of waiting for the other to come to us, we go towards him, as this man did.

VII

In the wake of the war, old enemies were brought closer together. As early as 1946, the American Secretary of State, James F. Byrnes, called in his memorable Stuttgart address for understanding in Europe and for assistance to the German nation on its way to a free and peaceable future. Innumerable Americans assisted us Germans, who had lost the war, with their own private means so as to heal the wounds of war. Thanks to the vision of the Frenchmen Jean Monnet and Robert Schuman and their cooperation with Konrad Adenauer, the traditional enmity between the French and Germans was buried forever.

A new will and energy to reconstruct Germany surged through the country. Many an old trench was filled in, religious differences and social strains were defused. People set to work in a spirit of partnership.

There was no "zero hour," but we had the opportunity to make a fresh start. We have used this opportunity as well as we could.

We have put democratic freedom in the place of oppression. Four years after the end of the war, on this May 8, in 1949, the Parliamentary Council adopted our Basic Law. Transcending party differences, the democrats on the council gave their answer to war and tyranny an Article 1 of our constitution: "The German people acknowledge inviolable and inalienable human rights as the basis of any community, of peace and of justice in the world." This further significance of May 8 should also be remembered today.

The Federal Republic of Germany has become an internationally respected state. It is one of the most highly developed industrial countries in the world. It knows that its economic strength commits it to share responsibility for the struggle against hunger and need in the world and for social adjustment between nations. For 40 years we have been living in peace and freedom, to which we, through our policy in union with the free nations of the Atlantic alliance and the European Community, have ourselves rendered a major contribution. The freedom of the individual has never received better protection in Germany than it does today. A comprehensive system of social welfare that can stand comparison with any other ensures the subsistence of the population. Whereas at the end of the war many Germans tried to hide their passports or to exchange them for another one, German nationality today is highly valued.

We certainly have no reason to be arrogant and self-righteous. But we may look back with gratitude on our development over these

40 years, if we use the memory of our own history as a guideline for our future behavior.

—If we remember that mentally disturbed persons were put to death in the Third Reich, we will see care of people with psychiatric disorders as our own responsibility.

—If we remember how people persecuted on grounds of race, religion and politics and threatened with certain death often stood before the closed borders with other countries, we shall not close the door today on those who are genuinely persecuted and seek protection with us.

—If we reflect on the penalties for free thinking under the dictatorship, we will protect the freedom of every idea and every criticism, however much it may be directed against ourselves.

—Whoever criticizes the situation in the Middle East should think of the fate to which Germans condemned their Jewish fellow human beings, a fate that led to the establishment of the state of Israel under conditions which continue to burden people in that region even today.

—If we think of what our Eastern neighbors had to suffer during the war, we will find it easier to understand that accommodation and peaceful neighborly relations with these countries remain central tasks of German foreign policy. It is important that both sides remember and that both sides respect each other. Mikhail Gorbachev, General Secretary of the Soviet Communist Party, declared that it was not the intention of the Soviet leaders at the 40th anniversary of the end of the war to stir up anti-German feelings. The Soviet Union, he said, was committed to friendship between nations. Particularly if we have doubts about Soviet contributions to understanding between East and West and about respect for human rights in all parts of Europe, we must not ignore this signal from Moscow. We seek friendship with the peoples of the Soviet Union.

VIII

Forty years after the end of the war, the German nation remains divided.

At a commemorative service in the Church of the Holy Cross in Dresden held in February of this year, Bishop Hempel said: "It is a burden and a scourge that two German states have emerged with their harsh border. The very multitude of borders is a burden and a scourge. Weapons are a burden."

Recently in Baltimore in the United States, an exhibition on "Jews in Germany" was opened. The ambassadors of both German states accepted the invitation to attend. The host, the President of the Johns Hopkins University, welcomed them together. He stated that all Germans share the same historical development. Their joint past is a bond that links them. Such a bond, he said, could be a blessing or a problem, but was always a source of hope.

We Germans are one people and one nation. We feel that we belong together because have lived through the same past. We also experienced the 8th of May 1945 as part of the common fate of our nation, which unites us. We feel bound together in our desire for peace. Peace and good neighborly relations with all countries should radiate from the German soil in both states. And no other states should let that soil become a source of danger to peace, either. The people of Germany are united in desiring a peace that encompasses justice and human rights for all peoples, including our own. Reconciliation that transcends boundaries cannot be provided by a walled Europe but only by a continent that removes the divisive elements from its borders. That is the exhortation given us by the end of the Second World War. We are confident that the 8th of May is not the last date in the common history of all Germans.

IX

Many young people have in recent months asked themselves and us why such animated discussions about the past have arisen 40 years after the end of the war. Why are they more animated than after 25 or 30 years? What is the inherent necessity of this development?

It is not easy to answer such questions. But we should not seek the reasons primarily in external influences. In the life span of men and in the destiny of nations, 40 years play a great role. Permit me at this point to return again to the Old Testament, which contains deep insights for every person, irrespective of his own faith. There, 40 years frequently play a vital part. The Israelites were to remain in the desert for 40 years before a new stage in their history began with their arrival in the Promised Land. 40 years were required for a complete transfer of responsibility from the generation of the fathers.

Elsewhere, too (in the Book of Judges), it is described how often the memory of experienced assistance and rescue lasted only for 40 years. When their memory faded, tranquility was at an end. Forty years invariably constitute a significant time span. Man perceives them as the end of a dark age bringing hope for a new and prosperous future, or as the onset of danger that the past might be forgotten and a warning of the consequences. It is worth reflecting on both of these perceptions.

In our country, a new generation has grown up to assume political responsibility. Our young people are not responsible for what happened over 40 years ago. But they are responsible for the historical consequences.

We in the older generation owe to young people not the fulfillment of dreams but honesty. We must help younger people to understand why it is vital to keep memories alive. We want to help them to accept historical truth soberly, not one-sidedly, without taking refuge in utopian doctrines, but also without moral arrogance. From our own history we learn what man is capable of. For that reason we must not imagine that we are quite different and have become better. There is no ultimately achievable moral perfection. We have learned as human beings, and as human beings we remain in danger. But we have the strength to overcome such danger again and again.

Hitler's constant approach was to stir up prejudices, enmity and hatred. What is asked of young people today is this: do not let yourselves be forced into enmity and hatred of other people, of Russians or Americans, Jews or Turks, of alternatives or conservatives, blacks or whites.

Let us honor freedom.

Let us work for peace.

Let us respect the rule of law.

Let us be true to our own conception of justice.

On this 8th of May, let us face up as well as we can to the truth.

Appendix: Definition of the SS as a "Criminal Organization"

Article 9 of the Charter [of the International Military Tribunal] provides: "At the trial of any individual member of any group or organization the Tribunal may declare (in connection with any act of which the individual may be convicted) that the group or organization of which the individual was a member was a criminal organization." . . .

SOURCE: "Judgment, 30 September–1 October, 1946," in *Trial of the Major War Criminals before the International Military Tribunal, Nuremberg, 1945–1946*, Official Text in the English Language, vol. 1, pp. 255–73.

... A member of an organization which the Tribunal has declared to be criminal may be subsequently convicted of the crime of membership and be punished for that crime by death. This is not to assume that international or military courts which will try these individuals will not exercise appropriate standards of justice. This is a far reaching and novel procedure. Its application, unless properly safeguarded, may produce great injustice.

Article 9, it should be noted, uses the words "The Tribunal may declare," so that the Tribunal is vested with discretion as to whether it will declare any organization criminal. This discretion is a judicial one and does not permit arbitrary action, but should be exercised in accordance with well-settled legal principles, one of the most important of which is that criminal guilt is personal, and that mass punishments should be avoided. If satisfied of the criminal guilt of any organization or group, this Tribunal should not hesitate to declare it to be criminal because the theory of "group criminality" is new, or because it might be unjustly applied by some subsequent tribunals. On the other hand, the Tribunal should make such declaration of criminality so far as possible in a manner to insure that innocent persons will not be punished.

A criminal organization is analogous to a criminal conspiracy in that the essence of both is cooperation for criminal purposes. There must be a group bound together and organized for a common purpose. The group must be formed or used in connection with the commission of crimes denounced by the Charter. Since the declaration with respect to the organizations and groups will, as has been pointed out, fix the criminality of its members, that definition should exclude persons who had no knowledge of the criminal purposes or acts of the organization and those who were drafted by the State for membership, unless they were personally implicated in the commission of acts declared criminal by Article 6 of the Charter as members of the organization. Membership alone is not enough to come within the scope of these declarations.

SS

Structure and Component Parts: The Prosecution has named Die Schutzstaffeln der Nationalsozialistischen Deutschen Arbeiterpartei (commonly known as the SS) as an organization which should be declared criminal. The portion of the Indictment dealing with the SS also includes Der Sicherheitsdienst des Reichsführer-SS (commonly known as the SD). This latter organization, which was originally an intelligence branch of the SS, later became an important part of the organization of Security Police and SD and is dealt with in the Tribunal's Judgment on the Gestapo.

The SS was originally established by Hitler in 1925 as an elite section of the SA for political purposes under the pretext of protecting speakers at public meetings of the Nazi Party. After the Nazis had obtained power the SS was used to maintain order and control audiences at mass demonstrations and was given the additional duty of "internal security" by a decree of the Führer. The SS played an important role at the time of the Röhm purge of 30 June 1934, and, as a reward for its services, was made an independent unit of the Nazi Party shortly thereafter.

In 1929 when Himmler was first appointed as Reichs Führer the SS consisted of 280 men who were regarded as especially trustworthy. In 1933 it was composed of 52,000 men drawn from all walks of life. The original formation of the SS was the Allgemeine SS, which by 1939 had grown to a corps of 240,000 men, organized on military lines into divisions and regiments. During the war its strength declined to well under 40,000.

The SS originally contained two other formations, the SS Verfügungstruppe, a force consisting of SS members who volunteered for four years' armed service in lieu of compulsory service with the Army, and the SS Totenkopf Verbände, special troops employed to guard concentration camps, which came under the control of the SS in 1934. The SS Verfügungstruppe was organized as an armed unit to be employed with the Army in the event of mobilization. In the summer of 1939, the Verfügungstruppe was equipped as a motorized division to form the nucleus of the forces which came to be known in 1940 as the Waffen SS. In that year the Waffen SS comprised 100,000 men, 56,000 coming from the Verfügungstruppe and the rest from the Allgemeine SS and the Totenkopf Verbände. At the end of the war it is estimated to have consisted of about 580,000 men and 40 divisions. The Waffen SS was under the tactical command of the Army, but was equipped and supplied through the administrative branches of the SS and under SS disciplinary control.

Beginning in 1933 there was a gradual but thorough amalgamation of the police and SS. In 1936 Himmler, the Reichsführer SS, became Chief of the German Police with authority over the regular uniformed police as well as the Security Police. Himmler established a system under which Higher SS and Police Leaders, appointed for each Wehrkreis, served as his personal representatives in coordinating the activities of the Order Police, Security Police and SD and Allgemeine SS within their jurisdictions. In 1939 the SS and police systems were coordinated by taking into the SS all officials of the Security and Order Police, at SS ranks equivalent to their rank in the police.

Until 1940 the SS was an entirely voluntary organization. After the formation of the Waffen SS in 1940 there was a gradually increasing number of conscripts into the Waffen SS. It appears that about a third of the total number of people joining the Waffen SS were conscripts, that the proportion of conscripts was higher at the end of the war than at the beginning, but that there continued to be a high proportion of volunteers until the end of the war.

Criminal Activities: SS units were active participants in the steps leading up to aggressive war. The Verfügungstruppe was used in the occupation of the Sudetenland, of Bohemia and Moravia, and of Memel. The Henlein Free Corps was under the jurisdiction of the Reichsführer SS for operations in the Sudetenland in 1938, and the Volksdeutschemittelstelle financed fifth-column activities there.

The SS was even a more general participant in the commission of War Crimes and Crimes against Humanity. Through its control over the organization of the Police, particularly the Security Police and SD, the SS was involved in all the crimes which have been outlined in the section of this Judgment dealing with the Gestapo and SD. Other branches of the SS were equally involved in these criminal programs. There is evidence that the shooting of unarmed prisoners of war was the general practice in some Waffen SS divisions. On 1 October 1944 the custody of prisoners of war and interned persons was transferred to Himmler, who in turn transferred prisoner-of-war affairs to SS Obergruppenführer Berger and to SS Obergruppenführer Pohl. The Race and Settlement Office of the SS together with the Volksdeutschemittelstelle were active in carrying out schemes for Germanization of occupied territories according to the racial principles of the Nazi Party and were involved in the deportation of Jews and other foreign nationals. Units of the Waffen SS and Einsatzgruppen operating directly under the SS main office were used to carry out these plans. These units were also involved in the widespread murder and ill-treatment of the civilian population of occupied territories. Under the guise of combatting partisan units, units of the SS exterminated Jews and people deemed politically undesirable by the SS, and their reports record the execution of enormous numbers of persons. Waffen SS divisions were responsible for many massacres and atrocities in occupied territories such as the massacres at Oradour and Lidice.

From 1934 onwards the SS was responsible for the guarding and administration of concentration camps. The evidence leaves no doubt that the consistently brutal treatment of the inmates of concentration camps was carried out as a result of the general policy of the SS, which was that the inmates were racial inferiors to be treated only with contempt. There is evidence that where manpower considerations permitted, Himmler wanted to rotate guard battalions so that all members of the SS would be instructed as to the proper attitude to take to inferior races. After 1942 when the concentration camps were placed under the control of the WVHA they were used as a source of slave labor. An agreement made with the Ministry of Justice on 18 September 1942 provided that antisocial elements who had finished prison sentences were to be delivered to the SS to be worked to death. Steps were continually taken, involving the use of the Security Police and SD and even the Waffen SS, to insure that the SS had an adequate supply of concentration camp labor for its projects. In connection with the administration of the concentration camps, the SS embarked on a series of experiments on human beings which were performed on prisoners of war or concentration camp inmates. These experiments included freezing to death, and killing by poison bullets. The SS was able to obtain an allocation of Government funds for this kind of research on the grounds that they had access to human material not available to other agencies.

The SS played a particularly significant role in the persecution of the Jews. The SS was directly involved in the demonstrations of 10 November 1938. The evacuation of the Jews from occupied territories was carried out under the directions of the SS with the assistance of SS Police units. The extermination of the Jews was carried out under the direction of the SS Central Organizations. It was actually put into effect by SS formations. The Einsatzgruppen engaged in wholesale massacres of the Jews. SS Police units were also involved. For example, the massacre of Jews in the Warsaw ghetto was carried out under the directions of SS Brigadeführer and Major General of the Police Stroop. A special group from the SS Central Organization arranged for the deportation of Jews from various Axis satellites and their extermination was carried out in the concentration camps run by the WVHA.

It is impossible to single out any one portion of the SS which was not involved in these criminal activities. The Allgemeine SS was an active participant in the persecution of the Jews and was used as a source of concentration camp guards. Units of the Waffen SS were directly involved in the killing of prisoners of war and the atrocities in occupied countries. It supplied personnel for the Einsatzgruppen, and had command over the concentration camp guards after its absorption of the Totenkopf SS, which originally controlled the system. Various SS Police units were also widely used in the atrocities in occupied countries and the extermination of the Jews there. The SS Central Organization supervised the activities of these various formations and was responsible for such special projects as the human experiments and "final solution" of the Jewish question.

The Tribunal finds that knowledge of these criminal activities was sufficiently general to justify declaring that the SS was a criminal organization to the extent hereinafter described. It does appear that an attempt was made to keep secret some phases of its activities, but its criminal programs were so widespread, and involved slaughter on such a gigantic scale, that its criminal activities must have been widely known. It must be recognized, moreover, that the criminal activities of the SS followed quite logically from the principles on which it was organized. Every effort had been made to make the SS a highly disciplined organization composed of the elite of National Socialism. Himmler had stated that there were people in Germany "who become sick when they see these black coats" and that he did not expect that "they should be loved by too many." Himmler also indicated his view that the SS was concerned with perpetuating the elite racial stock with the object of making Europe a Germanic continent and the SS was instructed that it was designed to assist the Nazi Government in the ultimate domination of Europe and the elimination of all inferior races. This mystic and fanatical belief in the superiority of the Nordic German developed into the studied contempt and even hatred of other races which led to criminal activities of the type outlined above being considered as a matter of course if not a matter of pride. The actions of a soldier in the Waffen SS who in September 1939, acting entirely on his own initiative, killed 50 Jewish laborers whom he had been guarding, were described by the statement that as an SS man, he was "particularly sensitive to the sight of Jews," and had acted "quite thoughtlessly in a youthful spirit of adventure" and a sentence of three-years imprisonment imposed on him was dropped under an amnesty. Hess wrote with truth that the Waffen SS were more suitable for the specific tasks to be solved in occupied territory owing to their extensive training in questions of race and nationality. Himmler, in a series of speeches made in 1943, indicated his pride in the ability of the SS to carry out these criminal acts. He encouraged his men to be "tough and ruthless", he spoke of shooting "thousands of leading Poles", and thanked them for their cooperation and lack of squeamishness at the sight of hundreds and thousands of corpses of their victims. He extolled ruthlessness in exterminating the Jewish race and later described this process as "delousing." These speeches show that the general attitude prevailing in the SS was consistent with these criminal acts.

Conclusions: The SS was utilized for purposes which were criminal under the Charter involving the persecution and extermination of the Jews, brutalities and killings in concentration camps, excesses in the administration of occupied territories, the administration of the slave labor program and the mistreatment and murder of prisoners of war. The Defendant Kaltenbrunner was a member of the SS implicated in these activities. In dealing with the SS the Tribunal includes all persons who had been officially accepted as members of the SS including the members of the Allgemeine SS, members of the Waffen SS, members of the SS Totenkopf Verbände, and the members of any of the different police forces who were members of the SS. The Tribunal does not include the so-called SS riding units. Der Sicherheitsdienst des Reichsführer SS (commonly known as the SD) is dealt with in the Tribunal's Judgment on the Gestapo and SD.

The Tribunal declares to be criminal within the meaning of the Charter the group composed of those persons who had been officially accepted as members of the SS as enumerated in the preceding paragraph who became or remained members of the organization with knowledge that it was being used for the commission of acts declared criminal by Article 6 of the Charter, or who were personally implicated as members of the organization in the commission of such crimes, excluding, however, those who were drafted into membership by the State in such a way as to give them no choice in the matter, and who had committed no such crimes. The basis of this finding is the participation of the organization in War Crimes and Crimes against Humanity connected with the war; this group declared criminal cannot include, therefore, persons who had ceased to belong to the organizations enumerated in the preceding paragraph prior to 1 September 1939.

Selected Further Readings

The following entries are chosen from English-language press and journal articles.

"A Question of Responsibility: The Search for Meaning at West Germany's Bitburg Cemetery" (A Discussion Guide). *Dimensions*, Fall 1985.

Buckley, William F., Jr. "On the Right." *National Review*, 31 May 1985.

Cockburn, Alexander. "Anti-Soviet Antecedents to the Cemetery Visit." *Wall Street Journal*, 2 May 1985.

Decter, Midge. "Bitburg: Who Forgot What." *Commentary*, August 1985.

Echikson, William. "French Government and Press Play Down WW II Anniversary." *Christian Science Monitor*, 3 May 1985.

Editorial, "Living by the Symbol." *Christian Science Monitor*, 17 April 1985.

Editorial, "Reagan's Loss in Germany." *Boston Globe*, 16 May 1985.

Eisenhower, Dwight D. "Face to Face with Nazi Brutality." Excerpt from autobiography, reprinted in *Boston Globe*, 22 April 1985.

Erlanger, Steven. "Germans Still Must Struggle." *Boston Globe*, 8 May 1985.

Friedlander, Albert H., ed. "Forgetting and Forgiving: The Post-Bitburg Controversy in Great Britain." *European Judaism*, Spring 1985.

Goldhagen, Daniel. "A Bitburg Footnote." *New Republic*, 13 May 1985.

Joffe, Joseph. "Germany's Undigested Past." *Washington Post*, 28 April 1985.

Lewis, Anthony. "Appointment in Bitburg." *New York Times*, 25 April 1985.

———."The Hollow Man." *New York Times*, 21 April 1985.

Markham, James. "West German TV Specials Spark Debate on Reconciliation with Nazi Era." *New York Times*, 24 April 1985.

"Reagan at Bitburg: Spectacle and Memory." *On Film*, no. 14 (Spring 1985). Several authors.

Reich, Walter. "Bitburg: Restored Honor, Evil Omen." *Los Angeles Times*, 2 May 1985.

Rentschler, Eric. "The Use and Abuse of Memory: New German Film and the Discourse of Memory." *New German Critique* 36 (Fall 1985).

Schwarz, Walter. "History—or Living Horror?" *Manchester Gaurdian*, 8 May 1985.

Shannon, William V. "Reagan and JFK: No Contest." *Boston Globe*, 15 May 1985.

Silberman, Charles E. "Speaking Truth to Power." Afterword to *A Certain People: American Jews and Their Lives Today*. New York: Summit Books, 1985.

Struminski, Wladimir. "Bitburg and German Nationalism." *Jerusalem Post*, 28 April 1985.

Sultanik, Kalman. "An Overview of 'Bitburg.' " *Midstream*, October 1985.

Tagliabue, John. "Rancor Is Evident in Commemorations of Dachau." *New York Times*, 29 April 1985.

————."SS Veterans Feel 'Rehabilitated' by Reagan Visit." *New York Times*, 3 May 1985.

Watt, David. "Bitburg Protest that Could Rebound." *London Times*, 3 May 1985.

Wilkinson, James D. "Remembering World War II: The Perspective of the Losers." *American Scholar*, Summer 1985.

Essayists

Theodor W. Adorno, who died in 1969, was a member of the "Frankfurt School" and a major philosopher.

William Bole is Washington correspondent for the Religious News Service.

A. Roy Eckardt, a Visiting Scholar in The Centre for Hebrew Studies at the University of Oxford, is Professor Emeritus of Religion Studies at Lehigh University and a clergyman in the United Methodist Church.

Saul Friedländer is Professor of History at the University of Tel Aviv and the University of Geneva.

Jürgen Habermas is Professor of Philosophy at the University of Frankfurt and has written widely on social and political thought.

Geoffrey H. Hartman is Professor of English and Comparative Literature at Yale University and Faculty Advisor to Yale's Video Archive of Holocaust Testimonies, which he helped found in 1982.

Raul Hilberg is Professor of Political Science at the University of Vermont and author of a definitive work on the Holocaust, *The Destruction of the European Jews*.

Primo Levi is a major Italian novelist, who has written many accounts based on his experiences as a survivor.

Alvin H. Rosenfeld is Professor of English and Director of the Jewish Studies Program at Indiana University.

Henry Rousso is an historian at the Institut d'Histoire du Temps Présent, Centre National de la Recherche Scientifique, in Paris.

James E. Young is Dorot Foundation Fellow and Assistant Professor of English at New York University.

editor: Risë Williamson
book designer: Sharon Sklar
jacket designer: Sharon Sklar
production coordinator: Marilla Schwomeyer
typeface: Baskerville
typesetter: J. Jarrett Engineering
printer and binder: Haddon Craftsmen, Inc.